ADVANCED   Solutions   Chris Speechley

The 1997 McGraw-Hill
Team and Organization
Development

CW00816285

Other McGraw-Hill Titles Edited by Mel Silberman

The 1997 McGraw-Hill Team and Organization Development Sourcebook

Mel Silberman, Editor

Assisted by
Carol Auerbach

McGraw-Hill

New York   San Francisco   Washington, D.C.   Auckland   Bogotá
Caracas   Lisbon   London   Madrid   Mexico City   Milan
Montreal   New Delhi   San Juan   Singapore
Sydney   Tokyo   Toronto

International Standard Serial Number:
The 1997 McGraw-Hill Team and Organization Development Sourcebook
ISSN 1084-1350

1 2 3 4 5 6 7 8 9 0   EDW/EDW   9 0 1 0 9 8 7 6   (Paperback)
1 2 3 4 5 6 7 8 9 0   EDW/EDW   9 0 1 0 9 8 7 6   (Looseleaf)

ISBN 0-07-057838-9 (Paperback)
PN 0-07-057937-7
PART OF
ISBN 0-07-057839-7 (Looseleaf)

*The sponsoring editor for this book was Richard Narramore, the editing supervisor was
Fred Dahl, the designer was Inkwell Publishing Services, and the production supervisor
was Suzanne W. B. Rapcavage.*

Printed and bound by Edwards Brothers.

CONTENTS

TOPICAL INDEX
Find a Tool for Your Specific Topic

In the place of a traditional index is the following classification by topic of the 40 tools found in *The 1997 McGraw-Hill Team and Organization Development Sourcebook*.

PREFACE

Welcome to the second year of *The McGraw-Hill Team and Organization Development Sourcebook,* an annual collection of practical tools to develop human resources. *The 1996 Sourcebook* was a huge success. *The 1997 Sourcebook* has another great lineup of resources for your professional use.

Along with its companion, *The McGraw-Hill Training and Performance Sourcebook, The McGraw-Hill Team and Organization Development Sourcebook* provides the latest cutting-edge advice and learning aids on topics important to today's public and private sector organizations. While *The Training and Performance Sourcebook* emphasizes development and support at the individual level of the organization, *The McGraw-Hill Team and Organization Development Sourcebook* focuses on organization-wide issues.

Having *The McGraw-Hill Team and Organization Development Sourcebook* available for instant reference allows you to select printed materials on team and organizational change written by leading experts. In addition, the *Sourcebook* serves as a state-of-the-art clearinghouse of ideas and new practices. It helps you keep up with the spiraling developments in the field of team and organization development.

The 1997 Sourcebook contains 40 team activities, assessment instruments, handouts, and practical guides ... creating a ready-to-use toolkit for consultants, trainers, and team leaders. It is also invaluable for team sponsors, managers, and other organizational representatives who are interested in team and organization development. Best of all, because these tools are reproducible, they can be shared with others.

Here are some of the topics you will find covered in *The 1997 McGraw-Hill Team and Organization Development Sourcebook:*

- ✓ Assessment of team and organizational functioning
- ✓ Conflict resolution
- ✓ Cooperation and trust building
- ✓ Creative problem solving
- ✓ Customer service
- ✓ Goal setting and planning
- ✓ Facilitating teams
- ✓ Managing and leading change

✓ Organizational initiatives

✓ Quality and continuous improvement

✓ Team development

I hope you will find *The 1997 McGraw-Hill Team and Organization Development Sourcebook* to be a one-stop resource you can draw upon again and again in your efforts to facilitate team and organizational effectiveness.

Mel Silberman
Princeton, New Jersey

The 1997 McGraw-Hill
Team and Organization
Development Sourcebook

TEAM ACTIVITIES

In this section of *The 1997 McGraw-Hill Team and Organization Development Sourcebook,* you will find sixteen team activities. They are designed to:

✓ Sell teamwork and cooperation
✓ Set goals
✓ Establish team trust
✓ Build cohesion
✓ Develop problem solving
✓ Increase facilitation skills
✓ Resolve conflicts

You can use these activities in a variety of settings:

✓ Team-building sessions
✓ Meetings
✓ Retreats
✓ Training programs
✓ Consultations

All of the activities featured here are highly participatory. They are designed in the belief that learning and change best occur through *experience* and *reflection.* As opposed to preaching or lecturing, experiential activities place people directly within a concrete situation. Typically, participants are asked to solve a problem, complete an assignment, or communicate information. Often, the task can be quite challenging. Sometimes, it can also be a great deal of fun. The bottom line, however, is that participants become active partners in the learning of new concepts or in the development of new ideas.

The experiences contained in the activities you are about to read can also be of two kinds: *simulated* and *real-world.* Although some may find them to be artificial, well-designed simulations can provide an effective analogy to real-world experiences. They also have the advantage of being time-saving shortcuts to longer, drawn-out activities. Sometimes, of course, there is no substitute for real-world experience. Activities that engage teams in actual, ongoing work can serve as a powerful mechanism for change.

Experience, by itself, is not always "the best teacher." Reflecting on the experience, however, can yield wisdom and insight. You will find that the team activities in this section contain helpful guidelines for reflection. Expect a generous selection of questions to process or debrief the actual activities.

All the activities have been written for ease of use. A concise overview of each activity is provided. You will be guided, step by step, through the activity instructions. All the necessary participant materials are included. For your photocopying convenience, these materials are on separate pages. Any materials you need to prepare in advance have been kept to a minimum. Special equipment or physical arrangements are seldom needed.

Best of all, the activities are designed so that you can easily modify or customize them to your specific requirements. Also, time allocations are readily adaptable. Furthermore, many of the activities are "frame exercises" ... generic activities that can be used for many topics or subject matters. You will find it easy to plug in the content relevant to your team's circumstances.

As you conduct any of these activities, bear in mind that experiential activity is especially successful if you do a good job as facilitator. Here are some common mistakes people make in facilitating experiential activities:

1. *Motivation:* Participants aren't invited to buy into the activity themselves or sold the benefits of joining in. Participants don't know what to expect during the exercise.

2. *Directions:* Instructions are lengthy and unclear. Participants cannot visualize what the facilitator expects from them.

3. *Group Process:* Subgroups are not composed effectively. Group formats are not changed to fit the requirements of each activity. Subgroups are left idle.

4. *Energy:* Activities move too slowly. Participants are sedentary. Activities are long or demanding when they need to be short or relaxed. Participants do not find the activity challenging.

5. *Processing:* Participants are confused and/or overwhelmed by the questions posed to them. There is a poor fit between the facilitator's questions and the goals of the activity. Facilitators share their opinions before first hearing the participants' views.

To avoid these pitfalls, follow these steps:

I. Introduce the activity.

1. Explain your objectives
2. Sell the benefits
3. Convey enthusiasm
4. Connect the activity to previous activities
5. Share personal feelings and express confidence in participants

II. Help participants to know what they are expected to do.
1. Speak slowly
2. Use visual backup
3. Define important terms
4. Demonstrate the activity

III. Manage the group process.
1. Form groups in a variety of ways
2. Vary the number of people in any activity based upon that exercise's specific requirements
3. Divide participants into teams before give further directions
4. Give instructions separately to groups in a multipart activity
5. Keep people busy
6. Inform the subgroups about time frames

IV. Keep participants involved.
1. Keep the activity moving
2. Challenge the participants
3. Reinforce participants for their involvement in the activity
4. Build physical movement into the activity

V. Get participants to reflect on the activity's implications.
1. Ask relevant questions
2. Carefully structure the first processing experiences
3. Observe how participants are reacting to the group processing
4. Assist a subgroup that is having trouble processing an activity
5. Hold your own reactions until after hearing from participants

SCENES FROM AN ORGANIZATION: AN EXERCISE FOR NEW TEAM MANAGERS

Deborah Hopen

Deborah Hopen (*6400 South Center Boulevard, Tukwila, WA 98188, 206-241-1464, debhopen@aol.com) has over twenty years of experience in total quality management. She has served as a senior executive with Fortune and Inc 500 companies and was the 1995-96 President of the American Society for Quality Control. Her varied experience includes general management, quality assurance and quality control, training, human resources, organizational development, and accounting. In addition to writing more than 50 publications and presentations, her consulting clients include Disney University, Weyerhaeuser, Microsoft, the city of Tacoma, and the state of Washington.*

Overview   When organizations begin to use teams in their workplaces, managers need to learn new roles. Managing a problem-solving or self-directed work team requires different skills than managing employees in a more traditional, hierarchical work setting. These three scenarios describe situations that teams and their sponsoring managers might face. As the participants consider the scenario questions and discuss their responses, they will discover ways to work effectively with teams.

Suggested Time   30 minutes.

Materials Needed

    ✓ Form A (Three Scenes from an Organization)
    ✓ Form B (Instructor Discussion Guide)

Procedure

1. Divide the participants into teams of two or three.
2. Give each team a copy of Form A.
3. Have them read the scenarios and formulate their responses.
4. Ask the teams to appoint a presenter to share and discuss their responses with another team. Thus, if there are two teams, the member appointed would visit the other team and share how his or her group viewed each scenario. If there are three or more teams, rotate "presenters" one time so that each team is visited once.

5. Reconvene the entire group. Share the key points on Form B and compare them with the views of participants.

Variation

1. Create three subgroups. Assign one scenario to each group.

2. Ask each subgroup to select a member to serve on a "panel" of group reporters.

3. Convene the panel and ask each reporter to discuss the scenario assigned to them and how they would respond.

THREE SCENES FROM AN ORGANIZATION

Scenario 1

The newly formed green team was having trouble making progress. The desired results were stated clearly, and management had given the team adequate resources and a reasonable amount of latitude in its approach to the task.

Nevertheless, they've been floundering from the beginning. They suffered through several false starts and directionless activities. They finally settled on an approach, but are now having trouble moving from one step to the next. They tend to postpone intermediate decisions or conclusions because they feel they need more information or more time or more resources.

How can you help the team get on track?

Scenario 2

In an effort to stimulate team activities, you establish a "Team of the Month" recognition program. Although there was a lot of excitement and many new teams formed during the first month of the program, the pace of business improvements associated with team activities has declined sharply in the past quarter.

Two months ago, you increased the reward from a $25 gift certificate for each team member to an overnight stay at a local resort hotel; however, this produced no noticeable improvement in results.

How can you best stimulate team performance?

Scenario 3

An ongoing team has been established in the food services department you manage. The first problem the team decided to tackle involved petty theft of utensils. You shared with the team at its formation that $650 of stainless steel flatware has disappeared since the beginning of the year. This constitutes a negative effect of 0.69% on the cafeteria profit margin. Everyone on the team is quite concerned about this situation. And as the department manager, you are experiencing significant pressure from the owners to solve this problem. On a recent business trip, your large key ring set off the metal detector at the airport. It immediately occurred to you that installing a metal detector in the exit door frame could quickly identify anyone leaving with stolen spoons. You suggested this approach at the next team meeting, but the team leader asked you to save your recommendation until the team had collected more data. You pointed out that the company's money was "walking out the door" while the team was wasting time when a perfectly good solution was staring it in the face. The team leader thanked you for your comment and the team returned to data collection planning.

What should you do now?

Scenario 1 Key Points

✓ *Ask the team members if they need any further clarification of or changes to the task agreement.*

Are the expected outcomes clear? Are the performance indicators easy to measure? Could they be better defined? Are the targets reasonable? Are the team members able to devote sufficient time to the task? Are more members or members with different skills needed? Is the team hampered by financial restrictions or management approval cycles?

✓ *Ask the team to identify and quantify exactly what is holding the group up.*

What needs to be increased? What needs to be decreased? What actions have been completely successful? What actions have been only partially successful?

✓ *Ask the team to examine its group process.*

Has the team established explicit norms? Is the team checking its behaviors against the norms? Does the team have any consistent behavioral issues?

✓ *Ask the team to review its progress.*

Has the team established a formal action plan? Is the team checking its progress against the action plan? If interim results fall short of targets, is the team recycling through the agreed-upon steps?

✓ *Ask the team how you can help.*

Scenario 2 Key Points

Have you considered the pitfalls of your current program?

✓ Creating competition instead of cooperation—rewarding teams or members who withhold information others could use in an effort to gain an advantage.

✓ Limiting the number of groups or employees that can be recognized at one time—when one team wins, the other teams all lose.

✓ Letting every team have its "turn"—it's difficult to recognize the same successful team over and over.

✓ Focusing on nuances—it's also often difficult to differentiate among performances.

What other reinforcement techniques are you using?

✓ Providing regular feedback—compliments for even small accomplishments.
✓ Recognizing milestones—public acknowledgment of intermediate results.
✓ Chatting informally with team members—listening with respect, not taking action, and recommending that any problems discussed be solved through the team structure.

Scenario 3 Key Points

Have you forgotten that you should leave your manager's hat outside the room when you are a member of the team?

✓ Do nothing.
✓ Honor the process.
✓ Participate as a cooperative member of the team and let the solution arise from the data and root cause analysis.
✓ Don't narrow your viewpoint prematurely.
✓ Build off other team members' suggestions.

Have you forgotten why the team was formed?

✓ Management wanted to tap into the creativity of a cross-section of the organization.
✓ Management perceived the problem was more complex than one person could permanently solve.
✓ Management felt that commitment could be built more effectively if the entire department participated in the process.

Are you worried that the team won't solve the problem: fast enough? cheaply enough?

✓ Trust—Do you have more faith in your own abilities than those of the team members?
✓ Respect—When the team is successful, do you think your superiors will lose respect for you as an individual?

JUMPING **2** THE GUN: HOW PATIENT IS YOUR TEAM?

Karen Lawson

Karen Lawson, *Ph.D. is the president of the Lawson Consulting Group (1365 Gwynedale Way, Lansdale, PA 19446, 215-368-9465), an organization and management development consultant firm. She has over twenty years of experience in the fields of management, training, consulting, and education across a wide range of industries. Karen is the coauthor of* **101 Ways to Make Training Active** *(Pfeiffer, 1995) and an editor of and contributor to* **20 Active Training Programs,** *vol. II (Pfeiffer, 1994).*

Overview   This exercise has three objectives: 1) to demonstrate how a team moves too quickly and too impatiently at times; 2) to assess how a team develops or fails to develop a process or method of operation; and 3) to determine how a team wants to change its process. It is designed for one or more teams of six or more members.

Suggested Time   45 to 60 minutes.

Materials Needed   ✓ Copies of Form A (Observer Sheet) for observers

Procedure   1. Place each team at a table. Obtain two observers from each team. Use a random method of selection such as the team members with the two earliest birthdays in the year or with the two first initials that come earliest in the alphabet.

2. Give copies of Form A to the observers. Provide them with a few minutes to read their instructions and get ready for the activity.

3. In the meantime, give the team(s) the following instructions:

   Your task is to set goals for the next 12 months. What would you like to accomplish in the next 12 months? You will have 30 minutes to begin this process. You are to assume that you will have more meeting time in the future to accomplish this task.

   If you are a new team, you will be setting goals for the first time. If you are an existing team, you may consider goals that have already been established as well as new ones.

Do not let anyone press you to clarify the task any further. It is purposely vague so that the observers can assess whether the team takes the time initially to clarify the task for itself. Also, do not tell them about the nature of the instructions given to the observers. Promise that they will be revealed at the end of the activity.

4. Begin the meeting. About two minutes before the time is up, give participants a two-minute warning.

5. Stop the meeting and ask observers to give their feedback. Encourage them to give feedback that is descriptive and specific rather than judgmental and general.

6. Allow the participants to clarify the feedback and obtain their reactions. Do everything in your power to keep the climate open and nondefensive. Accept "excuses" that participants give such as, "We assumed that we had to get the job done soon."

7. Debrief the activity. Ask the following questions:

   ✓ Do you think that teams "jump the gun" sometimes by not patiently setting up their process? by not clarifying what their task is? by debating ideas before hearing and clarifying all of them? by making decisions even if time hasn't been taken to establish that everyone agrees or can live with a decision even when they don't prefer it?

   ✓ How would you assess *your team's* "patience?"

   ✓ What would you like to do in the future to change the process of your team?

Variation

Videotape the meeting. Play back samples of it and allow the participants to observe themselves.

To the Observers: Do not reveal to your teammates what you are assessing. Your team has been given the following task:

Your task is to set goals for the next 12 months. What would you like to accomplish in the next 12 months? You will have 30 minutes to begin this process. You are to assume that you will have more meeting time in the future to accomplish this task.

If you are a new team, you will be setting goals for the first time. If you are an existing team, you may consider goals that have already been established as well as new ones.

Often, when teams are given this task, they "jump the gun" by proceeding too quickly with discussing and perhaps deciding upon goals before establishing how they will go about the task. Your job is to assess how impatient your team is. Specifically, consider the following:

1. Does the team take time in the beginning to clarify the task before them or does it just plunge into it?

   Notes:

2. Does the team develop a process or method of operation as to how it will proceed in working on the task? If so, what is the process they discuss?

   Notes:

3. Do participants take positions early on about the goals they want the team to set? Does this create a competitive climate in the team? What happens to the quality of team communication?

   Notes:

4. Do participants act as if they have to make decisions by the end of the meeting? If they do make any decisions, are they made by active consensus or is there an assumption that everyone agrees?

   Notes:

THE FOUR STAGES OF TEAM DEVELOPMENT: SMOOTHING OUT THE WRINKLES

3

Carol Harvey

Carol P. Harvey, *Ed.D. is an associate professor of management and marketing at Assumption College (500 Salisbury Street, Worcester, MA 01615-0005, 508-767-7459, charvey@eve.assumption.edu). Carol is the coauthor of* **Understanding Diversity: Readings, Cases, and Exercises** *(HarperCollins, 1995). A former manager with the Xerox Corporation, her current interests include workplace trends such as the changing nature of motivation in organizations, outsourcing of human resource functions, and the growth of the contingency workforce. Carol was also a contributor to* **The 1996 McGraw-Hill Training and Performance Sourcebook.**

Overview This exercise is designed to teach team members that many of the things that go wrong in the process of working together are normal and are often a function of the stage of the team's development. As team members learn to recognize these behaviors, they view them as evidence of progression in team maturity rather than as proof that effective teamwork is a myth. Because this exercise is nonthreatening, fun, and easy to relate to, it is a particularly effective way to get participants quickly involved in training activities and has been used successfully with a wide range of participants. The intended outcomes are "smoother" teamwork and fewer "wrinkles" in productivity. This exercise is suitable for groups of 8 to 30 members. Because so few materials are required, this exercise is particularly easy to do off-site.

Suggested Time 25 to 35 minutes, but additional time may be allowed for extended discussion.

Materials Needed ✓ Form A (Role Play: Smoothing Out the Wrinkles)
✓ Form B (Stages of Team Development)

Procedure

1. Break the group into four subgroups.

2. Give every participant copies of "Role Play: Smoothing Out the Wrinkles." (Form A)

3. Give the members of each of the four groups copies of "Stages of Team Development" (Form B) and assign them to read the description of one of the stages.

4. Give a brief introduction to the exercise in which you point out that most work teams go through somewhat predictable stages of struggle and development. Knowing what these should be like in advance prepares the team for this normal process.

5. Tell each group that they have 10 minutes to devise a 3-minute role play that demonstrates what the product development team's meeting might sound like at their assigned stage of team development.

6. After groups have prepared, each group *in the order* of the stages of team development, is told to present its role play. *What is particularly important is that the facilitator does not speak during the role plays and there is no class discussion until all four groups have presented. If the facilitator simply gestures to each group that it is their turn, it allows a "smoother" flow between the stages.*

7. After all of the groups have presented, conduct a brief discussion on the lifecycle of a team. As you progress through the stages, encourage members of the teams from *other stages* to cite behaviors that they saw at each stage that are typical of that stage of team development.

   During the discussion members often relate similar experiences to those demonstrated in the role plays and express relief that these are normal happenings as teams develop.

   If members regularly work together, the groups may be taped and the tape replayed at a later date to discuss the group's process and progression.

Assume that you are a member of a new product development team. Your team members all work for the same company but are from different departments and divisions and have never worked together before. As a team, you are responsible for the launch of a new, yet unnamed laundry detergent that smoothes out wrinkles during the wash cycle. Because this product will eliminate the need for ironing, your company is counting on it to be very successful.

As a group, develop a 3-minute role play that showcases the types of behavior typical in your assigned stage of team development. The setting should be a team meeting held to discuss the launch of this new product. What is important here is that you model the behaviors expected at your assigned stage.

STAGES OF TEAM DEVELOPMENT

STAGE I—FORMING

During this stage, group members are unclear about their roles and responsibilities as group members. They are often unsure of what to do, how they fit in, how to behave, and who is in charge. They are careful not to offend each other and, as a result, don't accomplish much.

STAGE II—STORMING

During this stage, team members struggle to define their contributions to the team effort. Subgroups may form, conflict and dissent surface, and there is a lack of unity. Members have not developed enough trust in each other to constructively solve problems.

STAGE III—NORMING

During this stage, team members resolve some of their differences in approaching a task by developing norms of behavior. The team takes more responsibility for leadership. Although members still struggle with their roles, there is more trust and group cohesion. Here being part of the group is important and a consensus about how to do things begins to develop. Although the group is still unstable during this stage, more work gets done because the group has come to agreement on its purpose.

STAGE IV—PERFORMING

During this stage, team members have a clear understanding about what needs to be done and how to do it. Members' roles are clearer, and people understand how to work with each other. Communication is free, people are less dependent on formal leadership, and they have established ways to deal with conflict. Here the group is focused on accomplishing its goals.

STUPID CONVERSATIONS IN TEAMS: ARE YOU READY TO BE HONEST?

Michael O'Brien

Michael O'Brien, *Ed.D. is president of O'Brien Learning Systems, Inc. (949 Woodcreek Dr., Milford, OH 45150, 513-831-8042), a human resource consulting firm that specializes in executive team development and executive coaching. The company offers products and services to help individuals, teams, and managers improve their ability to learn from experience, adapt to change, and manage their own development. Michael is author of* **The Learning Organization Practices Profile** *and* **Profit From Experience: How to Make the Most of Your Learning and Your Life.**

Overview   This activity helps promote team building and team communications by building awareness of "stupid conversations" people have with others at work. Participants learn what is meant by "stupid conversations," have a chance to explore their own recent stupid conversations, and discuss the implications for them on their jobs. With this activity, facilitators can boost team productivity by showing people the amount of time (and money) they waste daily in conversations that are not productive or satisfying. Team members also discover which of their relationships need immediate attention in order to produce the results for which they are responsible.

Suggested Time   40 minutes.

Materials Needed   ✓ Form A (Stupid Conversations Inventory)
     ✓ Flip charts/markers

Procedure   1. Introduce the exercise by telling the participants that far too often conversations between team members are not productive or very satisfying. What's more, all too often we become inured to this and we stop expecting our conversations to support effective work or satisfying relationships. There are many reasons for this. One of them is a norm of "politeness" that holds us back from honest communication.

     2. Have the participants close their eyes and ask them to reflect on the following:

"In the last week, how many people had conversations that needed to go somewhere with other members of your team, but didn't? Conversations, in other words, intended to produce understanding, commitment to action, and so forth, but that were somehow just left dangling? … How many people had conversations, or maybe meetings, that revolved around some point of conflict or difficulty that never got resolved? … How many of you in the last week had conversations in which you somehow never seemed to come right out and say what was really on your minds?"

3. After a minute of reflection, ask the participants to list the "stupid conversations" they had during the week on Form A. Tell them to make a rough estimate of the time involved. [E.g., "How many people spent more than an hour in such conversations? Two hours? Three? Four? More than six?"] Discuss how costly stupid conversations can be. [E.g., "What does it cost you, personally, professionally, economically?"] People who routinely spend six or more hours a week in stupid conversations at work would scream bloody murder if the actual cost of those conversations were deducted from their pay. You might even invite participants to calculate the actual annual dollar costs of their "stupid conversations."

4. Next, have the participants identify what stopped them from communicating clearly and completely. What were they afraid of that made them censor what they really wanted to say?

5. Have participants identify the "stupid conversations" they had last week that concern them the most. Again, ask participants to close their eyes and ask them to visualize what an alternative conversation would be like. Would they be willing to tell the other person (respectfully) what was really on their minds … including their *fear* of speaking their opinion? Would they be willing to inquire of the other person what they were really thinking and feeling?

6. Point out that having the courage to dialogue with others in this way is the alternative to "stupid conversations" and the path to productive relationships. Ask participants: What stops you from having this alternative, more honest conversation? Divide participants into pairs to discuss their answers.

7. Reconvene the entire group and invite participants to share the obstacles they have identified. Some obstacles that might be mentioned are:
   ✓ fear of reprisal
   ✓ not wanting to be critical of another person
   ✓ preferring to leave the situation as it is because it will take a lot of work to change it

8. Ask participants to weigh these obstacles against the expense of continuing to have "stupid conversations." Suggest that they select one time during the coming week to communicate more honestly and judge the value of doing so for themselves.

Incomplete conversations don't produce understanding or commitment to action, leave conflicts unresolved, feelings unexpressed, and upset unspoken.

The past week I had the following "stupid" conversations ...

<u>With Whom</u>   <u>About What</u>

✓

✓

✓

✓

✓

5
THE BALLOON FACTORY: DATA ANALYSIS IN TEAMS

Cindy Bentson

Cindy Bentson, *Ph.D. is an internal organization development consultant for the Federal Aviation Administration, Air Traffic Division, Northwest Mountain Region (ANM-503, 1601 Lind Ave. SW, Renton, WA 98055, 206-227-1116, bentsonc@grieg.seaslug.org). She consults with both union and management employees, facilitating organizational change, developing teams, aiding reorganization and redesign efforts, and facilitating labor-management collaborative problem solving and alternate dispute resolution methods. She was an external consultant in the private and public sectors prior to joining the FAA in 1992.*

Overview This activity is fun, high energy, intense, noisy, and often a little frustrating. The point that teams will understand by the conclusion of the activity is that data gathering and analysis, solution generation and selection, solution implementation, evaluation, feedback, and adjustment are all critical elements of a logical and systematic problem solving cycle.

Participants should be in teams of about 4 to 9. Standing or developing teams should be kept intact if at all possible to enhance the team development aspects of this activity. At least two teams are required to create opportunity for competition, excitement, and fun as well as opportunity for vicarious learning. The number of teams is unlimited except for physical space.

Suggested Time 45 to 90 minutes.

Materials Needed ✓ A work table (approximately 3′ × 8′) for each team

✓ A gross (144) of multicolored, 7″ round balloons for each team (keep a few gross more on hand if needed)

✓ One sharp object to pop balloons for each team (e.g., poultry skewers)

✓ 3 to 4 clear (so that teams can easily see from a distance or close-up what's inside of them) lawn-size trash bags for each team

✓ Whistle or bell for the facilitator to use to call time

✓ Glue, tape, sticks, paper plates, ribbon/yarn (these are distracters, so you can get creative with what you provide the teams—just make sure each team gets the same materials)

✓ Flip chart, easel, tape, and marking pens for each team for data gathering and analysis

✓ One chair for each team for "Quality Specialist" to sit on, placed at least 20 feet away from team table

Procedure

1. Before participants arrive, prepare each work table with the materials. Open the bag of balloons and dump it onto the table, and place the other (distracter) materials on the table. Place a flip chart and easel next to each work table.

2. Assign each team to a work table. Make sure there is space for participants to move around freely.

3. Have each team select a "Quality Specialist." Ask all of the "Quality Specialists" to go out of the room with one facilitator for "special training." Another facilitator should stay in the room with the teams to give them their instructions. (Note: If you only have a couple of small teams and you're the only facilitator, simply ask the nonspecialists to remain in the room relaxing while the specialists receive brief training.)

4. Out of earshot and view of the participants, explain to the quality specialists that their job is quality control. They will evaluate each balloon product as presented to them and either accept it as a quality product or reject it as a nonquality product. They may only accept or reject a balloon—they cannot in any way indicate why a balloon was accepted or rejected. If they accept the balloon, they place it in the large, clear garbage bag. If they reject it, they are to pop it with the sharp instrument. A quality product must be:

   ✓ fully inflated

   ✓ secured by a knot in the balloon

   ✓ presented to the Quality Specialist from the team member's left hand

   ✓ a different color from the previously presented balloon, regardless of whether it was accepted or rejected

   ✓ presented by a different team member each time, regardless of whether the balloon was accepted or rejected

   The Quality Specialists need to know these rules cold so they don't make a mistake. Any mistakes will cause the teams to not be able to collect accurate data on what makes a quality product. Keeping track is a lot tougher than it sounds!

5. Bring the Quality Specialists back into the room and have them take their places in their chairs. Each chair should be a good 20 feet (or more) from the table, in a relatively straight line from it.

You want the team members to have to travel a little bit during production times.

6. Explain that the teams are in a balloon factory and the product is an inflated balloon. The goal of each production unit (team) is to construct quality balloons using the raw materials at their work station. When a team believes it has a quality product, someone is to present the product to the Quality Specialist who will either accept or reject it. The Specialists are not allowed to talk or to indicate in any way why a balloon is accepted or rejected.

7. Indicate that they will have 5 minutes to plan their work . They are not allowed to inflate any of the balloons during planning time. They will then be given 3 minutes of production time. The beginning and the end of production will be indicated by a whistle.

8. After the first planning and production cycle, tell them that they'll have 10 minutes to plan for the next 3-minute production period. Again, use your whistle to indicate start and finish times.

Answer any questions they might have without giving anything away or telling them how they should plan their production.

9. There will be several rounds of planning and production times. Each planning session should be about 10 minutes, during which time the team members are not allowed to produce (inflate) any balloon products. They may rearrange their raw materials if they'd like. Each production session should be about 3 minutes. [These times may be adjusted according to the needs of the teams— longer planning sessions are encouraged if they're using the time to collect, analyze, and evaluate the data. On the other hand, I've discovered that longer production times increase the likelihood that teams use trial and error methods and focus only on turning out quantity, rather than slowing down to plan and produce quality products. Emphasis should be placed on planning rather than on production, though this is almost guaranteed to cause frustration and impatience for team members.]

10. During the first 10-minute planning session (just after the first production period), gather the Quality Specialists together so they can review the rules and calibrate their judgments. They're likely to be a bit overwhelmed and unsure of their ability to remember all of the rules and judge the balloon products fairly. They're also likely to be excited and wanting to talk about what has just happened, and maybe share their frustration at not being able to communicate with their own teams (or anyone else) during the production period. Make sure their discussions are out of earshot of the teams. Remind them that consistency is the key for successful data gathering and analysis by the teams.

11. Most of the time, the teams will start out in a pure trial and error mode, which is appropriate since they have no data yet.

Unfortunately, a lot of teams don't keep track very well of what is accepted or rejected (they have no clues so they'll try all sorts of interesting things), and some pursue a trial-and-error course all the way through the activity instead of carefully gathering data and analyzing it. If your teams are not getting the point of collecting data (what is rejected, what is accepted) and analyzing it by the third or fourth round, start gently facilitating them to think about how to figure it out. Some teams might get very frustrated and claim that the Specialists are using random (and malicious) judgments. You'll have to challenge that thinking and get them to think about how they could figure out what the characteristics of a quality product really are. If they think of it, they can go and examine all of the accepted balloon products (and the rejected balloons as well—the pieces will be scattered, though).

12. A team has successfully solved the quality product riddle when it can present several balloons (use your own judgment on the number) in a row and get them all accepted. After they have completed this task, have them tell you (out of earshot of the other teams) what the characteristics are. This will help you determine that their work was not simply a fluke. After a team has successfully completed the task, they can either be cheerleaders for the other teams or coach them, without directly telling the other teams the solution.

13. After all teams have completed the task or you run out of raw materials (balloons) or time, it's time for a little stress reducer! Dump out all of the accepted balloons and invite everyone to pop them in any way they want. This will be incredibly noisy, but it does reduce the frustration that may have built up. Then everyone needs to help pick up the balloon cadavers.

Variation
Before each team selects its "Quality Specialist," have them brainstorm the characteristics of an effective quality specialist as a team resource. Then have them match those characteristics to someone on the team who is then the "Quality Specialist." This variation simply adds another dimension to the activity if it's appropriate.

Debriefing
The debriefing really depends on what your teams needed to get from this activity and how it applies to their work situations. It also depends on how sophisticated they were at collecting and analyzing data and how that skill shows up at work. You might also have a discussion around their ideas of cheating versus vicarious learning (some of my teams have thought that learning from the successes and failures of another team was cheating). Another fruitful area of discussion is that of competition. They had separate workstations, raw materials, and quality specialists, but there never was any rule against collaboration.

Most teams will fall into the competitive mode instead of the collaborative mode. How does that relate to the work setting? Another area to discuss is the sharing of resources. Since they all work for the same company, did they share ideas, data, raw materials? Again, how does that show up at work? Another good area to debrief is their frustration around lack of communication from their Quality Specialists about a quality product. Let them discuss how poor communication, lack of clarity about goals, expectations, and so forth play a major part in frustration at work.

TEMPLE TREASURE: A TEAM CHALLENGE

Bill Matthews and Terry Swango

William R. Matthews *is a senior consultant/facilitator with Prism Performance Systems (37000 Grand River Ave., Suite 230, Farmington Hills, MI 48335, 810-474-8855, bmatt@msn.com). Bill's specialties include team, leadership and organizational development, systemic change, facilitation skills, and educational games and simulations. He is a member of the board of directors of the North American Simulation and Gaming Association. Bill is also an adjunct lecturer in Education at The University of Michigan-Dearborn, and coauthor of the book,* **101 Ways to Jump Start Your Job Search** *(McGraw-Hill, 1996).* **Terry Swango** *is a senior associate with Prism Performance Systems. Terry's specialties include systemic change, program development, design, and delivery. Terry has an ongoing interest in tools for affecting large systems change. Specifically, he has used search conferences, participative design workshops, and open spaces conferences to help organizations better involve key stakeholders in the process of charting their future direction.*

Overview   This activity has been very popular with our clients because of its simplicity and degree of challenge. It demonstrates pertinent issues relating to teamwork, paradigm challenges, cooperation *vs.* competition, leadership, followership, and more. Participants are challenged to work in teams to retrieve a treasure that is beyond their reach before time expires and the world explodes!

Suggested Time   45 to 60 minutes.

Materials Needed
- ✓ 2 pieces of rope approximately 30 ft. in length
- ✓ 2 buckets with removable handles (Rubbermaid makes good ones)
- ✓ 2 heavy duty bungee cords (use the heavy duty cords with molded, rather than wound metal, plastic ends for safety reasons)
- ✓ 8 pieces of rope about 8-10 ft. in length
- ✓ Form A (Temple Treasure Scenario)
- ✓ Form B (Keeper of the Company Store)
- ✓ Form C (Lead Archeologist)

Procedure

The Set-up

1. Take the two 20-ft. lengths of rope and form them into circles approximately 25-30 ft. apart.

2. Remove the handles from the buckets. Place one bucket in the center of each rope circle.

3. Off on the side somewhere, place the 8 smaller pieces of rope, 2 bungee cords, and the two bucket handles.

The Activity

1. You need at least 6 people for this activity, and preferably 8. Any number from 6 to 12 works well. With more than 12 people, set up an additional set of materials.

2. Gather the participants together and form them into two groups of approximately equal size.

3. Tell them the story of the Myth of the Temple Treasure. You may wish to use the role sheets (Forms B and C) if you decide to focus on the various team roles (See *Variations* and *Forms* for details). Otherwise, just read or describe the scenario (Form A) itself.

4. Remind them that they have 20 minutes to complete the task. Start the clock and observe what happens.

5. Monitor the play to make sure that no one inadvertently reaches or steps in the circles (if so, they lose the use of the offending limb). Here you may want to use extra participants as observers if you have any. If a "blowup" occurs, stop play briefly to mark the event but allow participants to continue to secure the treasure.

6. Call time after 20 minutes and debrief.

7. To increase the effect and add a little humor, throw a few rubber alligators, snakes, and other varmints into each circle.

The Debriefing

Use any of the following questions or others you develop to debrief, depending on your interests and desired outcomes.

✓ How successful do you feel you were in this activity? How did you define success?

✓ How did you go about planning your activities? How creative were you? How many times did you blow up?

✓ How did members of your team interact? How was work distributed?

✓ How did you work collaboratively with the other team? Or didn't you?

✓ What worked well during this activity? What would you do differently if you were to do it again?

✓ What if …

there was a real treasure?

one that couldn't be divided among the members?

there were real "toxins" to contend with?

Variations

1. If you want to add a focus on the various roles on an effective team, utilize Forms B and C, the role sheets for *Keeper of the Company Store* (champion/sponsor—one per activity) and the *Lead Archeologist* (team leader—one per team).

2. With this variation you can add the following debriefing questions …

    ✓ What was the nature of the interaction between the teams and the Keeper of the Company Store? Did the teams compete for the resources?

    ✓ What did the Keeper do that was helpful? Not helpful?

    ✓ How effective were the Lead Archeologists? What did they do that was helpful? Not helpful?

    ✓ What would you suggest be done differently by: a) the Keeper; b) the Lead Archeologists?

Many centuries ago, in a land not far from here, a great pharaoh decided to secure his place in history by leaving behind a treasure for future generations to reap.

The treasure consisted of two huge coffers overflowing with knowledge, wisdom, skills sets, and new paradigms—more valuable than the world's most expensive gems—that would make the owners successful in whatever business they desired.

Being concerned that his ancestors would be content to stay with the way things had always been done, the wise pharaoh planted the treasure in full view, so the masses would not have to search too hard to find it. But the pessimistic old pharaoh had another concern: that if the treasure was too easily within reach, people would not see the value in striving for it and not view it as worthy of their time or efforts.

So, he placed the two treasure coffers in the center of two small islets, just beyond arm's reach. Each of these islets was surrounded by a huge moat filled with crocodiles, alligators, poisonous snakes, and other rabid vermin; surrounded by water so vile that just reaching an arm, hand, or leg over the pool would cause the limb to immediately wither and fall off.

The pharaoh called forth his team of ageless master wizards to cast a spell over the treasure, protecting it from those known to be unworthy and unscrupulous.

Now, it is a well-known fact that every wizard worth his salt has a rather warped sense of humor. After much huddling, frenetic flailing about, and fits of frantic conjuring, the wizards came up with a spell to beat all spells.

A spell was cast such that to gain the treasure, one would have to pick up both treasure coffers at the exact same time, carry them to the opposite islet from where they came, and replace them back down in position again at the exact same moment. Failure to pick up or replace the two coffers at the exact same moment would result in an explosion powerful enough to blow up everything and everyone within a five-mile radius, but keeping the treasure safe for future expeditions. The ancient expression for this disaster is, "Sia Jai Luk Raboet," which roughly translates to, "Oops, ka-BOOM!!!"

Successfully completing the challenge of picking up the treasure coffers, exchanging them, and returning them at the same time, would break the spell, immediately drying up the vile pools, killing off all the nasty vermin and such, and allowing immediate access to the treasure, a safe return, and guaranteed success in business.

In one final mischievous act, the wizards cast a second spell, this one over the entire area surrounding the treasure isles; as soon as the challenge of the Temple Treasure has been accepted, the sands begin to fall from the hour glass, and in 20 minutes time, if the treasure has not been recovered, the entire area and everyone in it vaporizes. Dang Nan Sai Jai! (So Sorry!)

You are the keeper of the company store. As such, you have access to the many resources that could be used by any and all of the archeological expedition teams. Your current storehouse of resources includes:

- ✓ 8 lengths of rope of approximately equal size
- ✓ 2 bucket handles
- ✓ 2 bungee cords

These are the only supplies left in the store until the next fiscal year. The teams need not pay for these supplies; anything they use is just charged to their account (don't worry about the accounting).

Supply the teams with whatever they need, in any way you see fit. Just remember that these are the only supplies you and/or the teams have to work with (unless you can creatively use other things you can gather from the area about you).

As keeper of the store, feel free to offer any suggestions you think would help the teams accomplish their mission—to capture the treasure. You may make comments on the process being used and provide whatever direction, motivation, or guidance the teams are willing to accept. You can suggest that they think about the task or use resources differently, but you should not impose your will on a team.

Be as helpful as you can, without becoming overinvolved in actually picking up, moving, and replacing the treasure coffers. By the way, if any team is successful, you and the store get a bonus. If they fail, you also blow up with them!

As keeper of the company store, you have seen lots of unsuccessful teams come and go. You know that these unsuccessful archeological teams get so involved in trying to capture the treasure that they very often forget the following important information (which relates to their success criteria):

✓ Teams have 20 minutes from the start of the expedition to capture the treasure. At the 20-minute mark, everything (including the teams) vaporizes.

✓ Any member of the expedition team who reaches or steps into or over the moat area (surrounded by the rope) immediately loses the use of that extremity for the rest of the expedition.

✓ Failure to pick up both treasure coffers at the same time results in an explosion that devastates everything and everyone within 5 miles. (Participants will be allowed to continue the game after any explosions!)

Failure to replace the exchanged treasure coffers at the same time also results in an explosion that devastates everything and everyone within 5 miles.

As keeper of the company store, you have direct access to the g.o.d.'s (game overall directors) to answer any questions that may come up during the expedition. But don't be surprised if they don't always have an answer.

You are the head of an archeology team that has been charged by your company to get the secrets of the Temple Treasure for your organization. There is at least one other team that has been given the same challenge.

You need to bring your team together as quickly as possible to plan and execute how you will capture the treasure. Keep the following in mind at all times:

✓ You have 20 minutes from the start of the expedition to capture the treasure. At the 20-minute mark, everything (including your team) vaporizes.

✓ Any member of the expedition team who reaches or steps into or over the moat area (surrounded by the rope) immediately loses the use of that extremity for the rest of the expedition.

✓ Failure to pick up both treasure coffers at the same time results in an explosion that devastates everything and everyone within 5 miles. (Your team will be allowed to continue playing after any explosions.)

✓ Failure to replace the exchanged treasure coffers at the same time also results in an explosion that devastates everything and everyone within 5 miles.

You may obtain any supplies you need from the keeper of the company store. There is no charge up front, just put it on your account. Though some people are convinced that the storekeeper is senile, others suggest that the storekeeper could offer you some ideas on how to best proceed. It's up to you whether or not you ask for or listen to any advice given by the storekeeper.

The keeper of the company store also has direct access to the g.o.d.'s (game overall directors), who can answer any questions that may arise during your expeditions.

CREATING SUCCESSFUL TEAMS: A CARD SORT EXERCISE

Sophie Liebman-Oberstein

Sophie Liebman-Oberstein *is Senior Consultant for Key Managment Strategies (7906 Montgomery Avenue, Elkins Park, PA 19027, 215-635-6170, x131). She has published articles in* **Training and Development** *magazine on keeping participants enthusiastic and on designing creative training efforts. She is also an instructor in the training certificate program at Mercer County Community College.*

Overview This activity allows those thinking about forming a team in their organizations, or those involved in a team still in its initial stages, to become familiar with the factors that ensure a team's effectiveness. Rather than hearing a lecturer present a list of 20 items that would contribute to an effective team, participants come to their own understanding of the broad questions that every new team must address, making the content more memorable. The activity is intended as an introduction that will open the door for further discussion of the factors necessary to create a successful team.

Suggested Time 35 minutes.

Materials Needed ✓ 20 index cards, each containing one of the phrases from Form A
✓ Form B (Creating Successful Teams)
✓ Four pieces of chart paper
✓ Masking tape
✓ Markers

Procedure 1. Before beginning the activity, prepare four pieces of chart paper that each display one of the following questions:
✓ What organizational support is required?
✓ What must be established in the first team meeting?
✓ How does the team work together to achieve long-term success?
✓ What individual characteristics should team members possess?

43

Post the four prepared chart papers around the room, covering up the heading on each one until you are ready to reveal it.

2. Tell participants that this exercise will give them the opportunity to learn about the factors considered to be essential for successful teams.

3. Ask participants to assume the role of a member of senior management at a corporation. Explain that senior management has just created a team to help the corporation evaluate what new business directions to explore. Ask participants—in the role of senior managers—to respond to each of the following four questions one at a time. Chart their responses on the appropriately labeled chart papers.

    ✓ What organizational support will you provide to the team you are forming?

    ✓ What would you advise that the team try to establish in its first meeting?

    ✓ What advice would you give the team members about how they should work together to achieve long-term success?

    ✓ What individual characteristics should team members possess to create a productive team?

4. Explain that the questions you just asked the participants are the four broad questions that a team must address in order to be successful. Within each question, certain factors will positively impact a team's effectiveness, like the ones that they just provided.

5. Tell participants that they are going to compare their responses to factors identified by several experts on team development. Explain that the expert's suggestions are written on cards and that participants should work together to sort out the cards according to the four broad questions on the flip charts.

    If you wish to provide an example, ask participants: If the factor on the card is "Active Senior Management Support," which of the four broad questions would that factor answer? (Guide participants to the correct response: What organizational support is required?)

6. Shuffle the 20 cards you have created from Form A and evenly distribute them to each participant and ask each person to tape the card(s) received to the proper chart paper posted on the wall. Explain that when they have finished, there should be five cards taped to each chart. Encourage participants to work collectively. They have up to ten minutes to sort the cards.

7. Distribute Form B. Ask participants to review it.

8. Reconvene and discuss the significance of the answers. First, talk about the placement of the factors within the four broad question categories. Find out what was easy and what was more difficult about categorizing the factors. Then, compare participants' initial respons-

es to the factors identified on Form B. Be sure to reinforce the value of their own thoughts. Finally, solicit participants' opinions of the four broad questions and of the 20 factors for successful teams.

Variations

1. Instead of telling the group the four broad questions up front, introduce the activity by stating: "There are 20 factors that determine a team's effectiveness and these factors can be categorized into four broad categories." Without further explanation, distribute the cards to the whole group and ask participants to try to divide the cards into four distinct categories of five cards each. When they are finished, they should name the categories they've created and prepare to explain their categorizing rationale. Finally, distribute Form B and compare the group's responses to those provided.

2. Break the large group into four subgroups. Assign each subgroup one of the four broad questions and allow them ten minutes to brainstorm possible responses. Ask each subgroup to chart its responses on a flip chart and to be prepared to share its responses with the large group. After each subgroup has presented its responses, distribute Form B and compare subgroup responses with those identified. This variation is helpful if your group is larger (more than 20 participants) or if it is a group that does not put a great deal of credibility in solving puzzles or playing games as a training methodology.

Active senior management support

Problems to solve that matter immediately to the organization

Adequate budget and resources

Organizational systems that are compatible to working in teams

Necessary training for team members

Common goals

Team member roles

Clear rules of behavior/communication

Procedures

Immediate tasks to work on

Ensure equal participation and contribution of team members

Make feedback, recognition, and reward part of the regular team agenda

Become mutually accountable for results

Celebrate team accomplishments

Create opportunities for occasional socializing

A strong performance ethic

A cooperative, not a competitive, mindset

A high level of communication skills

A sense of empowerment; authority to act

Appreciation of complementary skills of team members

To be successful, a team must address four broad questions. Within each question, certain factors will positively impact a team's effectiveness.

What organizational support is required?	*What must be established in the first team meeting?*
Active senior management support	Common goals
Problems to solve that matter immediately to the organization	Team member roles
Adequate budget and resources	Clear rules of behavior/communication
Organizational systems that are compatible to working in teams	Procedures
Necessary training for team members	Immediate tasks to work on

How does the team work together to achieve long-term success?	*What individual characteristics should team members possess?*
Ensure equal participation and contribution of team members	A strong performance ethic
Make feedback, recognition, and reward part of the regular team agenda	A cooperative, not a competitive, mindset
Become mutually accountable for results	A high level of communication skills
Celebrate team accomplishments	A sense of empowerment; authority to act
Creat opportunities for occasional socializing	Appreciation of complementary skills of team members

BUILDING A COMMUNICATIONS TOWER: AN EXPERIENCE IN TEAMWORK

Thomas Baker

Thomas Baker *has been involved in education and training for over twenty years. He started his full-service training and development business, Thomas Baker Associates (31640 Wekiva River Road, Suite 100, Sorrento, FL 32776, 352-735-1030, tbaker@digital.net), in 1986 and personally specializes in stress management and communications. He has developed innovative training for national and international companies and various colleges and educational groups. Tom has developed and presented programs in Interpersonal Relations, Handling Difficult People, Time Management, Goal Setting, and Stress Management and has presented papers on training and personal development.*

Overview The Communications Tower can be used for many training experiences, including team training, communications classes, and supervisory and leadership programs. The discussion questions can be changed to focus the value of the experience. The discussion questions in this example are geared toward team training. The experience is always perceived as fun and meaningful. The Communications Tower becomes a significant symbol of the learning experience.

Suggested Time 45 to 60 minutes.

Materials Needed

✓ 7/64″ drill bits (stock up because they become dull)

✓ Safety glasses

✓ Electric drill

✓ Simple drill holder to simulate a drill press (not absolutely necessary, but useful)

✓ Box of craft sticks (purchase at hobby or crafts store)

[Drill holes at the ends of the craft sticks so that the holes are equidistant from the sides and the end of the sticks. Fifty-eight sticks are required for each team of the class. Teams of from four to seven are required for the exercise.]

✓ 31 4-40 round slotted stove bolts, 5/8″ (purchase at hardware store)

✓ 31 matching hex nuts

✓ Container to hold nuts and bolts (35 mm film containers work well)

✓ 1 copy of Form A (Communications Tower blueprint) for each team

✓ Copy of Form B (Discussion Questions) for each participant

✓ Copy of Form C (Flip Chart Activity) for each participant

✓ 1 bag of candy

✓ Sufficient table room for each team to work effectively (finished size of the Communications Tower is 33″ high by 20″ wide)

✓ Flip chart and markers

✓ Masking tape

Procedure

1. Make enough kits for the size of your class. Plan to put 4 to 7 people on each team. Each team needs a kit.

   Each kit contains:

   a. 58 prepared craft sticks bundled in rubber bands

   b. 31 4-40 round slotted stove bolts, 5/8″ (purchase at hardware store)

   c. 31 matching hex nuts

   d. Container to hold nuts and bolts (35 mm film containers work well)

2. Explain that you are going to divide participants into teams to build a Communications Tower.

3. Put 4 to 7 people on each team.

4. Ask each team to identify the person on the team who has the earliest birthday in the calendar year. These people will be the team leaders.

5. Meet privately with the team leaders to do the following:

   a. Give the team leaders the materials for building the tower—one kit including container with nuts and bolts, blueprint, and sticks in rubber band.

   b. Tell them their team must come up with a written secret bid on the amount of time that they will need to build the Communications Tower. **Stress the secrecy of the bid.**

   c. Explain that the facilitator must be able to pick up the Communications Tower and hold it. It must conform to the blueprint and be built within the time they have bid.

   d. Tell them they will have 10 minutes to decide on a bid.

   e. They may write on the blueprint but not on the sticks.

   f. Ask if they have any questions, but try not to give them any more information.

6. After 10 minutes, have the team leaders meet with you privately to compare written secret bids.

   a. Look at all bids without team leaders seeing each other's bids.

   b. Regardless of what they are, tell the team leaders that you will let them all build a tower, so long as they finish within the time they have bid. The winner will be the team that finished the tower first, so long as it is built within their bid time. Once their time is up, the team is disqualified. Tell them to build the Communications Tower so that it is rigid enough to pick up by the top stick and show to other teams.

   c. Tell them the starting time will be announced two minutes after team leaders get back to their teams. Team leaders need to explain the directions to their teams.

   d. Tell them that when the start time is announced, all craft sticks must be in their rubber bands and all nuts and bolts must be in their closed containers.

7. After two minutes announce the start time.

8. Wander around watching the action, but do not become a part of any of the teams. Do not answer additional questions. Just say, "You'll need to check with your team leader on that," or "The team will have to decide."

9. As the shortest bid time approaches, that team will be frantic. Once one team finishes, pick up the tower and compare it to the blueprint. Make sure it is sturdy. If all checks out, declare them the winners. Tell the others to quit. (They won't.)

10. Award the bag of candy to the winning team.

11. Have them take the Communications Towers apart and place the nuts and bolts in the containers and sticks in the rubber bands.

12. Debrief the exercise by asking the teams to select a spokesperson different from the team leader. The spokesperson will be giving the class a summary of what his or her team discussed.

13. Distribute Form B—**Discussion Questions.** Have participants discuss them within their teams.

14. Have spokespersons give reports for their teams.

15. Once the teams have discussed the questions on Form B, have them do Form C—**Flip Chart Activity.** Hand out a sheet of flip chart paper to each team. Then tell them to come up with two responses for the first two questions.

16. Explain that the third question will have as many different answers as there are people on the team and will be shared just in their teams. Each person needs to complete the sentence, "Because of what I learned from the Communications Tower exercise, the behavior I can change on the job is _____."

17. Have spokespersons share responses to the first two questions with the class. Give prizes to the team that volunteers to be first. Use masking tape to put their flip chart paper where everyone can see it.

Notes:

1. Put a tower together yourself first to be sure it works as planned.

2. Give directions very explicitly. If teams do not keep their bids totally secret, it can ruin the exercise.

3. In the many times the tower has been built, only one team tried to overlap the sticks exactly as they are on the blueprint. This is not necessary. You may want to include that fact in the directions.

4. The shortest time to actually build the tower can vary considerably with various groups, from 9 to 25 minutes.

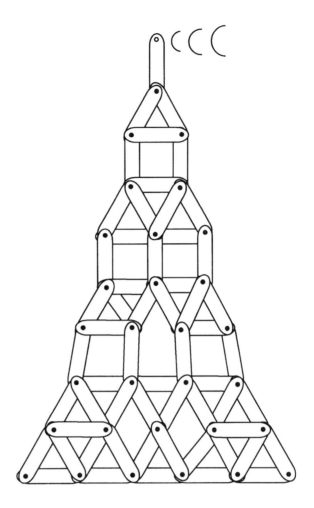

Team Building	Design Specifications for Bids	Materials Required for Tower # 14
Designers: Talk & Squawk	**Communications Tower # 14**	58 Girders (sticks) 31 Fasteners (assorted

Figure 8.1.

1. What are some of the things that your team did to be as effective as possible?

2. If you were to do the exercise again, what would you do differently?

3. What did the team leader do to help the process?

4. Who else served as leaders? How?

5. Did anyone not participate? Why?

6. What did you learn from this exercise?

1. What is the most important thing that you learned from the activity?

2. What would you do differently if you were to do the activity again?

[Question 3 is not answered on the flip chart. Instead each member of the team will answer the question to other members of the team.]

3. On the job, what change of behavior could you make as a result of what you learned today?

"Because of what I learned from the Communications Tower exercise, the behavior I can change on the job is _____."

DISCUSSING TEAM ISSUES BEFORE THEY BECOME PROBLEMS: CASE EXERCISES

9

Brenda Gardner and Sharon Korth

Brenda S. Gardner, *Ph.D. is Assistant Professor and Director of the Executive HRD Graduate Program at Xavier University (3800 Victory Parkway, Cincinnati, OH 45207-6521, 513-745-4287, gardner@xavier.xu.edu). She is on the board of the Academy of HRD and has extensive experience in training and organization development in public and private organizations.* **Sharon J. Korth,** *Ed.D. is Assistant Professor of HRD at Xavier University (513-745-4276, korth@xavier.xu.edu). She has chapters in* **In Action: Conducting Needs Assessment,** *edited by Jack Phillips & Elwood Holton, Alexandria, VA: ASTD, 1995, and* **ASTD Toolkit: More Needs Assessment Instruments,** *edited by John Wilcox, Alexandria, VA: ASTD, 1994. Sharon and Brenda were contributors to* **The 1996 McGraw-Hill Team and Organization Sourcebook.**

Overview   Many quality teams and long-term task forces/committees struggle with similar issues over extended time periods. This exercise is designed to help such teams address many of the common events that occur in the beginning, in the middle, and near the end of a project. By participating in these case exercises, team members have the opportunity to deal with these issues proactively and to voice their concerns and attitudes in a nonthreatening, neutral environment. The exercise will also help teams develop a list of team norms that can help them monitor their own behaviors.

Suggested Time   40 to 50 minutes for each round of cases.

Materials Needed   *For each team member:*

   ✓ A copy of Form A (for the first round at the beginning of the team's development), Form B (for the second round at some point after the fourth meeting or first month of the team's development), and Form C (for the third round after the midpoint of the team's lifecycle).

   ✓ For the third team meeting, a copy of the team norms developed at the second meeting of the team.

Procedure

1. As a facilitator/trainer/leader of an intact team that is just forming, discuss with team members the value of discussing issues that oftentimes occur when teams have to work closely together in problem-solving, task, or ongoing advisory situations. Depending upon your objectives and/or role within the team, you might want to provide them with an overview of a team development model such as Tuckman's (1965) "Forming, Norming, Storming, Performing," Francis & Young's (1992) "Testing, Infighting, Getting Organized, Mature Closeness," or Schutz's (1958) theory of group norms of "Inclusion, Control, Affection."

2. At the end of the first meeting, distribute Form A to each team member. Ask them to read the case and be prepared to discuss their responses to the questions for the next team meeting. Suggest that the issues raised in the case may not necessarily occur in their team but that discussing what reactions/solutions members have about the points raised in the case may help them learn about how members feel about these behaviors and situations. Reassure members that the cases are fictitious and were not written based upon any previous experience with a specific team in their organization/setting. Tell team members that this fictitious team will be followed through a lifecycle similar to theirs.

3. At the next meeting of the team, facilitate a discussion of the members' responses to the case questions. Depending upon the size of the team, you might want to break up the team into smaller teams of 4 to 6 members who can report back to the total team. During the discussion, be sure to steer comments away from members naming specific people in the organization who may exhibit similar behaviors. The goal of the discussion is for the team to air any concerns that they may have about teamwork and to develop a list of team norms that may be used throughout the team's lifecycle. Be sure to keep notes during the discussion so that you can facilitate discussion about team norms.

4. After the general discussion is over, ask members if you can summarize the issues the team discussed and their general consensus about the situations so that the team will have a list of norms that they can use to monitor their own behavior as their time together progresses. Post on a flipchart the major issues that may have surfaced:

   Attendance
   Consensus
   Role Clarity
   Minutes
   Agenda
   Conflict Management
   Disruptive Behavior
   Appropriate Leadership
   Commitment

Goal Agreement & Clarity
Participation Patterns
Constructive Feedback Mechanisms
Achievement Orientation
Follow-up Mechanisms
Problem-solving Techniques
Decision-making Techniques

Be sure that members agree with your summarization and understanding of how they perceive the situations. Volunteer to have the team norms typed and distributed at the next meeting. You might ask members if they'd like to have a large poster of the norms available at each of their meetings for reference/review.

5. At the next meeting of the team, distribute copies of the norms to all team members and leave time available to discuss any new thoughts/concerns that may have surfaced since the original discussion.

6. Depending upon how long the team will be in existence, distribute Form B to each team member at about the fourth team meeting (or after the first month) for discussion at the fifth team meeting. Remind members that the goal of the case is to help members voice concerns about how team norms are followed and how they suggest such situations be managed.

7. At the fifth team meeting, lead a discussion of the new issues that have surfaced in this case. Lead the discussion to a review of their team norms and how the case dealt with revisions/adjustments/observance of their own norms.

8. Depending again upon the length of the team's experience, distribute Form C to each team member after the midpoint of their time together or after the midpoint of a project they've been working on. Again, tell the team that this fictitious team has been dealing with a number of issues that may or may not have occurred in their own team and that the goal of following this case is to build a more effective and efficient team by addressing issues that commonly impede this process. Ask them to discuss their responses to the case and take the opportunity once again to review the team norms they developed/revised since the first team meeting.

Variations

✓ You might want to rewrite the cases to reflect common issues that occur in your own organization. Don't make the cases too realistic, however, or members will think that you are identifying "problem" team members, not fictitious people. Examples of other common issues in organizations may be supervisor-subordinate roles in the team, changing deadlines, inappropriate membership, union-management relations, and individual vs. team recognition and/or rewards.

✓ If your team has a major project it is working on, you might revise the cases to reflect milestones, and time the distribution and discussion of the cases according to these identified milestones.

✓ Instead of distributing the cases at the end of a meeting and having the team members discuss the questions at the next meeting, you could pass out the case, have the team read it, and have them discuss the case immediately.

✓ If the issue of changing membership (i.e., someone leaving the team due to promotion, leaving the organization, changed roles, etc.) will be part of your team, you might want to add this character to either Case B or Case C to substitute for Ambitious Ann:

Substitute Sam

__ 30-year-old male

__ 6 years' experience with the organization

__ has reported to Ambitious Ann for 3 years

__ is aware that Ann has played a leadership role with the team

__ concerned about how his facilitative style will be received by the team

__ feels much pressure to be successful

REFERENCES

Fisher, C. D., Shaw, J. B., and Ryder, P. (1994) Problems in project teams: An anticipatory case study. *Journal of Management Education, 18,* (3), 351-355.

Francis, D., and Young, D. (1992). *Improving Work Teams.* (Rev. ed.). San Diego: Pfeiffer & Co.

Osgood, T. Forming, norming, storming & performing: A card sort exercise. In M. Silberman (Ed.), *The 1996 McGraw-Hill Team and Organization Development Sourcebook* (pp. 5-10). New York: McGraw-Hill.

Schutz, W. C. (1958) *FIRO: A Three-dimensional Theory of Interpersonal Behavior.* New York: Holt, Rinehart & Winston.

Tuckman, B. (1965) Developmental sequence in small teams. *Psychological Bulletin, 63,* 384-399.

Read over the case, answer the questions individually, and be prepared to discuss your responses with your team members.

The team in the following case is being formed and will be working together for an extended period of time. During this time, the team will have responsibility for certain decisions, recommendations, and/or products and must report to their sponsors as requested. The team members in the case are fictitious and were not written based on any previous team in your organization/setting. Although the issues raised in the case may not necessarily occur in your team, discussing reactions and possible solutions for the case team may help your team learn how members feel about certain behaviors and situations throughout your team's life cycle.

The team consists of:

Intuitive Ike

___ 35-year-old male

___ 2 years with this organization; owned and managed a small business for 10 years

___ likes thinking about the "big picture" and looking at connections between various organizational systems

___ very well read on leadership and interpersonal issues

___ gets bored with the details of projects

___ thinks that this team should meet after hours into the evening

___ works best under pressure from a close deadline

Planful Pat

___ 27-year-old female

___ 8 years of experience in this organization; recently promoted

___ feels anxious about the pressure that comes with her new position

___ likes handling the details of a project; likes to plan and organize things

___ favors completing work comfortably ahead of the deadline

___ prefers to meet often, during work hours, to make sure that things are getting done

___ cannot stay after hours without prior planning due to child care arrangements

Ambitious Ann

___ 40-year-old female

___ 10 years of work experience with this organization; 10 years elsewhere in a similar function

___ often takes over the work of others to make sure that it meets her standards

___ is not particularly concerned with "people issues"

___ is impatient with people who do not make decisions quickly

___ has excellent project management skills

___ prefers to have lengthy meetings once a week, after work hours because it is more efficient

Supportive Sue

___ 26-year-old female

___ 3 years of experience with this organization

___ feels honored to be a part of this team, with her limited work experience

___ will do anything to help the team, especially behind-the-scene tasks

___ very quiet in team meetings; reluctant to speak in front of large teams

___ wants to make a good impression

___ afraid to admit that she does not understand something

___ uncomfortable with conflict; likes harmony

Political Paul

___ 50-year-old male

___ 25 years of experience in the organization

___ hoping that being on this team will help him get the promotion he thinks he deserves

___ wants to be involved in the roles that provide greater visibility in the organization

___ overlooks his responsibilities to the team if something else would benefit him more

___ his work experience gives him valuable information that will help the team succeed

___ is reluctant to set a regular schedule for meeting; likes to call impromptu meetings when needed

Case Team

1. What are the positive elements about this team that could help it be successful?

2. What issues are likely to limit the team's success?

3. What can the team do to get off to a strong start?

Your Team

1. How can you relate the issues of the case team to your current team?

2. What might your current team be able to do to enhance its ability to work together?

3. What are some norms that your team could develop that would help deal with these issues?

Read over the case, answer the questions individually, and be prepared to discuss your responses with team members.

It is now about a month after the team was formed and the first big milestone is coming soon. Ambitious Ann has been acting as the informal leader of the team and Planful Pat has been scheduling the meetings and keeping minutes. When Supportive Sue offered to take a turn with the minutes, Ann quickly told her that Pat has been doing that task very well and will continue throughout the project.

Whenever the team seems close to a decision on an item, Intuitive Ike offers several other options which throws the team back to the beginning. Both Ike and Political Paul have expressed that they think the team spends too much time on details and not enough on strategic issues. Over the past month, Supportive Sue has been very quiet in meetings, rarely speaking. The one time she offered a suggestion, Ann told her that the decision had already been made.

Political Paul has missed several meetings. Sue contacted him to see if he was planning to come to the next meeting and to ask about the progress on his portion of the project. After talking to Paul, Sue started doing the behind-the-scenes work for Paul and speaking in his behalf at the meetings.

As the deadline for the first milestone approaches, Ike has not completed his part of the project, but assures the team that he will have it by the deadline. Sue is working on both her part and Paul's. Ann volunteers to pull the whole project together, with the help of Pat. The team agrees to meet again one hour before their deadline to make sure that everything is ready.

Questions for Discussion:

Case Team

1. What issues have surfaced with this team?
2. How would you describe the situation from the perspective of each team member?
3. What suggestions do you have for this team to improve its effectiveness?

Your Team

1. How do the issues raised in the case team relate to your team's norms?
2. What are ways to revise, adjust, or observe your team norms that will help make your team more effective?

Read over the case, answer the questions individually, and be prepared to discuss your responses with team members.

It is now after the midpoint of the team's time together. The feedback from the sponsors has been generally positive, especially for Political Paul's part. Intuitive Ike's portion, completed at the last minute without feedback from others, was not consistent with the other parts of the project, which upset the other team members.

There is a significant amount of work yet to be completed by the team. Although they have had successes and continue to receive support and encouragement from the sponsors, the team has lost momentum. Ambitious Ann has been focusing her energy on another big project and she has missed the last two meetings. Pat has tried to take over the team leadership but her attempts to run the meetings do not seem to have the backing of Paul and Ike. Supportive Sue is becoming more confident in her role with the team because of Paul's support.

Pat is very worried that the team does not have the energy and commitment to meet the upcoming milestones and is frustrated because her attempts to make things happen have been to no avail. She leaves messages with each of the members expressing her concerns.

Questions for Discussion:

Case Team

1. What has happened to this team?
2. How have the roles changed?
3. What can they do to salvage the team?

Your Team

1. Has your team been following the norms it has developed?
2. How might you apply learning from the case team to your own team?
3. What can your team do to keep focused, healthy, and productive?

STRATEGIC SQUARES: IMPROVING THE QUALITY OF STRATEGIC PLANNING

10

Tom Devane

Thomas J. Devane *is president of Premier Integration Enterprises (317 Lookout View Court, Golden, CO 80401, 303-279-1099, tdevane@usa.net). Tom specializes in organizational development, Total Quality Management, fast cycle time, and activity-based costing. He is an author and international speaker on the topic of combining technical and human elements of large-scale change for knowledge work organizations. Tom is also a contributor to* **20 Active Training Programs,** *vol. III (Pfeiffer, in press).*

Overview Strategic Squares is a useful exercise for improving the quality of strategic planning in an organization. It's ideal to use in a newly formed or existing team, but can also be utilized as a simulation exercise in a training session. Any fan of "systems thinking" who has read Peter Senge's *Fifth Discipline* understands that in a complex system, it's more important to focus on the *interrelationships* of various components than it is to focus on selected *components* within the system. Strategic Squares provides a simple, easy-to-learn framework in which to apply this important principle.

Suggested Time 30 to 60 minutes.

Materials Needed ✓ Form A (Strategic Square), one copy per participant

Procedure 1. Explain that the purpose of this exercise is to create a relatively risk-free environment for team members to discuss and articulate ideas that will improve the organization.

2. Distribute Form A. Indicate that major ideas for change, ideally, improve the quality of services/products, lower costs, and show respect for the individuals who are affected by the change. In an ideal world, all three criteria are met. In a less than ideal world, some go by the wayside or actually conflict. Explain that the strategic square is designed so that a team can generate and/or assess change ideas by considering the interrelationships between these factors.

3. Ask the team to generate up to six change ideas that meet the two criteria suggested by each open box. Point out that no one factor should supersede the other. For example, a change idea that both improves the quality of service/product and, at the same time, shows respect for the individuals affected by the change would be placed in the box found in the first row, second column *or* in the box found in the second row, first column.

4. A team that has already developed some change initiatives can use the square to assess those initiatives. Which interrelationships do they support? They can also ask themselves how the interrelationships between any two factors could be maximized in the future.

Variation

When you want to use the strategic square in a training session in which intact teams do not exist, do the following:

1. Organize into subgroups. Each subgroup will represent a senior management team for an organization. Attempt to group people together who have similar industries, contexts, roles, and so forth.

2. Provide a copy of Form A to each subgroup. Explain that they are to assume the role of a senior management team that is charged with articulating a change strategy that maximizes the interrelationships suggested by the Strategic Square.

3. Ask each group to generate change ideas (appropriate to their common industry, context, or role) that meet the two criteria suggested by each open box.

4. Promote a sharing of ideas across groups and discuss their reactions to the exercise.

	Service/Product Quality	Respect for the Individual	Low Cost
Service/Product Quality			
Respect for the Individual			
Low Cost			

11
KEEP 'EM FLYING:
A TEAM DEVELOPMENT ACTIVITY

Ron Lawrence

Ron Lawrence *(48 Deer Creek Drive, Amelia, OH, 45102-2110, 513-752-7594) is an organization effectiveness mamager for Anthem Blue Cross and Blue Shield, a managed care organization serving Ohio, Kentucky, and Indiana. Ron has over ten years' experience in project management, organizational change and Total Quality Management.*

Overview This activity is designed to help team members realize the value of cooperation in planning and executing tasks, especially in project-heavy situations. Designed for quick use and processing, the activity offers safe, physical involvement that can be enjoyed by persons of any age or fitness level while providing a light opening to address serious, substantive content. It is most effective in teams of 8-12, though the activity is flexible and can be adapted for larger or smaller groups. For teams that are newly assembled or project teams that have just been chartered, the activity is a fun introduction to teamwork. A variation of the activity works equally well with strategic planning teams that are wrestling with issues of resource allocation. It is most useful when facilitating groups that are:

✓ Learning to work together as a team.
✓ Beginning to develop plans for managing and supporting numerous initiatives.
✓ Discovering the need for member interdependence.

Suggested Time 20 minutes.

Materials Needed
✓ 1 package of balloons
✓ Colored markers
✓ Flip chart
✓ Suitably large meeting room

Procedure

1. Explain that team members are usually individually responsible for a number of projects and/or tasks, and that like a juggler in a circus, each member "juggles these many priorities while trying to keep all of the balls in the air." State that it often becomes progressively more challenging for each individual to accomplish this juggling act alone.

2. Give each member of the team a number of balloons and a marker. Instruct the team members to inflate the balloons. Decide in advance if there might be members for whom inflating the balloons could be difficult; if so, give each team member preinflated balloons.

3. Instruct each member to write two- to three-word descriptors of tasks that they will need to accomplish in the setting, one descriptive phrase per balloon. For example, an executive planning session prioritizing company projects might yield balloons with the following phrases written on them:

   NEW PRODUCT #1, ACQUIRE CERTIFICATION, RETAIN LICENSURE, ENTER NEW MARKET, INSTALL NEW COMPUTER SYSTEM, NEW OFFICE SPACE, ADD GENERAL LEDGER SOFTWARE, etc.

   Encourage each team member to come up with at least five to ten items/projects that he or she "owns" and "champions."

4. Using the open floor space in the meeting room—you may have to create this space if there is a lot of furniture—gather the team members and their balloons in a wide circle. The circle's diameter should be determined by having each individual stand with both arms fully extended; no two members' outstretched hands should be touching.

5. Tell each member that they will be told to toss all of their balloons into the air and that they will have to keep "hitting" them to keep them flying. Instruct the team members that they may only hit "their" balloons, not each others'. Also, instruct the team members that they may not "catch" balloons; they may only "tap" the balloons to keep them airborne. State that each member is responsible for his or her balloons, because these balloons are his/her tasks. Warn that if a balloon hits the ground, it cannot be picked back up and tossed again. Remind the members to be careful not to hit each other when trying to tap balloons.

6. Have the team members toss their balloons into the air and follow the instructions from step five. Allow 1 minute for the team members to discover that some balloons have been "dropped."

7. Stop the team and ask each member to notice how many of their balloons "dropped." Have everyone gather their respective balloons and resume their original places in the circle. Tell them that now they can hit each others' balloons as well as their own, but

that each member is still responsible for keeping their own balloons flying. Remind them that if a balloon hits the ground, it cannot be picked back up and tossed again.

8. Have the team members toss their balloons into the air and follow the instructions from step seven. Allow 1 minute for the team to keep hitting the balloons. Watch to see if the members begin to help each other by "rescuing" each others' balloons before they drop, or if the members begin to pursue individual agendas and start "batting down" others' balloons.

9. Stop the activity and ask each team member to notice how many of their balloons "dropped." While the members remain standing, discuss the activity with the group. Ask questions such as the following:

    ✓ What did you notice that was different between the first and second times the team did the activity?

    ✓ Did you keep more balloons aloft when you were operating as individuals or when you were able to help each other?

    ✓ What did you do to create trust and cooperation within the team? What did you do that discouraged it?

10. Tell the team that now they have one common goal: to keep all or as many of the balloons aloft as possible. They can move closer together or farther apart, they can trade and/or share balloons, they can do whatever they want to do—but all of the balloons belong to the entire team, and the entire team is responsible for successfully keeping them flying.

11. Have the team members toss their balloons into the air and follow the instructions from step ten. Allow 1 minute for the team to keep hitting the balloons.

12. Stop the team and ask the members to notice how many of their balloons dropped. Have the team members go back to their seats and sit down.

13. Discuss the activity with the team. Use questions to guide the discussion, and record answers on a flip chart.

    ✓ *How did you feel as the activity progressed?* Answers may include: greater satisfaction when we were working together; easier to be successful when we had a clear, shared goal; it was more fun when I could help out my teammates.

    ✓ *How do you think this activity relates to what your team has been asked to do?* Answers may include: it shows the importance of teamwork; members may have to let others handle "their" tasks in order for the team to complete all of them; not all projects/tasks are equal, so team should focus on critical tasks first.

✓ *What barriers exist that may challenge your ability to work effectively as a team?* Answers may include: it's difficult for members to let go of projects/tasks in which they are personally/emotionally invested; company culture places higher value on some tasks than others, so members may not feel their tasks get equal consideration.

14. Conclude the activity by stating that it was meant to get them thinking about the advantages of teamwork, as well as the challenges that exist in learning to work together for the benefit of the team and not just the individual.

12

BUILDING BLOCKS: PRACTICE IN EFFECTIVE TEAM LEADERSHIP

Richard Whelan and Robert Merritt

Richard Whelan *is director of Associated Consultants for Training & Education (P.O. Box 5312, Deptford, NJ, 08096, 609-227-4273). He designs, develops and delivers training programs pertaining to human resource and mental health issues for organizations in both the public and private sectors.* **Robert Merritt,** *Ph.D. is a senior consultant with Associated Consultants for Training & Education. He is an applied social psychologist specializing in organization development and management training, working in both the private and public sectors.*

Overview Too often team leaders forget they are managing people and not just projects. Since people are the integral factor in any successful project or task, how they function in a team is crucial. An effective team leader needs to know how team members behave on an individual basis and how this affects team performance. This activity will provide team leaders with experience in recognizing and integrating team member performance into successful project completion. It can be used in intervening with problems in a work team or diagnosing team problems.

Suggested Time 45 to 60 minutes.

Materials Needed ✓ Easel
✓ Flip chart pad
✓ Note paper for each participant
✓ Markers
✓ Form A (What Successful Teams Do) for each leader
✓ Sets of Role Behavior Cards (from Text in Form B) for each team
✓ 5 boxes of wooden, multicolored, toy building blocks (each box should contain about 25-30 blocks of different size and shape)

Procedure 1. Have the participants count off so they are in groups of 5 or 6 depending on the total number in the class. (Six in a group is ideal.)

2. Give each group a box of building blocks and have them dump them out on a flat level surface (the floor or a table will work fine, as long as it is flat and level).

3. Show a flip chart page that has the following instructions:

   As a team, you are challenged to construct a sturdy, freestanding tower using all the blocks (and only the blocks) given to your group.

4. Choose one person randomly from each group. Announce that this individual will act as the "team leader."

5. Take the "leaders" out of the room and give them each a copy of Form A and tell them to read it. At the same time, tell them they are the leaders of a project group that is together for a short time—until this project is completed. Their role as leaders is to insure the teams' successful completion of the project in the time allowed, following the suggestions on Form A.

6. While the "leaders" are out of the room, have each participant take 5 minutes and **individually** plan out how the tower can be constructed, following the directions on the flip chart page. Remind them they are not to consult with other team members on their plans. You can give them note paper for this portion.

7. At the end of the 5-minute planning session, give each participant one "Role Behavior Card," insuring each member of each small group has a different card. Instruct the participants that this is to be their behavior style while working in the team. However, they should remember to be open to the influences around them, acting/changing accordingly. This means that they are not to be so adamant in their roles that they will never change. However, they should hold on to their role behavior unless convinced otherwise. **The "team leaders" are not to know their team members have received these cards and team members should not be sharing their roles with each other.**

8. Have the "leaders" rejoin their respective teams and start them on the task, allowing about 15 minutes for it. When time is up, acknowledge the product of each group but quickly segue to the debriefing of the exercise.

9. Have the team members read their behavior cards to each other and to the leader. Ask the groups to discuss the following questions:

   ✓ How well was the assigned task accomplished?

   ✓ How well did the leader diagnose the problems occurring in the group?

   ✓ What did the team leader do to form the individuals into a team, despite the conflicts that existed?

   ✓ What, if anything, would you do differently if you were the team leader?

10. At this point, the activity can be drawn to a close by asking for the "learning" from the exercise, helping participants transfer what they learned from the activity to actual team leadership challenges back on the job.

Variation

If the activity is going too "smoothly," certain "obstacles" can be added during the course of activity. Such obstacles could include:

✓ random elimination of certain shaped blocks

✓ disallowing certain color blocks

✓ height restrictions (announcing the tower can be no taller than 4′ since it is part of a larger structure)

✓ when the groups look like they are in the middle of completion, announce there are only 2 minutes left

✓ Clarify their goals.

✓ Clearly define team roles.

✓ Create ground rules.

✓ Engage in 2-way communication.

✓ Have a well-defined decision process.

✓ Balance participation.

YOU HAVE ALWAYS BEEN HIGHLY REGARDED FOR BUILDING THE HIGHEST TOWERS.

YOUR CONTRIBUTIONS ARE NEVER VALUED IN ANY TEAM PROJECT.

YOU HAVE ALWAYS SUCCESSFULLY BUILT TOWERS BY PLACING ONE SINGLE BLOCK HORIZONTALLY ON TOP OF ANOTHER.

YOU HAVE ALWAYS HAD THE LAST WORD IN HOW A TASK IS COMPLETED.

YOU SEE NO VALUE IN COMPLETING THIS TASK. IT'S ONLY AN EXERCISE.

13
FOLLOWING THE RULES: A MEASUREMENT EXERCISE

Laura Gregg

Laura Gregg *owns Wizard Textware (15600 NE 8th Street, Suite B1-167, Bellevue, WA 98008, 206-641-5951, wizeljay@aol.com). She specializes in the instructional design of quality training. She is a member of the American Society for Quality Control and serves as secretary of its Education Division. Her current interest is in the application of American archetype research to organizational efforts in quality, continuous improvement, and teamwork.*

Overview An understanding of measurement is fundamental to all quality improvement efforts. To solve problems, identify opportunities, and hold any gains, you must collect and analyze data. Furthermore, if you want meaningful results, whoever is collecting data must understand measurement. This active exercise teaches the following concepts:

✓ Precision—how close together individual measurements are

✓ Repeatability—how close multiple measurements are for a single observer

✓ Reproducibility—how close multiple measurements are among several observers

✓ Accuracy—how closely the average of several measurements matches the "real" value

✓ Bias—a consistent difference in measurement results

✓ Standardization—the process of measuring a unit of known result (a standard) and then determining if your measuring device gives you the expected answer

✓ Calibration—preparing or modifying the measuring device so that it gives you the expected answer

Suggested Time 30 minutes.

Materials Needed ✓ Form A (Measurement Recording Form), one copy per team

✓ Three 36-inch pieces of heavy-test fishing line for every learning team in the group

✓ One of three types of "12-inch" ruler. (Make the rulers yourself by photocopying a plastic ruler onto pieces of lightweight card stock, cutting them out and laminating them. Make one-third of the rulers the same size as the original, make one-third at 105% of the original size, and one-third at 95% of the original size.)

✓ An accurate ruler for the discussion following the exercise

Procedure
1. Divide the group into three teams.

2. Give each team three pieces of fishing line and a ruler. Give one team the full-size ruler, one the 105% ruler, and one the 95% ruler. Say to the teams, "All the fishing lines have a standard length."

3. Have each member on the team measure the three fishing lines as accurately as possible with the ruler while another member records the results of each measurement and who did the measuring.

4. Calculate and record the average and range of the three measurements for each team member on Form A (use the rows).

5. Calculate and record the average and range of the measurements for the entire team on Form A (use the columns).

6. When the teams have completed the exercise, reassemble the group and record on a flip chart or whiteboard the averages and ranges for each team member and for each team. Calculate and record the average and range of the measurements for the entire group.

7. Pose these questions to participants:

   ✓ How **precise** are these measurements?

   Answer: The fishing lines are all the same length. The results measured by any given ruler should be very close to one another. The group might notice, however, that some sets of measurements are significantly different than other sets.

   ✓ What do these results tell us about the **repeatability** of our measuring technique?

   Answer: There is some variability among the three measurements made by the same individual.

   ✓ What do these results tell us about the **reproducibility** of our measuring technique?

   Answer: There should be a lot of variability between the measurements made by individuals using rulers with different lengths. In other words, the measurement technique used does not seem to be very reproducible.

   ✓ How **accurate** are these measurements? In other words, how close are they to the actual length of the fishing lines?

   Answer: It depends on the accuracy of the measuring device—in this case, the rulers.

8. Ask the teams to compare their rulers with those of the other teams. Explain how the three rulers were made.

9. Pose the following questions:

✓ How could we have improved our accuracy? In other words, what could we have done to avoid getting these wrong answers to begin with?

✓ What measurement techniques would have improved repeatability?

✓ What measurement techniques would have improved reproducibility?

✓ What implications does this exercise have for the kinds of measurements you make in your organization?

MEASUREMENT RECORDING FORM

FORM A

Team Member	Fishing Line #1	Fishing Line #2	Fishing Line #3	Member Average	Member Range
Team Average:					
Range:					

WHAT WOULD YOUR MANAGEMENT TEAM DO? A CONSENSUS TASK

14

Catherine Penna

Catherine J. Penna *is an independent human resource development consultant (2516 22nd Drive, Longmont, CO 80503, 303-772-5185, cpenna@lamar.colostate.edu) and is currently pursuing a Ph.D. in Human Resources Development at Colorado State University. Catherine is preparing her dissertation on the effects of ethics on the bottom line in corporate America. She has been a corporate trainer specializing in needs analysis and course design and has published articles in the area of training transfer and negotiations skills. Catherine was a contributor to* **The 1996 McGraw-Hill Team and Organization Development Sourcebook.**

Overview
In today's dynamic business environment of right-sizing and layoffs, much emphasis has been placed on the profit margin or the bottom line. Types of leadership styles are changing due to pressures to maintain or obtain a profit percentage. Value once placed on the happiness and job satisfaction of the productive employee may seem lost in the increasing demand for greater monetary returns for the company.

This activity gives management teams an opportunity to view the vision of the company and make a holistic decision regarding what is ethically right or wrong. Obviously what is right for the individual employee may not be what is best for the corporation as a whole. This activity allows each person to evaluate his or her beliefs first as an individual and then together with others. It enables each individual to see how group processes impact individual thought processes and provides managers or employees an opportunity to examine their own actions as part of the company in making sound, profitable decisions.

In order for this exercise to work, the environment or setting needs to be nonthreatening. If your company is currently undergoing any downsizing activity or stressful change in management structure, then it might not be the right time to conduct this exercise.

Suggested Time
90 minutes.

Materials Needed
✓ Form A (Situation Sheet) for all participants
✓ Form B (Individual Worksheet) for all participants

✓ Form C (Group Worksheet) for all participants

✓ Flip chart and markers

Procedure 1. Explain to participants that this is an exercise in examining their beliefs as individual people, while providing an opportunity to enhance teamwork in a tough situation. Give them each copies of Forms A and B. Inform the participants that their own answers on Form B are confidential and that they can share, later on, with the group as much as or as little as they feel is appropriate.

2. After 20 minutes, ask participants to complete their individual reflection.

3. Hand out Form C. Give participants a few minutes to review the questions and then form one or more groups in a manner that best fits your circumstances. Ask each group to arrive at a consensus on how they are going to carry out their manager's orders. Anticipate agreement with management and hesitation from some who disagree but do not want to create controversy. This is why it is important to ensure a safe environment and to conduct this activity away from turbulent times within the company. Stay uninvolved but suggest some questions from Form B and C should the team reach an impasse. Allow the team 20 to 40 minutes to reach a consensus.

4. Ask the participants for feedback.

   ✓ How did they feel about the imposed situation?

   ✓ How were their individual responses different from what the group arrived at?

   ✓ How are ethics changing in their workplace and other environments in their lives?

5. Summarize this activity. Note any examples of conflict and frustration that you heard and generalize that to the fast-paced economy of today. Ask for other situations encountered by the group. Emphasize the following:

   ✓ Understand who you are and what personal mission you have at work.

   ✓ Acknowledge that there may be situations that you do not agree with and know which lines you can cross comfortably while not losing your self-concept.

   ✓ If it feels wrong, it probably is.

You belong to an operational unit within a large company. Your unit has approximately 100 people and you are one of the six managers within that group. All six managers report to the same director.

Your director has decided to lay off 20 people within the unit. The financial aspect of this process is that the company sets aside money for the payoff to those individuals who are being laid off. There are tax benefits to this in that it decreases profit for the year in which the payoff occurs. The employees have 60 days under the Warren Act to find a job within the company while still being on the payroll. If they don't find a job at the end of 60 days, then the 60 days plus the buy-out is a corporate expense. If the person finds a position within the 60 days, then those days are a unit expense, not a corporate expense. So if they find another job within the company but in a different unit, the unit that dismissed them will be charged with salary expense from dismissal date to new job date.

You are a first-line manager. Your director has explained to you how finding these people jobs will impact your specific department budget. The director has also reminded you that your performance appraisal (on which your pay is based) is influenced by your ability to keep your department within budget—or under budget. You have been encouraged not to find jobs for the people being laid off, as that will incur salary expense and threaten your budget. Several of your people have already had interviews and the outlook of finding a job within another unit is very good for some of your employees.

How do you feel about the actions taken by your director?

How would you feel if you, your best friend, or a member of your family were impacted by the director's actions?

Will you play an active role in finding people jobs?

If jobs are offered to employees, will you withhold that information or tell them about it?

If it is close to year-end, you may miss your year-end budget. How much of your salary can you afford to lose by being over budget?

Can you afford to lose your job by missing your target budget?

Can you afford to look for a new job at this moment in your life or will you have to stick with this one and "tough it out"?

It is important to note where your ethical line is—the line that you will not cross over to maintain your employment in the company. Would this situation be at that line? Where would your line be?

The rumor mill in your company is very fast and very accurate. It is important that your group work together so that you will appear as a unified, informed group. It is also important to act as a cohesive unit to avoid any legal issues.

Discuss the implications of this action. Is the unit cutting head count for monetary purposes, for elimination of a strategy, or for a boost in stock prices?

How will these specific actions of the director impact the remaining employees in the unit?

Does the process suggested by the director reflect an overall direction of the company? If so, does this change the company environment? What impact might that have?

Will the management team play an active role in finding people jobs?

If jobs are offered to people, will your team withhold that information, tell the individuals about it, or create a situation in which the employees cannot accept the positions?

Just for thought—How do the answers and processes arrived at by the group differ from your individual answers? Can you live with the group decision and still feel that you did the right thing for both the employees and the company?

THE COMPETITIVE GAME: A CONTINUOUS IMPROVEMENT EXERCISE

15

Gary Topchik

Gary S. Topchik *is a managing partner of SilverStar Enterprises (1659 Bel Air Road, Suite A, Los Angeles, CA 90077, 310-471-8489, gsilstar@aol.com), a consulting firm specializing in team building, organizational change, executive coaching, and management development. Gary is an adjunct faculty member in the Business and Management Department at UCLA and the author of* **Equity Checking: The Superordinate Management Skill.** *He was chair of the OD Network and selected the consultant of the year by the Training Directors' Forum. Gary was also a contributor to* **The 1996 McGraw-Hill Team and Organization Development Sourcebook.**

Overview The purposes of this exercise are to have a team experience the process of continuous improvement, recognize the specific factors that help/hinder teamwork, and identify how the diversity of work styles contributes to the team process. (The exercise can be a lot of fun for the participants and is ideally used at the beginning or conclusion of a team development session.)

Suggested Time 40 to 50 minutes.

Materials Needed
✓ Form A (Team Leader and Team Member Directions)
✓ Form B (Customer-Observer Directions)
✓ Form C (Debriefing Questions)

Procedure
1. Tell the participants that they will be playing a game in small groups. At the end of "playing" time, they will have to report certain information and observations to the large group.
2. Divide the larger group into teams of 6 to 8. (The exercise also works well when there is only one team.)
3. Tell the teams that they have 3 minutes to do the following:

✓ Select two members from your team who will have the dual role of "customers" and "observers."

✓ Select one member from your team who will be the team leader (the remaining are team members).

4. At the end of the 3 minutes, ask each team to identify who the customers, team leader, and team members are.

5. Distribute Form A (to team leader and team members) and Form B (to customers/observers) and allow at least 5 minutes for reading and clarification.

6. Tell the participants that they now have a total of 25 minutes to complete the exercise.

7. At the end of 25 minutes, have each team demonstrate its game to the entire group.

8. Distribute Form C to all teams and give the teams 5 to 10 minutes to answer the questions. Debrief the exercise. Start with the observations of the "customers"; then discuss the answers to Form C.

Variations

1. You can choose not to use Form C and lead the debriefing yourself.

2. Instead of having each team demonstrate its own game, have two participants from the other teams actually play the game (this increases involvement, intergroup interactions, and definitely, fun!)

3. The exercise can be done without assigning the role of the team leader. You may want to see how the teams handle this role on their own.

1. Clear the floor space in the middle of your circle or table.

2. Place several items from your pockets, handbags, or person on the table or floor.

3. In 15 minutes, develop an original competitive game that can be played by two people, using all or some of these objects. The game will be taught to your "customers" who will play the game in anticipation of purchasing it. They will give you feedback based on their experience of playing the game. Use that feedback to improve your game.

4. After your customers have made their comments and observations, you will have 10 minutes to improve the game.

5. You are responsible for the following specific actions:

   ✓ Plan the game.

   ✓ Direct customers on how to play the game.

   ✓ Evaluate the game by listening to customer feedback.

   ✓ Improve the game.

   ✓ Evaluate how your team worked together and listen to feedback from your observers.

1. You have two jobs: to serve as customers interested in a game being developed by the team to which you are assigned and to serve as group process observers.

2. Announce to the team that you are customers who are interested in their new product. Tell the team that at the end of a 15-minute time frame, you wish to play the game in anticipation of purchasing it. During that time, you will also be observing their process as a team.

3. Keep track of the time and record your observations about the following:

   ✓ What factors are helping the team to work together in planning the game?

   ✓ What factors are hindering them?

   ✓ Is there continuous improvement? Are they stuck in the same place?

   ✓ How do team members' different work styles help in the development of this product?

   ✓ What role does the team leader play and how do her/his actions help or hinder the team?

4. Announce when the first 15-minute period is about to expire. Play the game, and give feedback to the team on what you thought of the game. Was it:

   ✓ too complicated, too simplistic?

   ✓ difficult to understand?

   ✓ unoriginal, commonplace?

   ✓ too challenging, too easy?

   Offer recommendations for improvement.

5. Tell the team that they have 10 minutes to improve their product. Keep track of the time and record your observations.

6. Tell the team when their time is up.

1. How did you feel at the beginning of this exercise?

2. How did you feel at the end of the exercise, once the game was developed?

3. What factors helped and/or hindered the planning, decision making, and continuous improvement of the game?

4. How did the team leader help or hinder the project and the team?

5. What were the different work styles on the team? How did this help on the project?

6. What improvements did you make following the report from the customers?

7. How did this exercise parallel what happens in your work environments?

LEARNING ABOUT CHANGE: IS THE ZEBRA WHITE WITH BLACK STRIPES OR BLACK WITH WHITE STRIPES?

16

Carol Harvey

Carol P. Harvey, *Ed.D. is an associate professor of management and marketing at Assumption College (500 Salisbury Street, Worcester, MA 01615-0005, 508-767-7459, charvey@eve.assumption.edu). Carol is the coauthor of* **Understanding Diversity: Readings, Cases, and Exercises** *(HarperCollins, 1995). A former manager with the Xerox Corporation, her current interests include workplace trends such as the changing nature of motivation in organizations, outsourcing of human resource functions, and the growth of the contingency workforce. Carol was also a contributor to* **The 1996 McGraw-Hill Training and Performance Sourcebook.**

Overview   This exercise is designed to teach participants that individuals react to change quite differently and that these differences need to be understood and acknowledged in the formulation and implementation of major organizational changes. It is designed for approximately 20 participants. If you have fewer or more participants, adjust the directions accordingly.

Suggested Time   30 to 45 minutes.

Materials Needed   ✓ Form A (Reaction to Change Sheet)
✓ Form B (Tan Team Instructions)
✓ Form C (Gray Team Instructions)
✓ Form D (Red and Green Team Instructions)

Procedure   1. Give every member of the group a copy of the Reaction to Change Sheet (Form A).

2. Tell the participants that they have 5 minutes to list as many words or phrases as they can that describe their individual feelings about change. (At first this seems easy, but as the time goes on they struggle with this.)

3. Call time at the end of 5 minutes.

4. Tell participants to rate each of their descriptions as positive, negative, or neutral and then to count the number in each category. List the totals at the bottom of the Reactions to Change Sheet (Form A).

5. Form four groups in the following manner:

   ✓ Divide the total number of participants by four. Use that number to assign quartiles to the participants' scores on Form A. For example, if there are 16 participants, 4 participants will be in each quartile. (The numbers in each quartile do not have to be exactly the same.)

   ✓ Designate the quartile with the *highest number of negative scores* the Red team and the quartile with the *highest number of positive scores* the Green team.

   ✓ Artbitrarily divide the participants in the two middle quartiles into two teams. Name one of these groups the Tan team, and name the other group the Gray team.

6. Conduct a brief discussion about why people think they had such different lists. Participants usually cite work experiences, perceptions, frames of reference, etc.

7. Give copies of Form B to the **Tan** team and Form C to the **Gray** team.

8. Give Form D to the **Red** (negative about change) team and to the **Green** (positive about change) team.

9. Allow at least 15 minutes for the teams to prepare their plans for the change.

10. Ask the Tan team to report their best plan for informing the positive people about the change. Follow this with a report from the actual high positive scorers, the **Green Team,** about how they wanted this change to be communicated and implemented. [Those who are positive about change often focus on the need for closure and ceremony such as a cake, etc.]

11. Repeat the procedure by having the Gray team report their plan for implementing the change for people who are more negative about change. Follow with the report from the actual high negative scorers, the **Red Team.** [Those who are more fearful about change often cite a need for more time to get used to the idea, want a say in how their peers are told, etc.]

12. In the discussion, all participants learn that there is *considerable* difference among managers' own attitudes about change, especially the way that it is communicated and implemented and the expectations of subordinates. While much of this is a product of personality and experience, it needs to be taken into account when announcing and implementing changes that employees will accept.

13. Participants learn that their development of change strategies is heavily influenced by their own attitudes toward change. This is particularly important when these are different from those of their subordinates. While changes may be inevitable in organizations, *how* managers implement change may be a determining factor in the more successful transformations. This exercise is a powerful way to experience change from another's perspective.

In the space below, describe your feelings and reactions to the idea of change. Your answers should be limited to a word or a short phrase. In the time allotted try to list as many reactions as possible.

	Rating		Rating
1. _____ _____		20. _____ _____	
2. _____ _____		21. _____ _____	
3. _____ _____		22. _____ _____	
4. _____ _____		23. _____ _____	
5. _____ _____		24. _____ _____	
6. _____ _____		25. _____ _____	
7. _____ _____		26. _____ _____	
8. _____ _____		27. _____ _____	
9. _____ _____		28. _____ _____	
10. _____ _____		29. _____ _____	
11. _____ _____		30. _____ _____	
12. _____ _____		31. _____ _____	
13. _____ _____		32. _____ _____	
14. _____ _____		33. _____ _____	
15. _____ _____		34. _____ _____	
16. _____ _____		35. _____ _____	
17. _____ _____		36. _____ _____	
18. _____ _____		37. _____ _____	
19. _____ _____		38. _____ _____	

#P _____   #N _____   #Nu _____
(Positive)   (Negative)   (Neutral)

As a group, devise a specific plan for explaining the following situation to an employee who has *positive* feelings about change.

> *Your employee's office is going to be relocated to another building at a nearby site. All that you know about this move is that the other members of his/her department will not be going along, the employee's job will essentially remain the same, he/she will still report to you, and you don't know why the employee has been asked to move.*

Your plan should include but is not limited to:

1. Details about how you tell the person (how, when, where, etc.).

2. Exactly what you would say.

3. Any other implementation actions you would like to include.

As a group, devise a specific plan for explaining the situation to an employee who has *negative* feelings about change.

Your employee's office is going to be relocated to another building at a nearby site. All that you know about this move is that the other members of his/her department will not be going along, the employee's job will essentially remain the same, he/she will still report to you, and you don't know why the employee has been asked to move.

Your plan should include but is not limited to:

1. Details about how you tell the person (how, when, where, etc.).

2. Exactly what you would say.

3. Any other implementation actions you would like to include.

As a group, devise a specific plan for how you would like your supervisor to handle the following situation.

Your employee's office is going to be relocated to another building at a nearby site. All that you know about this move is that the other members of his/her department will not be going along, the employee's job will essentially remain the same, he/she will still report to you, and you don't know why the employee has been asked to move.

Your plan should include but is not limited to:

1. Details about how you are told (how, when, where, etc.).

2. Exactly what is said to you.

3. Any other implementation actions that you would like included that might make this change easier for you.

ASSESSMENT INSTRUMENTS

In this section of *The 1997 McGraw-Hill Team and Organization Development Sourcebook,* you will find five assessment instruments. With these instruments, you will be able to answer questions such as:

✓ What motivates your leadership style?

✓ How successful is your total quality management program?

✓ How committed is top management to developing human resources?

✓ How do you perform a pre-team-building flight check?

✓ How empowered is your management style?

The instruments are designed both to evaluate team/organizational issues and to suggest areas for improvement. Most are not for research purposes. Instead, they are intended to build awareness, provide feedback about your own specific situation, and promote group reflection.

In selecting instruments for publication, a premium was placed on questionnaires or survey forms that are easy to understand and quick to complete. Preceding each instrument is an overview that contains the key questions to be assessed. The instrument itself is on a separate page(s) to make reproduction more convenient. All of the instruments are scorable and may contain guidelines for scoring interpretation. Some include questions for follow-up discussion.

Many of these instruments are ideal to utilize as activities in training sessions. Participants can complete the instrument you have selected prior to or during the session. After completion, ask participants to score and interpret their own results. Then, have them compare outcomes with other participants, either in pairs or in larger groupings. Be careful, however, to stress that the data from these instruments are not "hard." They *suggest* rather than *demonstrate* facts about people or situations. Ask participants to compare scores to their own perceptions. If they do not match, urge them to consider why. In some cases, the discrepancy may be due to the crudeness of the measurement device. In others, the discrepancy may result from distorted self-perceptions. Urge participants to open themselves to new feedback and awareness.

Other instruments will help you and others to assess future training needs. Again, it would be useful to show and discuss the data that emerges with others involved in the area under evaluation.

You may also wish to use some instruments as a basis for planning retreats or staff meetings. Have participants complete the instruments prior to the session. Then, summarize the results and open it up to team discussion.

If you choose this option, be sure to state the process clearly to respondents. You might want to use the following text:

We are planning to get together soon to identify issues that need to be worked through in order to maximize our future effectiveness. An excellent way to begin doing some of this work is to collect information through a questionnaire and to feed back that information for group discussion.

I would like you to join with your colleagues in filling out the attached questionnaire. Your honest responses will enable us to have a clear, objective view of our situation.

Your participation will be totally anonymous. My job will be to summarize the results and report them to the group for reaction.

You can also share the instruments with others in your organization who might find them useful for their own purposes. In some cases, merely reading through the questions is a valuable exercise in self and group reflection.

17
HOW SUCCESSFUL IS YOUR TOTAL QUALITY MANAGEMENT PROGRAM?

William J. Rothwell

William J. Rothwell, *Ph.D. is president of Rothwell & Associates (647 Berkshire Drive, State College, PA 16803, 814-234-6888, WJR9@psu.edu), a full-service international consulting firm that specializes in all facets of Human Resource Development, Organization Development, Human Resource Management, and Human Performance Improvement. Author, coauthor, editor, or coeditor of over 12 books and a frequent conference presenter, he is also an associate professor of Human Resource Development at The Pennsylvania State University.*

OVERVIEW

A Total Quality Management (TQM) program is an organized effort leading to continuous improvements in an organization. Many organizations have established such efforts.

Unfortunately, many organizations implement TQM programs without careful consideration of the most important issues associated with them. These important issues are called *success factors,* and they are the keys to establishing, implementing, and evaluating successful TQM programs. The perceptions of key stakeholders about a TQM program are important since the stakeholders must assume program ownership for it to be successful.

How do key stakeholders rate your organization's TQM program? What do they consider to be the most important issues associated with the program? What do they consider to be the most effective areas of an existing TQM program in the organization? How successfully is the organization's TQM program matching up to the perceptions of the key stakeholders? The following *Total Quality Management Program Survey* should help you answer these questions.

TOTAL QUALITY MANAGEMENT PROGRAM SURVEY

Prepare for administering this survey by first selecting a committee representing key stakeholders inside and outside your organization. For instance, you may wish to form a committee that includes a top manager, a middle manager, a supervisor, a professional, a technical worker, a salesperson, a skilled tradesperson, an hourly worker, a customer, a distributor, and a supplier. Modify the committee membership as necessary so it represents the most important groups inside and outside the organization. Choose no more than one person to represent each group.

Assemble this group for one hour. If you cannot find one hour when everyone is available, or if geographical separation makes a meeting prohibitively expensive to arrange, then pick an hour when all can be available either personally or by audioconference. Send out the following survey in advance to all participants. Ask the participants to complete the survey based on their individual perceptions about the organization's TQM program. (This survey assumes that your organization has already implemented a TQM program in some form.)

Participants should read each issue appearing in the left column below and then circle numbers in the center and right columns to indicate:

✓ *How important* they believe the issue to be for the organization's TQM program's success.

✓ *How effectively* they believe the organization's TQM program is addressing the issue.

To rate importance, the participants should use the following scale:

SCALE FOR IMPORTANCE	1	=	Not at all important
	2	=	Somewhat important
	3	=	Very important

To rate effectiveness, the participants should use the following scale:

SCALE FOR EFFECTIVENESS	1	=	Not at all effective
	2	=	Somewhat effective
	3	=	Very effective

Issue	Importance			Effectiveness		
	Not at all Important	Somewhat Important	Very Important	Not at all Effective	Somewhat Effective	Very Effective
In this organization, the Total Quality Management (TQM) Program …	1	2	3	1	2	3
1. Enjoys strong, visible top management support	1	2	3	1	2	3
2. Has clearly established responsibilities	1	2	3	1	2	3
3. Is supported by continuing training	1	2	3	1	2	3
4. Is implemented in the design of products OR the delivery of services	1	2	3	1	2	3
5. Has established a continuing effort to clarify, meet, and exceed customer requirements	1	2	3	1	2	3
6. Has established clear requirements for suppliers	1	2	3	1	2	3
7. Holds suppliers accountable for meeting or exceeding requirements established by the organization	1	2	3	1	2	3
8. Has established the means by which to improve work processes or work methods continuously	1	2	3	1	2	3
9. Has established a clear definition of quality in the organization so that managers and employees alike understand what it means	1	2	3	1	2	3
10. Has clearly established ways of collecting information about the cost of the TQM program and of feeding that information back to the key groups affected by the TQM program	1	2	3	1	2	3
11. Is tied to an employee involvement or employee empowerment program	1	2	3	1	2	3
12. Leads to continuing improvement in the organization	1	2	3	1	2	3

Total the Scores from the Center and Right Columns and place the Scores in the boxes at right:	**Importance Score:**	**Effectiveness Score:**

Score the survey by asking each participant to add up the scores in the center and right columns and place their total scores in the boxes at the end of the survey.

Using a flip chart, record the scores from each participant for importance and effectiveness. When all scores have been received, arrange them in order from high to low for importance and effectiveness. Then pose the following questions to participants:

✓ How important are the "issues perceived to be the most important" for the Total Quality Management program of the organization, based on the collective scores?

✓ What issues scored highest on importance? (Lead participants to discuss which issues they scored as most important and why. Try to narrow down the list of most important issues to no more than three.)

✓ Do the participants agree that the issues scoring the highest on the survey would probably be identified as most important by others in the organization? (If so, ask why. If not, ask why.) If uncertainty exists about the issues of greatest importance, ask participants how they feel the issues could be resolved. (Would it be advisable to administer a shortened survey to everyone in the organization in order to clarify the most important issues associated with the TQM program? A sample of people in the organization?)

✓ How effectively is the TQM program addressing the issues perceived to be the most important, based on the collective scores?

✓ What issues scored highest on effectiveness? (Lead participants to discuss which issues they scored as most effective and why. Try to narrow down the list of most effective issues to no more than three.)

✓ Do the participants agree that the issues scoring the highest on the survey would probably be identified as most effective by others in the organization? (If so, ask why. If not, ask why.) If uncertainty exists about the issues of greatest effectiveness for the TQM program, ask participants how they feel the issues could be resolved. (Would it be advisable to administer a shortened survey to everyone in the organization in order to clarify the most effective issues associated with the TQM program? A sample of people in the organization?)

✓ *How can the results of this activity be used to establish an action plan to improve the organization's TQM program?* Lead participants to establish an action plan for improving the organization's TQM program and gain support for implementing it.

18

HOW COMMITTED IS TOP MANAGEMENT TO DEVELOPING HUMAN RESOURCES?

Jack Phillips

Jack J. Phillips, *Ph.D. has served in managerial and executive positions for over twenty-five years, including HRD manager and bank president. He is currently the president of Performance Resources Organization (P.O. Box 1969, Murfreesboro, TN 37133-1969, 615-896-7694), a consulting firm that provides human resource accountability services to a wide range of clients in ten countries. Jack has written or edited seven books and over 75 articles. He was also a contributor to* **The 1996 McGraw-Hill Team and Organization Development Sourcebook.**

OVERVIEW

Top management commitment to the training and development and human resource development function is very critical to the overall success of an organization. Top management commitment goes deeper than a pledge or promise. It includes the action of top management to allocate the resources and lend support to the training and development effort. Each chief executive officer (CEO) or other top administrator or executive at a particular location, division, or subsidiary company has some degree of commitment to training and development for his or her area of responsibility. The extent of commitment will usually vary with the style, attitude, and philosophy of the top executive. A high level of commitment to training and development usually correlates with a successful training function and organization.

How do you know if your top management is committed to HRD? The following commitment checklist presents a self-test for the top executive. In just a few minutes, a CEO can examine the extent to which the organization is committed to the training and development function. Guidelines found in the interpretation section that follows the assessment instrument will help the executive know the extent of his or her commitment to the HRD function. It is recommended that this instrument be administered to the top executive group in an organization in addition to the CEO. The process can have a favorable impact on the thinking of the chief executive, particularly if there has been little effort to secure additional commitment to the training and development effort previously.

This instrument can be used in the following ways:

✓ It can initiate discussion about the current scope and success of programs and the extent of executive commitment that is needed in the future. This is usually at the beginning of a discussion in which the goal is to enhance overall commitment.

✓ It can measure changes over time as the organization allocates more resources and attention to the training and development function.

✓ It can alert a top executive group that their efforts for supporting the function are not where they should be. An information session built around this checklist shows executives what significant behavior changes are needed to reap the necessary rewards from the training and development effort.

CEO COMMITMENT CHECKLIST

Directions: Respond by placing a checkmark in either the yes or the no column next to each of the statements below.

YES   NO

❑   ❑   1. Do you have a corporate policy or mission statement for the HR function?

❑   ❑   2. Do you hold managers accountable for the training, education, and development of their subordinates?

❑   ❑   3. Does your organization set goals for the extent of employee participation in formal HR programs?

❑   ❑   4. Is your involvement in HRD more than written statements, opening comments or wrap-up sessions?

❑   ❑   5. Did you attend an outside development program in the past year?

❑   ❑   6. Do you require your immediate staff to attend outside development programs each year?

❑   ❑   7. Do you occasionally audit an internal HRD program conducted for other managers?

❑   ❑   8. Do you require your managers to be involved in the HRD process?

❑   ❑   9. Do you require your managers to develop a successor?

❑   ❑   10. Do you encourage line managers to help conduct HRD programs?

❑   ❑   11. Do you require your management to support and reinforce HRD programs?

❏   ❏   **12.** Do you require your top managers to have self-development plans?

❏   ❏   **13.** Is your HRD manager's job an attractive and respected executive position?

❏   ❏   **14.** Does the top HRD manager report directly to you?

❏   ❏   **15.** Does the HRD manager have access to you regularly?

❏   ❏   **16.** Do you frequently meet with the HRD manager to review HRD problems and progress?

❏   ❏   **17.** Do you meet with the HRD manager to review HRD programs at least annually?

❏   ❏   **18.** Do you require a proposal for a major new HRD program?

❏   ❏   **19.** When business declines, do you resist cutting the HRD budget?

❏   ❏   **20.** Do you frequently speak out in support of HRD?

❏   ❏   **21.** Do you often suggest that HRD personnel help solve performance problems?

❏   ❏   **22.** Do you require the HRD department to have a budget and cost control system?

❏   ❏   **23.** Is the HRD department required to evaluate each HRD program?

❏   ❏   **24.** Do you ask to see the results of at least the major HRD programs?

❏   ❏   **25.** Do you encourage a cost/benefit evaluation for major HRD programs?

Number of Yes Responses	Interpretation
More than 20	Excellent top management commitment, usually tied to a very successful organization.
More than 15	Top management commitment is good, but there is still room for additional emphasis.
More than 10	Poor top management commitment, with much improvement necessary for the HRD department to be effective.
Fewer than 10	Almost no top management commitment; HRD barely exists in the organization, if at all.

19

HOW DO YOU PERFORM A PRE-TEAM BUILDING FLIGHT CHECK?

C. R. Parry and Robert Barner

C. R. Parry *and* **Robert Barner** *are president and vice president of Parry Consulting Services, Inc. (P.O. Box 224, Jupiter, FL 33468-0224, 407-744-1762, ibscribe@aol.com), an international training and consulting company. Bob is a well-known public speaker and writer. He is the author of* **Crossing the Minefield: Tactics for Overcoming Today's Toughest Management Challenges** *(AMACOM, 1994) and* **Lifeboat Strategies: How to Keep Your Career Above Water During Tough Times— Any Time** *(AMACOM, 1993). Bob was also a contributor to* **The 1996 McGraw-Hill Team and Organization Development Sourcebook.**

OVERVIEW

Ineffective team building sessions are rarely the fault of either unskilled facilitators or uninterested team members. Instead, sessions that lack effectiveness may be missing a pre-workshop flight check—a list of questions that can uncover problems that have the potential to derail a team-building session. *The Pre-team Building Workshop Flight Check*, while not intended to substitute for an in-depth team assessment, can help you to better focus your team-building activities and identify issues that should be resolved before embarking in team building. The interpretation section that follows the checklist provides guidelines for further processing of the types of information yielded by this assessment instrument. Use the checklist the next time you need to insure that your team will be flying right.

PRE-TEAM BUILDING WORKSHOP FLIGHT CHECK

1. **History.** Is the team newly formed or well established?
    - ❏ Newly formed
    - ❏ Well established

2. **Experience.** Has this team previously participated in a team building workshop?
    - ❏ First time
    - ❏ Prior experience

3. **Life Cycle.** Is this a permanent or temporary (project, customer action, product development) team?
    - ❏ Permanent
    - ❏ Temporary

4. **Structure.** Is this team intact (a single team leader and members) or is it a cross-functional team?
    - ❏ Intact
    - ❏ Cross-functional

5. **Composition.** Is this team single-layered (a team leader with immediate team members) or multilayered (a composite team made up of different management levels)?
    - ❏ Single-layered
    - ❏ Multilayered

6. **Location.** Is this team co-located or dispersed across locations or shifts?
    - ❏ Co-located
    - ❏ Dispersed

7. **Leader's Role.** What term would best describe the degree of leader control and member autonomy exercised by this team?
    - ❏ This is a leader-directed team
    - ❏ This is a leader-coached team
    - ❏ This is a self-directed team

8. **Scope of Review.** Has the team already clearly identified a series of issues for review that are a) within the team's direct control, and b) targeted enough to be covered within the time available for team building?

   ❏ Issues have been identified

   ❏ Issues have not been identified

   ❏ There is disagreement among members regarding the relative priority that should be assigned to certain issues

9. **Drivers.** Who initiated the request for team building?

   ❏ The team

   ❏ The team leader

   ❏ A third party (internal customer/human resources manager, team leader's manager)

10. **Leader's Position.** Which of the following best describes the team leader's position regarding the planned team-building activity?

    ❏ Highly supportive

    ❏ A little skeptical, but willing to explore the issues

    ❏ Highly skeptical or a little hostile

11. **Facilitator's Role.** Do the team leader and members have a clear understanding of the role that you will play as a team-building facilitator?

    ❏ Yes

    ❏ No

12. **Follow-up.** What prior commitment has been made for following up on the action items generated during the team-building process?

    ❏ None. Such a process isn't necessary.

    ❏ A follow-up process is needed, but has not yet been developed.

    ❏ As the team building facilitator, I will manage follow-up.

    ❏ The team leader will manage follow-up.

    ❏ Follow-up will be a shared responsibility among team members.

1. *History.* Is the team newly formed or well established?

   Newly formed teams often have to deal with such issues as goal clarity, structure optimization, and the establishment of members' roles before they can proceed. Established teams, on the other hand, are often able to immediately zero in on selective issues that can help them better leverage their performance.

   Another difference between the two teams is that those that are established have developed a history that can be used as part of their learning process. For example, if the performance issue to be reviewed is team decision making, part of the team-building session might involve having members evaluate previous decisions the team has reached against an ideal model of team decision making provided by the facilitator. Lacking this history, newly formed teams must often rely on synthetic exercises as the basis for their team-building session. A related example would be the use of one of the many commercially available team consensus decision-making exercises to help members evaluate their team's processes.

2. *Experience.* Has this team previously participated in a team building workshop?

   If this will be the team's first workshop experience, you have the advantage of starting with a clean slate. If the team has previously completed a team-building workshop, it's important to determine how the team viewed the outcomes of that workshop and the assumptions they hold for you as a facilitator. Many teams have undergone a number of unusual and ineffectual group interactions that have been umbrellaed under the term "team building." If the team building process you are undertaking differs significantly from one that the team has previously experienced, be certain to clarify these differences.

   In addition, ask questions that can help you determine whether the team itself has changed significantly—their charter, membership, or leadership—since their last workshop experience. How are these changes likely to affect the team-building workshop you want to implement?

3. *Life Cycle.* Is this a permanent or temporary (project, customer action, or product development) team?

   Keep in mind that teams with a relatively short life cycle can't afford to extend team building over a long period of time. They need to compress team building and experience it at the earliest possible point in their life cycle.

4. *Structure.* Is this team intact (a single team leader and members) or is it cross-functional?

Cross-functional teams usually need to focus in on *process directed issues* such as "How can we best organize ourselves to maximize our efficiency?" and "How can we, as internal suppliers, more carefully define the performance requirements of our internal customers (the other members of our team)?" Intact teams, on the other hand, often surface such *relationship issues* as "How can we balance our members' needs for greater autonomy with our leader's need for effective team management?" and "How can we effectively resolve conflicts among members?"

5. *Composition.* Is this team single-layered (a team leader with immediate team members) or multilayered (a composite team made up of different management levels)?

   As a rule, the members of multilayered teams tend to have greater concerns regarding the open disclosure of issues and concerns. The reason is that nonmanagerial team members may feel intimidated by the presence of senior-level managers in the team-building workshop. One way around this is through the use of the nominal group technique or breakout sessions by management level employees—techniques that allow members to anonymously share their initial concerns without fear of reprisal from their managers.

6. *Location.* Is this team co-located or dispersed across locations or shifts?

   Teams that are scattered across shifts, time zones, or locations will often find it difficult to follow up on action items generated during the team-building workshop. In such situations, you may have to look for ways to establish a sturdier follow-up process, such as the use of groupware software programs that enable team members to engage in the on-line sharing of documentation, or the posting of requests for information or assistance to other members.

7. *Leader's Role.* What term would best describe the degree of leader control and member autonomy exercised by this team?

   There are really two questions here. The first is, "How is the team *currently* performing?" while the second is "*Ideally,* how would the team like to perform?" An overriding issue is whether both the team members and their leader are committed to moving their team toward member self-management, and whether they see the team-building workshop as a vehicle for moving them toward this goal.

   A second related issue involves control. The leaders of leader-directed teams sometimes assume that they can stand apart from the team-building process or that they should exert a high level of control and direction over that process. When working with such team leaders, it's important to clearly state up front that the essence of team building involves establishing each member as an equal owner in the team's success. It is also important that the team leader recognize that to fulfill this aim she must support the basic ground rules of team building—no censorship, an equal say by all members, insuring a sharing of time, and giving each other mutual respect. Unless the team leader is willing to support these ground rules, team building is inevitably doomed to fail.

8. *Scope of Review.* Has the team already clearly identified a series of issues for review that are a) within the team's direct control, and b) targeted enough to be covered within the time available for team building?

It is usually risky to walk into a team-building session without having first established an up-front agreement with members regarding their goals for the team-building workshop. You can easily obtain such agreement by conducting individual interviews or a team survey approximately two to three weeks in advance of the workshop. If there is disagreement among members regarding the relative priority of issues for review, use a multiple voting method to have members establish priorities among issues before the start of the workshop.

When answering this question, be careful of situations in which members define the goals for team building in a very abstract and global way. For example, while all members may agree that the goals of the workshop are "to help the team increase its efficiency," a probe into this area may quickly reveal that some members define "increasing efficiency" as correcting cumbersome and ineffective work processes, while others are looking at the way work is scheduled and coordinated among members. The best way to pin members down on this question is to ask the secondary question, "Give me an example of what this issue looks like in terms of your team's day-to-day performance?"

9. *Drivers.* Who initiated the request for team building?

The point to be made here is that it's important to determine the real "owners" of the team-building process. Team building is sometimes mandated for a team by a third party, such as a company's human resources manager or the team leader's manager. If this is the case, be careful that a) the team and team leader are actually supportive of the team-building process, b) that they agree with the third party regarding the criteria that will be used for defining the success of the team-building process, and c) that team building is not being used by the third party as a means of correcting a performance deficiency on the part of the team leader. *Team building should never be used as a substitute for performance coaching!*

10. *Leader's Position.* Which of the following best describes the team leader's position regarding the planned team-building activity?

This question is closely related to question 9. There are many situations in which team leaders who were officially "supportive" of team building later confess (after some honest questioning) to some concerns or hesitations about the process. When team leaders voice initial resistance to team building it is often because a) they are under the mistaken idea that the facilitator is going to try to subvert their control, or b) they have had past experiences with team building that were very unsuccessful.

To address these concerns, take the time to carefully explain the approach that you intend to use in the team-building process, as well as your role as the facilitator. Ask the team leader if he would be willing to suspend judgment and walk into the session with an open mind. Also, find out if there is anything you can do in advance of the session—such as conducting individual data gathering interviews with team members—that can help you to lower the leader's risk level for the process.

11. *Facilitator's Role.* Do the team leader and members have a clear understanding of the role that you will play as a team-building facilitator?

It's important that the team recognize and accept that as a team-building facilitator your role involves encouraging balanced discussion and a full review of issues, not making decisions, providing technical advice, or functioning as an arbitrator of internal disputes.

12. *Follow-up.* What commitment has been made for following up on the action items generated during the team-building process?

When team building fails, it's often because no process has been developed for translating the decisions that fall out of the workshop into a set of achievable objectives. Every action item selected by the team should designate:

a) the time period for completion,

b) who is going to be involved,

c) who outside the team needs to be notified of the action,

d) how the team is going to evaluate the successful implementation of the action,

e) who on the team will play the lead role in completing the action, and

f) how and when that team member will agree to follow up with the team on the status of the action item.

Be careful of placing yourself, as the team facilitator, in the role of watchdog for insuring follow-up on action items. Ideally, all team members should share in this responsibility.

HOW EMPOWERING IS YOUR STYLE?

Barbara Pate Glacel and Emile Robert

Barbara Pate Glacel, *Ph.D. is CEO and* **Emile A. Robert, Jr.,** *Ph.D. is COO of VIMA International (5290 Lyngate Ct., Burke, VA 22015, 703-764-0780). They are coauthors of* **Light Bulbs for Leaders—A Guide Book for Team Learning** *(John Wiley, 1996). VIMA International works with clients in the United States, Europe, Africa, and the Pacific Rim. Services include executive and organizational development, team learning, and strategic leadership. Both authors are on the adjunct faculty of the Center for Creative Leadership. They each have extensive experience in human resource development and administration with such organizations as Lockheed Martin, MITRE, NASA, Atlantic Richfield, and MCI as well as not-for-profit agencies.*

OVERVIEW

The Empowerment Style Questionnaire is a self-administered questionnaire designed to assess the organizational environment and its receptivity to practices of empowerment. Clearly, the level of empowerment in an organization is related to both management and follower practices. The atmosphere must be promoted by supervisors and managers in order for followers to feel safe in practicing empowered actions and decisions. However, at the same time, followers must accept the responsibility and accountability of acting in an empowered manner. Empowerment is not abdication. Neither is it chaos. It is the result of training, experience, trust, and practice in operating an organization and its functions.

The Questionnaire's results will reveal whether individuals operate within an empowered environment as created by others. It also reveals whether individuals themselves practice the behaviors associated with self-empowerment and create an environment in which others are empowered. Leaders and followers alike are responsible for creating an environment in which empowerment is the preferred behavior.

By comparing your results with the norms, you can determine whether your score is above, within, or below the mean. By looking at those behaviors that result in the lowest scores, you can choose those practices that have the greatest impact in increasing the level of empowerment in the situation in which you work. Team members or coworkers can assess the environment together and discuss the behaviors with both the highest and lowest scores in an effort to increase the group's overall effectiveness.

THE EMPOWERMENT STYLE QUESTIONNAIRE

Select the answer below that applies most often to your own situation. Use the score sheet that follows the questionnaire to record your answers.

1. I prefer working
   a. as part of a team.
   b. alone.
   c. in charge of a team.

2. I prefer to make decisions
   a. on my own.
   b. with guidance from my superior.
   c. by consulting my subordinates.
   d. based on the team's consensus.

3. My relationships with others at work include
   a. involvement only with the job to be done.
   b. interest in others' personal lives.
   c. social events together.

4. When conflict occurs on the job, I usually
   a. confront the individual(s) in the conflict.
   b. ignore it and hope it will go away.
   c. feel badly that someone may be hurt in the conflict.
   d. feel annoyed that the conflict is occurring.

5. The level of trust in the team I manage would be characterized as
   a. high, based on competency and authority of individuals.
   b. high, based on affiliation and affection among individuals.
   c. enough trust to get the job done.
   d. low, based on lack of competency and authority of individuals.
   e. low, based on lack of affiliation and affection among individuals.

6. The working relationships within the team I manage would be characterized as
   a. very positive and friendly.
   b. sufficient to get the job done.
   c. conflicted, getting in the way of the mission.

7. I would characterize my work style as

   a. delegating the appropriate responsibility and authority to others.

   b. taking on too much work myself.

   c. delegating actions, but maintaining control.

8. My colleagues/subordinates would characterize my work style as

   a. perfectionist.

   b. micro-manager.

   c. delegator.

   d. role model.

9. My work and my personal life are

   a. coordinated into a balanced whole.

   b. inextricably linked together and out-of-balance.

   c. separate and equal.

   d. separate and out-of-balance.

10. I am

   a. tolerant of others' work.

   b. respectful of others' work.

   c. impatient with others' work.

   d. critical of others' work.

11. The people on my team

   a. work in the way I suggest to them.

   b. prefer to work according to their own style.

   c. check with me on the way I want jobs performed.

   d. ask forgiveness (if necessary) rather than permission.

12. I discuss the vision and mission of the organization with my team

   a. often.

   b. once in a while.

   c. never.

   d. We have no clear vision and mission.

13. Decisions in my organization are made by

   a. the boss.

   b. the person doing the work.

   c. the team.

   d. the policy guideline.

14. Decisions in my organization are made based on
    a. reason and logic.
    b. effects of the decision on people.
    c. both a and b.

15. Information is
    a. shared freely (with the exception of sensitive information).
    b. shared with a need to know.
    c. guarded as a source of power.

16. The atmosphere in my organization is
    a. high stress.
    b. high fun.
    c. task-oriented.
    d. enjoyable.

17. Feedback about performance is delivered
    a. annually with performance reviews.
    b. more often than annually in a written format.
    c. continuously in both written and verbal form.
    d. once in a while when needed, usually verbally.
    e. never.

18. Humor is expressed at work
    a. often.
    b. in a positive, stress-relieving manner.
    c. in a critical, biting manner.
    d. seldom or not at all.

19. My own boss provides me with
    a. sufficient latitude to do my job.
    b. micro-management.
    c. empowerment with both responsibility and authority.

20. I provide my subordinates with
    a. sufficient latitude to do their jobs.
    b. micro-management.
    c. empowerment with both responsibility and authority.

THE EMPOWERMENT STYLE QUESTIONNAIRE

SCORE SHEET

NAME: _____ DATE: _____

Use this answer sheet to record your responses to the Empowerment Style Questionnaire.

1. _____   11. _____

2. _____   12. _____

3. _____   13. _____

4. _____   14. _____

5. _____   15. _____

6. _____   16. _____

7. _____   17. _____

8. _____   18. _____

9. _____   19. _____

10. _____   20. _____

SCORING THE EMPOWERMENT STYLE QUESTIONNAIRE

Score your own questionnaire by choosing the number that corresponds to your answer and then adding the results. Transfer the grand total amount to the next page to determine where your style falls within this questionnaire's norms.

	LINE 1			LINE 2			LINE 3	
1.	**a.**	10	**8.**	**a.**	3	**15.**	**a.**	10
	b.	3		**b.**	3		**b.**	7
	c.	5		**c.**	7		**c.**	3
				d.	10			
2.	**a.**	3				**16.**	**a.**	3
	b.	5	**9.**	**a.**	10		**b.**	7
	c.	7		**b.**	5		**c.**	5
	d.	10		**c.**	5		**d.**	10
				d.	3			
3.	**a.**	3				**17.**	**a.**	5
	b.	10	**10.**	**a.**	7		**b.**	7
	c.	5		**b.**	10		**c.**	10
				c.	3		**d.**	3
4.	**a.**	10		**d.**	3		**e.**	0
	b.	3						
	c.	7	**11.**	**a.**	3	**18.**	**a.**	7
	d.	3		**b.**	7		**b.**	10
				c.	5		**c.**	5
5.	**a.**	7		**d.**	10		**d.**	3
	b.	10						
	c.	5	**12.**	**a.**	10	**19.**	**a.**	7
	d.	3		**b.**	5		**b.**	3
	e.	3		**c.**	3		**c.**	10
				d.	3			
6.	**a.**	10				**20.**	**a.**	7
	b.	5	**13.**	**a.**	3		**b.**	3
	c.	3		**b.**	7		**c.**	10
				c.	10			
7.	**a.**	10		**d.**	3			
	b.	3						
	c.	5	**14.**	**a.**	5			
				b.	7			
				c.	10			

SUBTOTAL
LINE 1 _____

SUBTOTAL
LINE 2 _____

SUBTOTAL
LINE 3 _____

GRAND TOTAL _____

YOUR GRAND TOTAL _____

POSSIBLE RANGE: 59-200

YOUR QUARTILE: _____

The norms presented here are based on a sample of 213 leaders from Aerospace, Biotechnology, Financial Services, and Government Officials. You may choose to use these as a comparison to your responses or compare your results to others in the same organization.

N:	213	Possible Range:	59-200
Mean:	148	Actual Range:	92-183
Median:	153	Range for Top Quartile:	164-183
Mode:	144	Range for Second Quartile:	154-163
		Range for Third Quartile:	134-153
		Range for Bottom Quartile:	92-133

WHAT MOTIVATES YOUR LEADERSHIP STYLE?

21

James Thompson and George Mizzell

James Thompson, *Ph.D. currently works as an Associate Management/-Organizational Psychologist with Somerville and Company, Inc. of Denver, CO (303-380-0900). His previous assignment was Manager and Principal Consultant at Alabama Power Company where he had responsibility for the development and testing of selection and assessment processes and instruments. Jim refines existing and new instruments to assist companies in placing employees into positions that maximize their strengths.* **George Mizzell** *owns Engineered Concepts (Canyon Rd., Birmingham, AL 35216, 205-823-0751), a business consulting firm specializing in developing customized corporate surveys and employee assessment instruments, conducting complex analysis of data, developing employee feedback reports, and multimedia executive presentation.*

OVERVIEW

This survey instrument, *The Profile of Motives,* assesses an individual's leadership ability through the eyes of peers and direct reports. It is designed to combine items from the behaviors that were found to best correlate to overall leadership effectiveness.

The Profile of Motives is a way of measuring "Why" leaders might behave the way they do. Identifying why leaders operate the way they do provides greater insight into an organization's performance. Primarily, the very best leaders share common motives that employees respect. Typical surveys capture what a leader does, but *The Profile of Motives* survey goes beyond that to the heart of a leader. People can usually sense a leader's motives even if the leader is a good actor. This survey sees through the facade.

The results of this survey can be helpful in determining employee development opportunities or in matching a team with complementary individuals.

PROFILE OF MOTIVES

The purpose of this survey is to provide the rated individual with feedback on his/her behavior as a leader compared to other leaders. In order to provide the person with the most meaningful information, please respond carefully and candidly to each item.

Rater Classification—Choose the statement that best describes your relationship to the person being rated.

(S) I am the person being rated (Self)

(P) I work with the person being rated (Peer)

(I) My supervisor works directly for the person being rated (Indirect)

(D) I work directly for the person being rated (Direct)

(B) The person being rated works directly for me (Boss)

(C) The person being rated provides services to my organization (Client)

Organization Code: (0) (1) (2) (3) (4) (5) (6) (7) (8) (9)
(0) (1) (2) (3) (4) (5) (6) (7) (8) (9)
(0) (1) (2) (3) (4) (5) (6) (7) (8) (9)
(0) (1) (2) (3) (4) (5) (6) (7) (8) (9)

Person being rated: **Date rated:**

_____   _____

Please indicate the degree to which the items below characterize the person being rated.

Not at All Characteristic	Rarely Characteristic	Slightly Characteristic	Occasionally Characteristic	Fairly Characteristic	Frequently Characteristic	Very Characteristic
(1)	(2)	(3)	(4)	(5)	(6)	(7)

Carefully read the following descriptions of each human need. Consider how the person you are rating may display evidence of having each need. Think of examples when these motives have produced the following behaviors and how intense the behavior was. Taking both the frequency and intensity into consideration, mark your rating of this person using the scale of 1 to 7 to indicate how strongly you believe this need is manifested.

1. **Humility:** This need is characterized by the willingness to accept responsibility—especially for failures: to feel personally liable when things go wrong and to quickly accept ownership for the troubles of others; a tendency to avoid praise or recognition for success.

Almost always accepts the credit for success, but avoids taking the blame for mistakes ① ② ③ ④ ⑤ ⑥ ⑦ *Almost always accepts blame for mistakes, avoids praise*

2. **Achievement:** This need is evidenced by a desire to achieve significant things, to outperform others, to win the competition; usually a collector of symbols of achievement (e.g., trophies, awards, plaques, membership in organizations).

Avoids competition, recognition, or Win-Lose positions ① ② ③ ④ ⑤ ⑥ ⑦ *Almost always seeks out competition to test skills; seeks to win at all costs; seeks recognition for successes*

3. **Affiliation:** People with this need want to belong, to have a sense of being a member in good standing with one or more groups, e.g., family or sports teams. They require reassurance of their acceptance and may also require symbols of their membership such as team colors, hats, or logos. Symbols of status are likely to be important, e.g., badges, rings, jackets, etc.

Prefers working alone; avoids membership in groups; indifferent to what others think of him/her; may ruffle the feathers of others ① ② ③ ④ ⑤ ⑥ ⑦ *Almost always seeks out groups to join; strongly desires to be liked by everyone; avoids making waves or causing conflict or controversy*

4. **Aggression:** This needs is characterized by a desire to dominate others, to have one's way at all costs, to put others in a position of weakness, to criticize others publicly, to actively disagree with positions or ideas not of one's making; apparent pleasure derived from putting others down; enjoyment in having and using authority over others.

Avoids arguments & disagreements with others; avoids using authority to get way; dislikes putting others in "one-down" positions or taking unfair advantage of people ① ② ③ ④ ⑤ ⑥ ⑦ *Quickly assumes control; takes charge & issues orders; belittles those who disagree; uses power to get way; enjoys having control over others*

5. **Autonomy:** This need is characterized by a desire to operate independently; to have relative freedom from rules, regulations, policies, and close supervision, etc.; to not be held back in any way; to not depend on others for anything of importance; to set one's own agenda and priorities.

Seeks guidance, asks persmission, requests directions, enjoys working under close supervision, uncomfortable with unclear directions ① ② ③ ④ ⑤ ⑥ ⑦ *Doesn't ask permission, or seek guidance, enjoys working on own relying on own resources, self-directing and independent*

6. **Change:** This need is characterized by a requirement for a lot of variety in daily life; a desire for regular changes in duties, location, and people with whom to interact; changing job responsibilities, new challenges thrust upon them; opportunities to use their wits to cope with novel problems and situations.

Always finds change upsetting; seeks consistency & predictability; prefers following rules & procedures without question; enjoys routine	① ② ③ ④ ⑤ ⑥ ⑦	*Always seeks new challenges, surrounding, tasks, & people; uncomfortable with constancy; enjoys unpredictability*

7. **Structure:** Characterized by a desire to understand the rules governing the work or situation; to be able to predict outcomes with relative certainty; to have little ambiguity in formation required in decision making; to organize the work & put everything in its place; to have most things of importance fit neatly into either the "black" or "white" box—no shades of "gray."

Happy with unclear or ambiguous situations; seems to thrive on chaos and disorder; sees situations in shades of gray, not black and white	① ② ③ ④ ⑤ ⑥ ⑦	*Always organizes work; defines roles; establishes rules and procedures; avoids chaos and disorder in people and work*

8. **Influence:** Characterized by a strong desire to exert an influence on people and events; to obtain some degree of control of the future; to believe he or she is having a major impact on the course of work or events; to be in a position to determine what is to be done and who is to do it through persuasion, leadership, and salesmanship; to make a real difference in the outcome of initiatives.

Dislikes being in a position of selling ideas to others; shies away from positions of influence; prefers to go along with others or take a back seat	① ② ③ ④ ⑤ ⑥ ⑦	*Always tries to have an influence on the course of events; willing to take a stand and persuade others; enjoys a good debate on the issues*

9. **Endurance:** Characterized by need to complete any journey begun regardless of the personal sacrifice required; desire to have their resolve tested; to persevere in the face of adversity; to tough out situations to which others yield; to push ahead when others give up; to test their will against the elements; to overcome insurmountable barriers and obstacles.

Tries to avoid obstacles and frustrations; dislikes activities that test one's endurance; prefers smooth sailing to fighting rough seas	① ② ③ ④ ⑤ ⑥ ⑦	*Readily take on even the most difficult challenges; enjoy putting their own toughness to the test; want to prove that they can do what others cannot*

10. **Exhibition:** This need is characterized by a desire to be the focus of people's attention; to have the admiration of others, to be entertaining to others; to be sought after; to have fame, to perform in front of an audience of some sort.

Prefers remaining out of the spotlight; yields to others when given a chance to perform in front of groups; prefers "blending in" to "standing out"

Quickly takes "center stage"; enjoys being the life of the party; seeks opportunities to perform in front of groups

11. **Risk Taking:** Enjoys taking chances; gambling on his/her ability to achieve a desired end; finds the stimulation of risking losing it all exhilirating; seeks out opportunities to "best the odds" and succeed where others have failed; has a knack for transforming setbacks into new opportunities for success.

Almost never puts himself in a position where he can fail; procrastinates when confronted with decisions involving some risk of failure

Jumps at new opportunities regardless of risk; readily assumes risk of trying something new & untested; is not discouraged in the face of setbacks

12. **Introspection:** Characterized by a desire to examine one's own motives & emotions; to understand her personal impact on others and their impact on her; a requirement to use her internal reactions to people and events as information to help understand the dynamics of the situation; to strive to understand her relationships with people, principles, and organizations.

Uninterested in examining own feelings & reactions to events; insensitive to her impact on others; little interest in exploring relationships

Always considers how things are affecting her; tries to sort out the ethical issues & clarify her values; seeks to understand herself

13. **Nurturance:** Characterized by a desire to care for the needs of others; to give of herself to provide help to those in need; to be seen as a provider & counselor to others; to help others grow spiritually, emotionally, & intellectually; to be viewed as one upon whom others can depend.

Not interested in being helpful to others; seems relatively unconcerned about the plight of others; seems to look down on those who ask for help

Among the first to lend a helping hand; enjoys being in the role of caretaker; encourages others; keeps commitments to others

14. **Understanding:** Needs to grasp the meaning of events and behavior; to develop theoretical or philosophical ideas explaining the relationships between complex variables, events, and issues; to use systematic approaches to gathering information to get to a deep understanding of what causes what and why.

Not particularly interested in understanding the world around her; shows little curiosity; satisfied with having only the facts—not necessary to have the "whys"; believes "ours is not to reason why, but simply to do or die"

Stubbornly persists until a full understanding of the issue is achieved; cannot rest until all the pieces of the puzzle fit together; uses all available resources to find explanations for events; must understand something before she is willing to do it

1. When surveys are returned, average each item for each rater category. Spreadsheets are wonderful for doing this step. After you have your average score for each item by rater group, use the appropriate percentile table (Peers or Directs, below) to obtain your percentile score.

Percentile Lookup Table for Direct Reports

	1.0	1.5	2.0	2.5	3.0	3.5	4.0	4.5	5.0	5.5	6.0	6.5	7.0
M1	1	1	1	1	2	6	12	23	37	54	70	83	91
M2	1	2	5	9	15	24	35	47	59	71	81	88	93
M3	1	2	4	7	14	23	36	51	64	76	86	92	96
M4	10	16	25	35	46	58	69	79	86	92	95	98	99
M5	1	1	1	3	6	11	19	31	44	58	72	83	90
M6	1	1	1	1	2	5	12	22	36	53	69	82	91
M7	1	2	3	6	11	18	27	39	51	63	74	83	90
M8	1	1	1	1	1	1	3	8	17	32	51	68	82
M9	1	1	1	1	2	5	10	19	31	46	62	76	87
M10	3	5	10	16	25	35	47	59	71	81	88	93	96
M11	1	1	1	2	4	8	16	26	40	54	68	80	89
M12	1	1	1	2	4	8	15	26	40	55	70	81	90
M13	1	1	1	1	2	5	10	18	30	44	59	73	84
M14	1	1	1	2	4	8	15	26	40	55	69	81	89

Percentile Lookup Table for Peer Raters

	1.0	1.5	2.0	2.5	3.0	3.5	4.0	4.5	5.0	5.5	6.0	6.5	7.0
M1	1	1	1	3	6	12	21	34	49	64	77	87	93
M2	1	2	5	9	16	26	37	51	64	75	85	91	96
M3	1	2	4	8	14	24	36	49	62	74	84	91	95
M4	10	16	25	35	47	59	71	80	88	93	96	98	99
M5	1	1	3	6	11	18	28	41	54	67	78	87	93
M6	1	1	2	4	8	15	25	37	52	66	78	87	93
M7	1	1	2	4	7	14	23	34	48	62	75	84	91
M8	1	1	1	2	4	9	17	27	41	56	70	81	89
M9	1	1	1	3	6	12	20	31	45	59	72	82	90
M10	2	5	9	15	24	35	48	61	72	82	89	94	97
M11	1	1	2	4	8	15	24	36	51	64	76	85	92
M12	1	1	2	3	7	14	23	35	49	63	76	86	92
M13	1	1	1	2	4	8	15	25	37	51	65	77	87
M14	1	1	1	2	5	10	19	32	47	63	76	87	93

Example: An employee has 7 directs and 5 peers. Look at some sample data and how to calculate the average score and look up the percentile score.

Item M1 is the question on Humility. Lower scores indicate a tendency to be less humble and higher scores indicate greater humility.

Item M1—Directs: 5, 5, 6, 7, 4, 7, 5   average = 39/7 = 5.6

Item M2—Peers: 6, 6, 6, 7, 7   average = 32/5 = 6.4

2. Now take these numbers and look up the percentile scores. Note that it is only necessary to simply round to the nearest value from the table. From the table for item M1 on directs we get a 54 which means this score is better than 53 percent of the people who have taken the survey. Look up the 6.4 in the Peers table to get a score of 87. This means that 86 percent of the people in the database have scored lower in peer ratings. Repeat this for all 14 items.

3. Notice that depending on the item and type of rater the percentile score may vary significantly for the same numerical score. This is based purely on how other people have been rated. Further, the scores are not meant to be interpreted as "good" or "bad"; it is just how others perceive you. It is also very dependent upon your present position. For example, a high score on structure is very desirable for a quality assurance manager at a nuclear plant. However, it would not be as desirable for a manager with responsibility for graphic design artists or advertising professionals. This survey facilitates the matching of people with jobs and circumstances to achieve the best results.

4. After determining the percentile score for each item for the Direct Reports and Peers, refer to the form on page 177 and use a highlighter pen to make a bar that extends to approximately the same point as the percentile score for Directs. Then take a regular pen and write a "P" at the approximate point of the Peers score.

PROFILE OF MOTIVES

Employee: _____

*Use a highlighter pen to draw a bar to represent the average of your Direct reports in percentile ranking. Use a pen to write **P** to indicate the Peers rating.*

1. **Humility:** *This need is characterized by a willingness to accept responsibility for failures; to feel personally liable for the trouble.*

Almost never accepts blame—
especially for things others do,
deflects it to others

0 10 20 30 40 50 60 70 80 90 100

Almost always accepts blame for
mistakes & avoids praise for a job well
done

2. **Achievement:** *This need is evidenced by a desire to achieve significant things, to outperform others, to win the competition at any cost.*

Almost never becomes involved in
competition, avoids recognition for
achievements

0 10 20 30 40 50 60 70 80 90 100

Almost always seeks out competition;
desires to win at all costs; seeks
recognition for successes

3. **Affiliation:** *People with this need want to belong to one or more groups of people—families, sports teams, organizations, etc.*

Almost never seeks out membership
in groups; prefers working alone

0 10 20 30 40 50 60 70 80 90 100

Almost always seeks out one or more
groups to join; evidences a desire to be
liked by everyone

4. **Aggression:** *Characterized by a desire to dominate others, to have one's way at all costs, to put others in a position of weakness, or criticize others publicly.*

Almost never tries to dominate
others in any way or avoids
arguments or using authority

0 10 20 30 40 50 60 70 80 90 100

Almost always assumes a dominant
position; takes charge & issues
orders; belittles those who disagree

5. **Autonomy:** *Characterized by a desire to operate independently; to have relative freedom from rules, regulations, policies, & close supervision, etc.*

Almost always asks for permission,
seeks guidance or requests direction;
enjoys close supervision

0 10 20 30 40 50 60 70 80 90 100

Almost never asks for permission or
guidance; enjoys working on own,
relying on own resources

6. **Change:** *This need is characterized by a requirement for a lot of variety in daily life; a desire for regular changes in duties or opportunities.*

Almost never welcomes change of
any sort, seeks consistency, follows
existing rules or procedures

0 10 20 30 40 50 60 70 80 90 100

Almost always seeks new challenges or
surroundings; uncomfortable with
constancy; thrives on novelty

7. **Structure:** *Characterized by a desire to understand the rules governing the work or situation or be able to predict outcomes with relative certainty.*

Thrives on chaos, sees circumstances
as shades of gray; enjoys ambiguous
or changing rules

0 10 20 30 40 50 60 70 80 90 100

Almost always structures work; defines
roles, establishes rules & operating
procedures; uniformity

8. **Influence:** *Characterized by a strong desire to exert an influence on people and events or to obtain some degree of control of the future.*

Almost never seeks out opportunities
to sell ideas; avoids being in a
position to influence events

0 10 20 30 40 50 60 70 80 90 100

Almost always attempts to influence the
course of events; enjoys debates; and
persuades others

9. **Endurance:** *Characterized by a need to complete any journey regardless of the personal sacrifice required; perseveres in the face of adversity.*

Almost never overcomes obstacles,
avoids tough tests of stamina &
perseverence, prefers smooth sailing

0 10 20 30 40 50 60 70 80 90 100

Almost always takes on the most
difficult challenges; enjoys "toughness"
tests; loves to try the impossible

10. **Exhibition:** *This need is characterized by a desire to be the focus of people's attention; to have the admiration of others; or to entertain others.*

Almost never seeks out opportunities
to be the center of attention; prefers
to blend in

0 10 20 30 40 50 60 70 80 90 100

Almost always takes "center stage";
enjoys being the life of the party;
behaves in ways that draw attention

11. **Risk Taking:** *Enjoys taking chances; gambling on his/her ability to achieve a desired end; finds the stimulation of risking losing it all exhilarating.*

| Almost never places himself/herself in a position where he/she could fail; avoids risk of failure | 0 10 20 30 40 50 60 70 80 90 100 | Almost always jumps at new opportunities; readily assumes the risk of trying new approaches |

12. **Introspection:** *Characterized by a desire to examine one's own motives & emotions and to understand their personal impact on others.*

| Almost never concern themselves with their own feelings & reactions to events; avoid looking at own motives | 0 10 20 30 40 50 60 70 80 90 100 | Almost always considers how things are affecting others; tries to clarify ethics & values issues |

13. **Nurturance:** *Desires to care for the needs of others; to give of oneself; to provide help to those in need; to be a provider or counselor to others.*

| Almost never tries to find ways to help; seems relatively unconcerned about the plight of others | 0 10 20 30 40 50 60 70 80 90 100 | Almost always is among the first to lend a helping hand; enjoys being the caretaker or encourager |

14. **Understanding:** *Needs to grasp the meaning of events & behavior; to develop theoretical or philosophical ideas; uses systematic approach to data gathering.*

| Almost never shows an interest in reaching a deep understanding; is satisfied with having only the facts | 0 10 20 30 40 50 60 70 80 90 100 | Almost always persists until a full understanding of the issue is achieved; searches for explanations |

HELPFUL HANDOUTS

In this section of *The 1997 McGraw-Hill Team and Organization Development Sourcebook,* you will find seven "helpful" handouts. These handouts cover topics such as:

✓ Team facilitation
✓ Virtual teams
✓ Organizational and team assessment
✓ Focus group meetings
✓ Sharing accomplishments

These handouts can be used as:

✓ Participant materials in training programs
✓ Discussion documents during meetings
✓ Coaching tools or job aids
✓ Information to be read by you or shared with a colleague

All the handouts are designed as succinct descriptions of an important issue or skill in performance management and development. They are formatted for quick, easily understood reading. (You may want to keep these handouts handy as memory joggers or checklists by posting them in your work area.) Most important of all, they contain nuggets of practical advice!

Preceding each handout is a brief overview of its contents and uses. The handout itself is on a separate page(s) to make reproduction convenient.

It is helpful to read these handouts *actively.* Highlight points that are important to you or push you to do further thinking. Identify content that needs further clarification. Challenge yourself to come up with examples that illustrate the key points. Urge others to be active consumers of these handouts, as well.

EIGHT TOOLS TO FACILITATE TEAM MEETINGS

Mary Margaret Palmer

Mary Margaret Palmer *is president of Facilitation Technologies, a consulting firm that provides facilitation and training services, and Paperless Boarding Systems, Inc., a manufacturer of paper-free meeting and training materials. Mary Margaret is a member of the International Association of Facilitators, founder of the Internet newsgroup, misc.business.facilitators, and a frequent contributor to* **The Facilitator.** *Mary Margaret can be contacted at 5400 Freidrich Lane, #61, Austin, TX 78744, 512-912-8147 or at mmpalmer@onr.com.*

OVERVIEW

At the heart of team facilitation lie the many processes and techniques used to help members achieve their meeting goals. While many processes can be used to achieve the same end, successful facilitators know what process or technique to apply to any given situation. Factors that influence the selection of a process include: the desired end result, group size, meeting room set-up, time constraints, personalities of participants, their level of expertise, documentation requirements, and the facilitator's intuition. Eight of the more commonly used processes and techniques are described in this helpful handout.

EIGHT TOOLS TO FACILITATE TEAM MEETINGS

1. Brainstorming

The most widely known and universally applied group process in use today. Also known as Idea Generation or Blue Sky. The purpose of brainstorming is to rapidly generate ideas, solutions, or issues relating to a particular topic, situation, or problem. During a brainstorming session ideas are generated and recorded without discussion or judgment. The ideas put forward are then discussed, clarified, and organized. Duplicates or inappropriate input are eliminated and the results documented.

2. Clustering and Affinity Diagramming

Processes for organizing ideas and issues collected during a brainstorming session. Each idea must be written separately on some type of note card that can be easily attached, moved, and re-attached to a wall or board. With Clustering, the facilitator posts and groups the cards one at time at the direction of the participants. With Affinity Diagramming, all the cards are randomly posted on the wall and the participants silently move and organize them themselves. No guidelines for grouping are given. After all cards are grouped, each cluster is assigned a meaningful label.

3. Role Playing

Gives participants the chance to try on new or different roles. Role playing helps to resolve misunderstandings and provides an experiential opportunity to function in an unfamiliar role or situation. Team-building simulations are the best sources for this technique.

4. Small Group Work

Expedites the generation and evaluation of creative ideas when working with a large group. Participants are divided into small groups of four to six. These groups are then given either the same or different tasks to perform, e.g., develop a mission statement or come up with five ideas for improving customer service. When the whole group comes back together, each small group presents its results for discussion and validation by the larger group.

5. Round Robin and Talking Stick

Facilitates discussion and provides a forum in which everyone can speak. In Round Robin, each participant is given a chance to speak in turn. One person is selected to start. When he or she is finished speaking, it becomes the turn of the next person to speak. The Round Robin is finished when everyone has had a chance to express themselves. Usually a time limit for speaking is set. During this process no one can interrupt the speaker and no discussion is allowed between speakers.

Talking Stick is a variation of Round Robin that has its origins in Native American traditions. During this process the group sits in a circle and an object such as a ball or stick is passed from speaker to speaker. However, unlike Round Robin, participants can pass the object to anyone of their choosing. Moments of silence between speakers are observed.

6. Straw Man

A written example or sample created prior to a workshop or meeting. The Straw Man serves as a starting point for discussion, thereby providing the group with something to edit, change, accept, or reject. An example of a Straw Man might be a company's mission statement. Sometimes several Straw Men are presented for comparison purposes.

7. Force Field Analysis

A framework for problem solving advanced by Kurt Lewin. This technique examines both supporting and resisting forces to a change or solution. A strategy for accomplishing the change is developed from the insights that result. The steps of Force Field Analysis are:

✓ Define the problem and write out a problem statement.

✓ Define the objectives: the desired results if the problem were solved.

✓ Define the driving forces: those conditions, actions, events that promote or will promote change.

✓ Define the resisting forces that inhibit change.

✓ Develop a solution strategy given the identified drivers and resisters.

✓ Compare the strategy to the objectives.

8. Decision-Making Scale

Determines what will constitute agreement or consensus among a group of participants. Visually the scale is a line with six evenly spaced points end to end. Each point represents a number from zero to five, where five is the most desired and zero the least. Participants define in their own words what each point means. For example, a five might be characterized by the expression, "To die for" and zero by "Over my dead body." Participants also decide what will constitute consensus, that is, what will be the minimum votes needed for a decision to pass. For example, a group of 15 might decide that at least 10 of the votes must be a five and that none of the remaining votes can be below a three. Voting is accomplished by a showing of hands where a fist represents zero.

FIVE STAR POINTS OF INTEGRATION

Cynthia Solomon

Cynthia Solomon, *Ph.D. is a technical program specialist for FERMCO, an environmental restoration company in Ohio (6469 Fountains Blvd., West Chester, OH 45069, 513-777-5435). Cindy has led or designed organizational and professional development projects for her employer, the health care industry, and professional and private organizations. She authored* **TQM in Dietetics and Nutrition Services,** *and has designed several training and management documents. She also manages a private human resources development practice. Cynthia was a contributor to* **The 1996 McGraw-Hill Team and Organization Development Sourcebook.**

OVERVIEW

Here is a handout that simplifies the process of integration for those who work in complex environments. The *Five Star Points of Integration* is an easy way for employees to remember how they can tie in their work with other individuals or groups. The "STAR" is most helpful for complex work processes, or for work processes that have many affecting or affected points of integration.

Anyone who performs work that affects the work of others, or whose work is affected by others, should be constantly asking how they can best integrate their work into the entire work process in their organization. In the absence of properly integrated work, individual efforts may be fragmented and never achieve full potential within the organization.

The "STAR" is a simple way to remind all workers to check five questions about their individual tasks, and to address all five points, as necessary, to ensure that their individual effort becomes an integrated part of a larger whole effort. The "STAR" helps to avoid the following errors:

✓ Failure to use corporate knowledge to achieve excellence.

✓ Creation of a work process or system that is cumbersome or unnecessary for others to follow.

✓ Resistance of a work process by others.

✓ Rejection of individual work by those whose approval or acceptance is necessary to support it and help make it successful.

FIVE STAR POINTS OF INTEGRATION

WHOSE WORK DO I AFFECT?

❏ Whose work will change as a result of my work?

(Consider changes in work procedures, materials used, regulations that have to be followed, people who must be involved, for example.)

WHO SHOULD I INVOLVE?

❏ Who has experience with my task who could help me perform my work?

❏ Whose advice should I seek?

❏ What corporate knowledge can I use to achieve excellence?

WHO SHOULD I TELL?

❏ Who should I tell about my work—at its inception, during its creation, and at its completion?

WHOSE APPROVAL DO I NEED?

❏ Who is my customer, and what does my customer want?

❏ What external stakeholders must be satisfied with my work?

(Consider members of the local community, professional organizations, government regulators, taxpayers, for example.)

❏ What level of management must approve my work?

WITH WHOM MUST I COLLABORATE IN PLANNING?

❏ Who else uses the same resources I need?

❏ How can we make decisions about the most effective use of those resources?

❏ How does my work schedule affect the schedule of other projects?

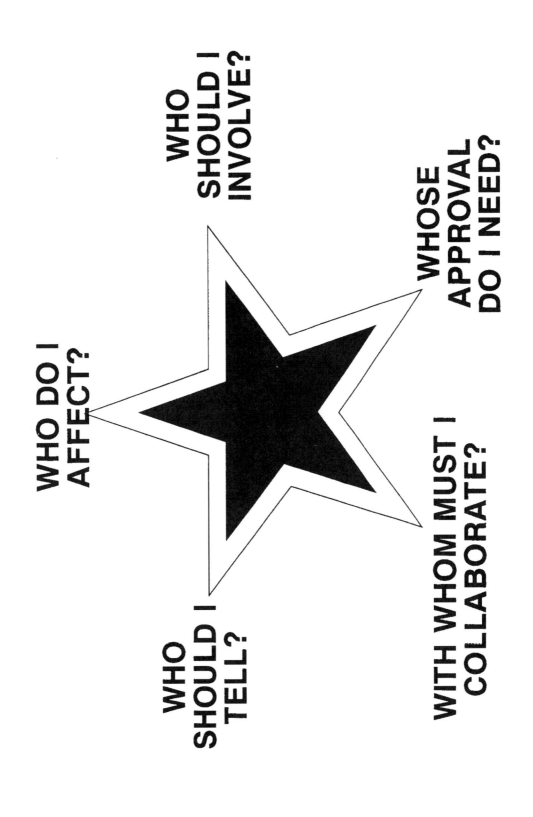

WHO SHOULD I INVOLVE?

WHOSE APPROVAL DO I NEED?

WHO DO I AFFECT?

WHO SHOULD I TELL?

WITH WHOM MUST I COLLABORATE?

TIPS FOR VIRTUAL TEAMS

Barbara Pate Glacel and Emile Robert

Barbara Pate Glacel, *Ph.D. is CEO and* **Emile A. Robert, Jr.,** *Ph.D. is COO of VIMA International (5290 Lyngate Ct., Burke, VA 22015, 703-764-0780). They are coauthors of* **Light Bulbs for Leaders—A Guide Book for Team Learning** *(John Wiley, 1996). VIMA International works with clients in the United States, Europe, Africa, and the Pacific Rim. Services include executive and organizational development, team learning, and strategic leadership. Both authors are on the adjunct faculty of the Center for Creative Leadership. They each have extensive experience in human resource development and administration with such organizations as Lockheed Martin, MITRE, NASA, Atlantic Richfield, and MCI as well as not-for-profit agencies.*

OVERVIEW

"The relationships among the partners in a virtual organization must include trust, open and honest communication, and compatible management styles."

Goldman, Nagel, and Preiss

Virtual reality. Virtual space. Virtual organizations. Virtual teams. The word *virtual* is today's buzzword. What does it really mean? How does it impact organizations? Simply, it means "in essence or in effect, but not in fact." Operationally, however, there seems to be a struggle for a common definition.

Virtual organizations exist in disparate locations but are interconnected. Work must be accomplished by people and resources who are geographically separated but somehow joined together to add purposeful value. Sometimes people in different locations never see each other; nor might they understand and view the whole process of creation from beginning to end.

In other cases, the members of this virtual organization must find synergies among themselves in order to improve their products, services, and information. Advances in technology help make this possible without face-to-face interaction.

The question is: Can **virtual teams** exist? Perhaps this question is academic. At the very least, it is semantic. Given the strict definition of team, it is probable that virtual teams exist only with great difficulty, if at all. In fact, a firm foundation of nonvirtual, face-to-face relationship-building is an essential prerequisite for virtual teaming.

A team is different from a group of people who work together. The team is absolutely interconnected, adding value because of their connectedness, mutuality, complementary skills, and diverse outlooks. Those four tenets demand that the team work its way through the often difficult process of formation. This demands time for sorting out and bartering over who does what and who is in charge, the establishment of mutually agreed-upon values and practices, and the continuous attention to what is important for achieving the goal. Only by giving time and credence to this process can the team be high-performing.

Geographic dispersion eliminates the possibility of learning through osmosis. When the core team works together, it is continuously learning by hearing and observing what is going on around it. Even package deliveries and ringing phones are inputs to the awareness of what's happening. While electronic and real-time communications may be good, they don't substitute for being in the next room.

Handling conflict and emotionally charged issues is difficult in virtual space. And, in fact, one doesn't always know there is a conflict or an emotion attached until an issue has worked its way through several e-mails. By then, frustrations and concerns can overwhelm a team's performance.

Nothing beats face-to-face communication, not even the combination of video-teleconference, telephone conference, electronic mail, or the more mundane fax, phone, and written communications. Despite all those technologies, **virtual teams** demand proximity. Virtual work groups where products and services are "thrown over the wall" are a "piece of cake," but teams have different requirements in order to take advantage of connectedness, mutuality, complementary skills, and diverse outlooks. Use the following tips to help your virtual team be successful.

TIPS FOR VIRTUAL TEAMS

✓ **Find** time early on in the process to get together face-to-face.

✓ **Learn** something personal about each member of the team so you can exchange a bit of small talk when you begin an interaction.

✓ **Post** pictures of the team members near your computer screen or next to the telephone so you can envision your teammates when you are interacting.

✓ **Be aware** that team members have other priorities and obligations that you may be interrupting. Since you can't see them in person, you don't know what is in front of them when you call.

✓ **Use** frequent process checks to assess how the relationship is going and how the work is progressing.

✓ **Communicate** often, even if nothing is pressing in your work together.

✓ **Rely** on more personal communication rather than less, especially if something seems wrong. Try to solve problems first through face-to-face interactions. If this is not possible, work through other communications options in this order: video-teleconference, telephone conference, e-mail, fax, and last by letter.

✓ **Be attuned** to heightened emotions when using electronic mail. If you feel frustrated or angry after reading a written communication, take a process time-out before sending an e-mail response.

✓ **Share responsibility** to get the team back on track if virtuality—or anything else—is getting in the way of meeting the team's overall goal.

FOUR ORGANIZATIONAL ASSESSMENT TOOLS

25

Cathleen Smith Hutchison

Cathleen Smith Hutchison *is Managing Partner of Metamorphosis Consulting Group (P.O. Box 1147, Cedar Crest, NM 87008, 505-281-4496), a full-service human resources consulting firm specializing in managing corporate change. She is the coauthor of* **Instructor Competencies: The Standards,** *vol. I and vol. II and numerous professional articles. She is a past officer of the International Society for Performance Improvement at international and chapter levels and of the International Board of Standards for Training Performance and Instruction. Cathleen was a contributor to* **The 1996 McGraw-Hill Team and Organization Development Sourcebook.**

OVERVIEW

There are a number of data collection and analysis tools that can provide information about the status of the organization. Some of these tools are:

1. A Climate Survey or Attitude Survey
2. An Operational Audit
3. A Culture Audit
4. An Organizational Scan

Each of these tools differs in its scope and perspective. The following handout characterizes each of the four methods and identifies their key strengths and uses. The organizational assessment tools are then compared and contrasted in an easy-to-read column format for quick reference.

FOUR ORGANIZATIONAL ASSESSMENT TOOLS

1. The Climate or Attitude Survey

This is a method of assessing the current feeling(s) and opinion(s) within the organization regarding particular topic(s), issue(s), initiative(s), or action(s). The climate survey collects data related to "what it feels like" to work in this organization. While the climate of a country reflects things like the temperature, amount of rain and sun, and the length of the growing season, the climate of an organization reflects the same type of quantifiable surface characteristics. You can experience the climate of a country at poolside in a resort hotel while sipping Mai Tais and never meet the natives. You can obtain climate and attitude information with a survey sent out from a comfortable corner office and never know there are unaddressed issues beneath the surface or relating to other issues. However, you do not raise expectations that action will be taken to address issues other than those specifically being surveyed. *If the organization is interested in what employees feel about one or more specific issues, topics, initiatives, or actions, it should conduct a climate or attitude survey.*

2. The Operational Audit

This is a method of assessing the processes, procedures, methods, and activities of the organization. The operational audit gathers data on both the actual processes and procedures that are being followed and also those that are specified and prescribed in manuals, handbooks, rules and regulations, and guidelines. It compares the two to assess the level of variance or compliance between them. This method provides a snapshot of what the organization is actually doing to achieve its results. An operational audit of a country would look not only at the laws and regulations on the books, but also at the way the citizens work around those laws and the level of consistency with which they are applied. Similarly, an organization would analyze the processes and procedures that actually occur and compare them to "the rules." This audit determines the level of consistency of procedures in actual practice throughout the organization. *If an organization is interested in the level of compliance with prescribed and documented policies, procedures, and methods, it should conduct an operational audit.*

3. The Culture Audit

This is a method of assessing the behavioral practices in place within the organization and the manner in which the organization conducts its business on a day-to-day basis. As with the culture of a country, the culture of an organization is comprised of how and why people in the culture behave as they do, follow the practices, dress, rituals, and have the heroes and myths, values and beliefs that they do. Understanding the culture of either a country or an organization allows the observer to understand the beliefs behind and underneath surface behaviors. It allows for behavioral understanding of an organization, and may yield the ability to broadly predict reactions and behaviors in future situations. *If the organization is interested in identifying current values, beliefs, behaviors, and practices, it should conduct a culture audit.*

4. The Organizational Scan

This is a method of assessing both *what* is occurring in the organization and *how* the organization conducts its business. This method deals with all aspects of the organization as a system. The organizational scan is, in some ways, a combination of an operational audit and a culture audit. While the breadth of the assessment is increased, the depth is somewhat reduced. The organizational scan does not usually collect data in either of the two areas to the level of detail that the individual audits do. However, a key feature is that the organizational scan does address the level of alignment between the culture and the operations of the organization and their alignment with support systems within the organization. *If the organization is interested in an overall picture of the alignment of culture and operations and how they support and interact with each other, it should conduct an organizational scan.*

	Climate/ Attitude Survey	Operational Audit	Culture Audit	Organizational Scan
Purpose	To determine the feelings and opinions that employees have at a given time about a given issue/initiative or set of issues/ initiatives.	To determine the processes, procedures, methods, and activities that occur throughout the organization for comparison to those that are documented and/or dictated.	To determine the values, belief systems, and behavioral practices in place throughout the organization that govern the way people behave with one another and how they get their work accomplished.	To determine what the issues are in the organization. To determine the strengths, weaknesses, values, and practices that operate throughout the organization and the level of of both horizontal and vertical alignment throughout the organization on these issues.
Scope	Either limited to a specific issue or set of related issues or aimed at a broad spectrum of potential issues of "what it feels like" working within the organization. The methodology limits data collection to a surface level and makes follow-up difficult.	A broad and deep data gathering effort to identify the processes, procedures, methods, and activities the organization undertakes to achieve its results. It may be targeted at operations regarding a specific function or segment of the organization or it can address the entire organization.	A broad and deep data gathering effort to identify all behavioral aspects of *how* and *why* the organization operates as it does to achieve its results. It may be targeted at a specific function or segment of the organization or it can address the entire organization.	A very broad data gathering effort to identify not only how the organization operates, what processes and procedures it uses, but also issues around individuals or groups within the organization. The main focus is the level of alignment of all elements within the organizational system.

	Climate/ Attitude Survey	Operational Audit	Culture Audit	Organizational Scan
Methodology	Survey of questions identified prior to data collection. Usually requires choice of predetermined responses to most questions with one or more open-ended questions to elicit data broader than specified in the body of the survey.	A combination of facilitated focus groups, interviews, work site observations, review of artifacts (tools, equipment, and documents), questionnaires, and instruments. These can be modified during the process to follow up on unexpected data.	A combination of facilitated focus groups, interviews, questionnaires, and instruments. These can be modified during the process to follow up on unexpected data.	A combination of interviews, facilitated focus groups, work site observations, review of artifacts (tools, equipment, and documents), questionnaires, and instruments. These can be modified during the process to follow up on unexpected data.
Target Population	Usually the entire employee population. Sometimes a representative sample.	Key operators of specified and/or critical processes, procedures, methods, and activities. Also the users of the outputs of these processes, procedures, methods, and activities.	Either all or key representatives of the senior management group, plus representatives of all areas of the organization.	Either all or key representatives of the senior management group, plus representatives of all areas of the organization. Key operators of specified and/or critical processes, procedures, methods, and activities. Also the users of the outputs of these processes, procedures, methods, and activities.

	Climate/ Attitude Survey	Operational Audit	Culture Audit	Organizational Scan
Place in the Organizational System	Analyzes the feelings and opinions elicited on a given issue/ initiative or set of issues/initiatives.	Analyzes the procedural operation of the organization.	Analyzes the behavioral norms, values, and belief systems throughout the organization.	Analyzes all aspects of the organizational system and their alignment with each other.
Strengths	It collects quantifiable data that can be statistically manipulated to reflect how people feel about specific issues and initiatives.	Identifies what is actually happening within the ranks of the organization. Identifies bottlenecks, barriers, and enhancers to processes and procedures. It identifies problems and opportunities related to processes and procedures. It collects anecdotal data that can be probed as needed and can be followed up on later. Can include both quantitative and qualitative data.	Identifies values, beliefs, behavioral norms, and practices of how people interact and work with or around each other. Describes people's feelings about each other and the organization. It identifies problems and opportunities related to behaviors. It collects anecdotal data that can be probed as needed and can be followed up on later. Can include both quantitative and qualitative data.	It collects comprehensive data on the alignment of what the organization is doing and how people are doing it. It looks at both sides of the organizational alignment model and at the support systems in place to maintain them. It identifies alignment, nonalignment, and related problems and opportunities. It collects anecdotal data that can be probed as needed and can be followed up on later. Can include both quantitative and qualitative data.

	Climate/ Attitude Survey	*Operational Audit*	*Culture Audit*	*Organizational Scan*
Potential Problems	It often does not collect data that is actionable. It is difficult to use as a management tool. It is difficult to follow up on unexpected data.	It does not address relevant behaviors and norms that affect how things are accomplished. It may miss barriers caused by the people side of the organization or cultural misalignment.	It does not address what processes and procedures are in place. It may miss issues around what is being done that is inappropriate for the strategy.	Ordinarily it does not delve as deeply into issues on either side of the organizational alignment model as either of the individual audits. Because it is not as deep as the individual audits, the scan may uncover problems and opportunities that will require more detailed research or analysis for full understanding.
Uses	Identify how widespread generic feelings and opinions are held. To broadly determine if problems exist that may require additional analysis or intervention.	Determine the level of compliance with rules and regulations and if processes are adequate to achieve the strategy or if process engineering or continuous improvement interventions are needed. It can identify operational priorities for intervention.	Determine culture strength, characteristics, and strategic fit. It can identify the need for cultural change or interventions. It can identify behavioral priorities for intervention.	Determine alignment of the organization as it is operating today. Determine need for organizational alignment interventions. It can identify organizational priorities for a wide variety of potential interventions.

	Climate/ Attitude Survey	Operational Audit	Culture Audit	Organizational Scan
Products	An academic style report of quantifiable segments of the organization and opinions about specific issues or initiatives.	A descriptive report on what processes, procedures, and activities are actually operating within the organization and a comparison to those in guideline, rules and regulations, and handbooks.	A descriptive report on how people throughout the organization interact and communicate with each other to accomplish their tasks and achieve their results and a description of the values and beliefs held by segments of the population.	A descriptive report on both what processes, procedures, and activities are actually operating within the organization and how people throughout the organization interact and communicate with each other to accomplish their tasks and achieve their results. Additionally how the two align with each other and with the support systems in place throughout the organization.

SHARING TEAM 26 ACCOMPLISHMENTS

Sophie Liebman-Oberstein

Sophie Liebman-Oberstein *is Senior Consultant for Key Managment Strategies (7906 Montgomery Avenue, Elkins Park, PA 19027, 215-635-6170, x131). She has published articles in* **Training and Development Magazine** *on keeping participants enthusiastic and designing creative training efforts. Sophie is also an instructor in the training certificate program at Mercer County Community College.*

OVERVIEW

Two factors that contribute to successful teams are spending a lot of time together and making rewards and recognition part of the regular team agenda. Too often, however, time constraints get in the way of team meetings. Busy executives and managers may minimize the time that teams spend together due to the belief that it is an unproductive use of the sponsoring organization's money. When they do meet, teams often get right down to business and ignore their prior intentions to recognize group accomplishments.

To ensure that infrequent team sessions achieve their full impact, time must be set aside to review past team successes. The following handout lists creative suggestions for using periodic team meetings to share team accomplishments. The ideas on the list are meant to go beyond the idea of simply starting every meeting off by having members review their achievements. Some of the ideas take longer than others or require advance preparation. These are grouped accordingly. Use them as written or use them as springboards for your own creative approaches to team building.

SHARING TEAM ACCOMPLISHMENTS

In fifteen minutes or less:

1. Ask: What Good Things Are They Saying About
   Us Behind Our Backs?

   > Start a team meeting by asking members to toot their own horns in an unconventional way—from an outsider's point of view. Ask participants to think of good things that other people in the organization are saying about the team and its output since the last time the team met.

2. Ask: What Team Accomplishments Did You
   Share with Your Loved Ones?

   > Very few people share the details of every project they work on with their loved ones. The projects they do discuss with family and friends, therefore, are the ones that are the most exciting or interesting. Asking this question highlights the results of which the members are most proud. It also lends a necessary social dimension to team interaction when members introduce each other to the people important to them outside of work.

3. Post Key Accomplishments on Flip Charts.

   > Before team members arrive, hang flip charts throughout the room. Put a provocative heading on each flip chart such as "My contribution to the team's output this month," "Why we deserve a day off," "How we earned our salaries," or "What worked this week." As each team member enters, hand her a marker and ask her to write responses to the headings on the charts posted around the room. Review the charts before beginning the meeting.

If you're willing to prepare in advance:

4. Give Team Awards.

   > Ask a different team member to come to each session prepared to present a team achievement award. The award should summarize the successes of the team since its last meeting. The award can be as creative as the giver would like (e.g., it could have a fun title, it could be in the form of a certificate/trophy, or it could be presented via video).

5. Create a Results Collage.

Ask each team member to bring in one item that shows that they have been successful (e.g., a letter from a satisfied "customer," a cost savings report, or a finished product). Put all of the items together to create a collage of the team's accomplishment. Keep it on display somewhere between meetings as a source of inspiration.

6. Create a Success Tracking Mechanism.

Fund-raising groups are well known for the giant "thermometers" they use to chart their advancement towards a goal. Let the team create its own symbolic way of measuring successes. Start each subsequent meeting off by using the device to track achievements.

If you have an hour or more:

7. Develop a Yearbook.

At key meetings (e.g., year or project end), the time is ripe for reviewing accomplishments in the form of a yearbook. The yearbook might include sections like extracurriculars where members can list their outside interests, superlatives where every team member is assigned a "best" title, or a year-in-review page. It is especially motivating if you can hold on to the yearbook until a particularly stressful time later in the year and then distribute copies to all team members.

8. Produce a Newsletter or Press Release.

Why not let the team create a tool that is both motivating and practical as a means of communicating the team's accomplishments externally? Have the team create a newsletter of their accomplishments or write a press release for the sponsoring organization's newsletter.

9. Invent a Team Logo.

Having a consistent symbol that represents what your team has accomplished and what it brings to the sponsoring organization is a very effective ongoing motivator. It is especially useful for internal or external team communications. Let the logo represent the contributions of all team members to ensure more cohesive relationships.

10. Write a Team Member Job Description.

If you really want to know how much you have accomplished, write it all down. When we create job descriptions, we learn the true scope of our own responsibilities and value. Having a team member job description can also be practical when you want to recruit new team members or form new teams in the future.

TAKING THE TEAM'S TEMPERATURE

27

Bill Matthews

William R. Matthews *is a senior consultant/facilitator with Prism Performance Systems (37000 Grand River Ave., Suite 230, Farmington Hills, MI 48335, 810-474-8855). Bill's specialties include team, leadership, and organizational development, systemic change, facilitation skills, and educational games and simulations. He is a member of the board of directors of the North American Simulation and Gaming Association. Bill is also an adjunct lecturer in Education at The University of Michigan-Dearborn, and coauthor of the book,* **101 Ways to Jump Start Your Job Search** *(McGraw-Hill, 1996).*

OVERVIEW

Taking the team's temperature is a practical, constructive way to help team members check out and deal with what's going on here and now. The purpose is to focus in on what *is* or *will be* happening to the team that needs attention or information right away. It's an important tool to circumvent many of the problems that can occur "living together" as a team, just as they would living together as a family. The information surfaced by the temperature check can help the team eliminate any potential roadblocks and move forward without leaving members behind.

The technique can be used periodically to take a snapshot of what the team looks like in the eyes and minds of its members. The format makes it possible to surface and deal with sensitive issues and achieve more positive, productive results with fewer stressful feelings.

Each member of the team fills out the one-page temperature check, writing in only those areas on which they have a personal opinion. The information from all team members is combined and presented back to the team with the expectation that they will clarify issues and develop actions where appropriate. *It's important that the team take ownership for resolving any outstanding issues.*

Create a flip chart page for each of the five categories of the temperature check and post them on the training/meeting room wall for very large groups. Ask each person to circulate from one chart to another and add their comments as desired. When everyone has had a chance to contribute, place the charts together at the front of the room for the team or group to inspect as a means of starting a meaningful discussion.

The Team Temperature

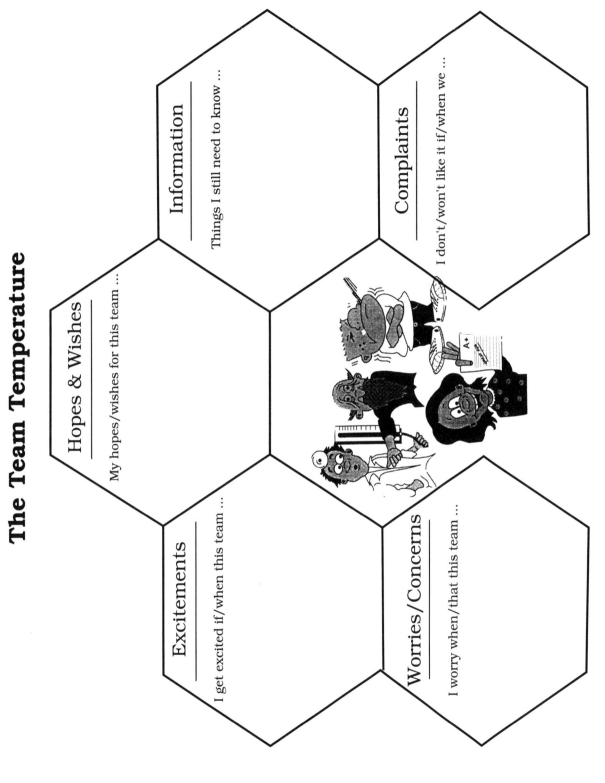

Information

Things I still need to know …

Complaints

I don't/won't like it if/when we …

Hopes & Wishes

My hopes/wishes for this team …

Excitements

I get excited if/when this team …

Worries/Concerns

I worry when/that this team …

TWELVE STEPS TO SUCCESSFUL FOCUS GROUP MEETINGS

Brooke Broadbent

Brooke Broadbent *(867 Explorer Lane, Orleans, Ontario, Canada KIC 2S3, 613-837-3924, broadb@magi.com) is a training consultant specializing in instructional design, technical writing, and project management. Brooke is the author of numerous courses, articles, books, and brochures about computer-related training, training methods, and workplace safety. Brooke was also a contributor to* **The 1996 McGraw-Hill Training and Performance Sourcebook.**

OVERVIEW

Focus group meetings, which are ad hoc gatherings to discuss specific topics, have become popular data capturing tools for task analyses and competency studies. They are also used in the business improvement process and to guide human resource practitioners in other activities.

The popularity of focus group exercises can lead to negative feelings among participants who give up their time for such activities and do not reap any benefits. What would you do if a participant in one of your focus groups introduced herself by saying that she has yet to see any results from the numerous focus groups she has attended in the past? Brush it off as cynicism? Wonder if all participants are thinking the same way?

The best approach to dealing with unenthusiastic focus group participants is to be proactive. Use the tips on this handout to develop strategies for positive and productive meetings. By adapting the following ideas to your particular situation, you will increase the likelihood of collecting accurate data from all focus group members, even those who are reluctant to participate.

TWELVE STEPS TO SUCCESSFUL FOCUS GROUP MEETINGS

Steps	Why?	Examples
PLANNING		
1. Carefully plan what you are looking for before the meetings start.	Knowing your priorities before the meetings start will help you zero in on pertinent data when it is raised and capture it for your report.	Establish a need to identify infrequent and critical tasks since they may become a focus in training at a later time.
2. Set up a method to chunk the data you plan to collect in the focus group exercise.	Up-front categorization of data provides a framework for analysis.	In conducting a task analysis, you could use several levels such as: jobs, main responsibilities, tasks, perhaps sub-tasks, knowledge, and skills.
3. Allocate ample time to conduct the focus groups.	During the focus group meetings, people may need to come to grips with a new way of seeing their work. This may precipitate time-consuming discussion.	Plan a day-long meeting for each focus group meeting.
4. Collect your data from people who perform the work being analyzed.	People who do the job know it best.	Arrange to hold structured meetings with mixed groups of people who perform the work you are analyzing.
CONDUCTING		
5. Explain the process to the participants.	Participants may have been in other similar but slightly different processes and they may expect a process other than the one you have in mind.	Prepare flip chart pages listing the components of the process, post them on the wall, and explain the process using your sheets as a reference.
6. Use a flexible way of collecting data.	Focus group members may get new insight as the exercise progresses, forcing you to modify your approach.	Collect data on flip chart pages. Post them on the wall. Move and regroup the sheets as required.

Steps	Why?	Examples
7. Sell the utility of the exercise.	Participants may be skeptical about whether the exercise will lead to anything productive, especially if they have been through a similar exercise that did not produce positive results.	Explain how you think the data you collect should be used and what you, personally, will do to achieve that end.
8. Concentrate on maintaining the credibility of the focus group process.	The success of the exercise depends on participants perceiving it as credible.	Consult with representatives from all stakeholder groups and incorporate their input into your report; if some of these stakeholders are not available for focus group activities, meet with them separately.
9. Concentrate on end results.	Focusing on end results helps to give a clear meaning to the exercise and moves participants' energies in a specific direction.	Openly discuss the nature of your final report with participants, its distribution, and examples of good results from other focus groups.
10. Acknowledge the value of participants' contributions.	Chances are that nobody is doing the participants' work while they are meeting with you. Recognize that they are making a personal sacrifice to help you conduct your focus group meeting.	Thank people both during and after the meeting.
ANALYZING AND REPORTING		
11. Validate data.	Calm reflection on the data will often lead to a higher level of analysis.	Meet with a second group of people who perform the work being analyzed, provide them with the results of the earlier focus group meeting, and invite their comments.

Steps	Why?	Examples
12. Thoroughly review your data and draft your report.	A clear, concise report will be easier to understand and will therefore be more credible.	Compare, contrast, analyze, synthesize, use tables and flowcharts—do whatever it takes to produce a pertinent, easy-to-understand analysis of the data.

REFERENCES

Friesen, Kaye and Associates. 1996. *Designing Instruction Workshop: Course Manual.* Ottawa.

Harrington, H. James. 1991. *Business Process Improvement.* New York: McGraw-Hill, p. 242.

Rummler, Gary. 1987. "Determining Needs," *Training and Development Handbook.* New York: McGraw-Hill, pp. 217-248.

PRACTICAL GUIDES

In this section of *The 1997 McGraw-Hill Team and Organization Development Sourcebook,* you will find twelve practical guides. These "how to" guides are short articles containing useful ideas and guidelines for implementing training and performance support initiatives.

You will find advice about such topics as:

✓ Organizational motivation

✓ Building quality, participatory organizations

✓ Downsizing

✓ Organizational learning

✓ Customer advocacy

✓ Teleconferencing

✓ Task agreements

✓ Organizational assessment

✓ Brainstorming

✓ New leadership

Each guide contains step-by-step advice. Several have examples, illustrations, charts, and tables to enhance your understanding of the content. You will find that these guides are clearly organized and easy to read.

Here are four possible uses for these practical guides:

1. Guidelines for your own consulting, facilitating, and training interventions.

2. Implementation advice to be shared with peers and people who report to you.

3. Recommendations to senior management.

4. Reading assignments in team building and organizational consultations and training programs.

HOW TO REDUCE THE DEMOTIVATORS IN YOUR ORGANIZATION

29

Dean Spitzer

Dean R. Spitzer, *Ph.D. is president of Dean R. Spitzer & Associates, Inc. (Suite 316, 5150 S. Florida Avenue, Lakeland, FL 33813, 941-648-2754 , drspitzer@aol.com), a firm specializing in enhancing organizational motivation. He is a past vice-president of the International Society for Performance Improvement (ISPI), author of numerous publications, and contributor to the* **Handbook of Human Performance Technology.** *Dean's latest book is* **SuperMotivation: A Blueprint for Energizing Your Organization from Top to Bottom** *(AMACOM Books, 1995). He was also a contributor to* **The 1996 McGraw-Hill Team and Organization Development Sourcebook.**

Do you think that your organization is doing all that it can to support and reinforce its employees? Read this guide to discover the surprising ways that you may actually be sabotaging your organization's best human resource policies. A list of five action steps will help you to reduce negative motivational factors and create a much improved organizational climate.

Surveys have indicated that motivation in organizations is at an all-time low. Eighty four percent of employees report that they are not working up to their full potential, and, most shockingly, 50% say that they are only putting enough effort into their work to hold on to their jobs (Spitzer, 1995)!

The problem is, in large part, due to the prevalence of hidden and generally ignored, negative motivational factors called "demotivators." Demotivators are nagging, daily occurrences that frustrate employees and cause them to reduce, either consciously or unconsciously, the amount of productive energy they use in their jobs. It is a sad fact that demotivators are draining the motivational life out of employees, undermining morale, and wasting the most valuable resource we have—human talent and creativity.

But demotivators are not necessarily egregious wrongs. They are simply counterproductive practices (such as the ones listed below) that have crept into an organization and become part of its normal operations—more a result of neglect than design. Demotivators exist because they are allowed to, and they remain because little or nothing has been done about them.

Common Demotivators

Politics	Unfairness
Unclear expectations	Discouraging responses
Unnecessary rules	Criticism
Poorly designed work	Capacity underutilization
Unproductive meetings	Tolerating poor performance
Lack of follow-up	Being taken for granted
Constant change	Management invisibility
Internal competition	Overcontrol
Dishonesty	Takeaways
Hypocrisy	Being forced to do poor-quality work
Withholding information	

Many organizations take great pride in touting their humane treatment of employees and their employee-centered work environments. Other companies pat themselves on the back for the great salaries and benefits they offer. However, when employees find themselves excluded from important decisions, deprived of information, bored in useless meetings, and given the same rewards as poor performers, these demotivating forces negate much of the hoped-for positive impact of the benevolent treatment.

No matter how generous an organization is to its employees, demotivators will be around long after they have forgotten the act of generosity. And, no matter how interesting or challenging employees' jobs might be, demotivators leave them feeling helpless and disappointed.

One worker summed up the problem well by wistfully observing, "This could be such a wonderful place to work—*if it weren't for all the demotivators!*"

The Insidious Impact of Demotivators

Too many managers are isolated from the daily frustrations of the rank-and-file workforce and simply do not appreciate the seriousness of the demotivation problem. They underestimate the importance of what they consider to be "minor irritations" in their organizations, not realizing how large these irritations loom in the subjective experience of employees. To employees stuck in the middle of them, they are not minor at all. Demotivators tend to affect people far out of proportion to their actual size.

Not only do demotivators trigger negative emotions, but they also elicit negative behaviors—such as withholding effort, absenteeism, tardiness, extended breaks, criticizing management, theft, conflict, and even violence, vandalism, and sabotage—that cost American companies an estimated $170 billion each year (Sprouse, 1992)!

In addition, demotivators adversely affect the health of American workers. Research has shown that work-related ailments (in no small part due to demotivators) account for 100,000 deaths and 340,000 disabilities each year and cost American industry another $150 billion (Levering, 1988).

Any way you look at it, the human and financial cost of demotivators in the workplace is truly staggering—and they could be costing your organization a bundle. This is why *all* organizations must declare war on demotivators!

Estimating the Cost of Demotivators in Your Organization

If you want to estimate the cost of demotivators in your organization, try using this approach:

Ask a sample of employees how much productivity they lose when they encounter a demotivator (such as one of those listed on the prior page). The figure will probably range from one to three hours (depending on the emotional impact of the event). Some employees don't regain their productivity for weeks following a particularly serious demotivating event (like an adverse performance appraisal). Assume that employees experience just one demotivator per day (although you would probably have to admit that demotivators are even more prevalent than that).

Now assume that the actual loss of productivity per demotivator is one hour (a very low figure) at an average of $20 per hour (including indirect costs). Multiply this by the number of employees in your organization (say, 500) and by the number of working days per year (230). The estimated loss of productivity due to demotivators for your organization in one year would be $2,300,000. And, that's just assuming one demotivator per day and only accounting for the immediate loss of productivity (not other negative effects, such as poor quality, poor customer service, turnover, possible retaliatory actions, stress, associated impact on health, etc.).

Defeating Demotivators: A Strategic Approach

If your organization is serious about reducing its demotivational "mine field," then the following five-step strategy will provide the methodology for doing so:

1. *Identify the highest priority demotivators.* Trying to address all demotivators at once is unrealistic. It is far better to attack demotivators one (or a few) at a time, starting with the ones that have the greatest impact. There are many ways to prioritize demotivators. Ultimately, the best way to identify and prioritize demotivators is just to ask the employees, perhaps in focus groups. After all, employee perception is at the root of all demotivators, and most employees are "demotivator experts."

When you ask employees about demotivators, solicit their responses to the following three questions:

1) What demotivators are most prevalent in the organization?

2) How does each demotivator affect employee morale and performance?

3) How widespread is it?

Based on the answers to these questions, a prioritized list of demotivators can be developed. If you want to formalize the process, you can establish a cross-functional "Demotivator Reduction Team" to coordinate the demotivator reduction process. This will give the process more continuity and credibility with employees.

2. *Identify demotivating practices.* When first identified, you will notice that demotivators are often rather vague and subjective. It is vital that you describe how the highest priority demotivators currently manifest themselves in your organization, and do so as specifically as possible. Identify specific examples of demotivating practices in your organization. For example:

Politics: "Personnel decisions are perceived as subjective; selection criteria for posted positions are unclear; the reasons for selection are not communicated."

Unnecessary rules: "The policies and procedures manual hasn't been revised for several years; many rules are obsolete; some rules are perceived as barriers to effective customer service."

Unproductive meetings: "Meetings are at least twice as long as they should be; there are no written agendas; a few people dominate."

3. *Define desired practices.* Identify the practices that *should* be occurring in place of the demotivating ones. For example:

Politics: "Make sure the criteria for all personnel actions are clearly communicated so that everyone understands them."

Unnecessary rules: "Remove all obsolete rules from the policies and procedures manual. Review rules and procedures for organizational contribution at least once a year."

Unproductive meetings: "Train all meeting leaders in meeting facilitation skills."

4. *Eliminate support for demotivating practices.* Most demotivators persist because they are being inadvertently reinforced. A well-established psychological principle indicates that when rewards for any behavior are removed, the behavior will generally extinguish. Make it clear that demotivating practices will no longer be rewarded—or tolerated.

5. *Provide support for desired practices.* Not only do rewards for negative behaviors need to be eliminated, but support for positive behaviors must also be established. Two crucial support factors are *training* and *example.* For instance, if you want to reduce unproductive meetings in your organization, senior managers should be the first to be trained for, and then demonstrate, productive meeting behaviors. This is why meeting leadership skills training should always begin at the top, and then be expanded throughout the organization. In fact, changes in any practice should always begin at the top.

The Importance of Management Commitment

For better or for worse, it is senior management that sets the motivational climate in any organization. The rest of the organization generally follows what it sees at the top—and what is tolerated. Almost without exception, once organizations start focusing *real attention* on addressing the problem, demotivators promptly decrease. When management clearly and unambiguously states that particular demotivating conditions are no longer acceptable—and sets an appropriate example to that effect—the rest of the organization will usually get the message, and follow the lead.

Nobody expects demotivators to be eliminated completely or overnight. Some have been around for a long time and are just too deeply entrenched. However, when management makes a committed effort to reduce them, people will take notice.

In some companies managers are using dramatic actions to show their seriousness about demotivator reduction—for example, taking such actions as reducing their own salaries and perks, and admitting their own responsibility for the demotivation problem. One CEO showed his personal commitment by having lunch in each department, explaining the plan for demotivator reduction to startled employees. In an even more dramatic gesture, another CEO publicly shredded his company's twenty-two-inch policy manual and replaced it with a one-page statement of philosophy!

Although demotivator reduction must be led from the top, employee involvement is an essential ingredient in any organizational improvement process. Therefore, it can be extremely beneficial to empower a team to coordinate the effort. Any such team should be broad-based, with a diverse, cross-functional membership representing all major areas and levels of the organization.

When employees perceive that the war on demotivators is credible, and is actually being fought with vigor, they will begin to see a ray of hope. Although skeptical, they will feel that something might actually be done about the nagging demotivators that have frustrated them for so long. If you do attack the demotivators in your organization, you will see a big difference in the motivational climate ... and, ultimately, in your bottom line.

Another Use of Demotivator Reduction

One of the factors that sabotages most performance improvement interventions is the prevalence of demotivators. If you are involved in designing a new project or initiative (such as training, safety, customer service, or quality management), you should make sure that demotivators will not undermine its success. Demotivators in the context of your organization or those that are inadvertently allowed to creep into your intervention can lead to its ultimate failure. Many technically well-conceived projects fail because the motivational aspects were ignored.

Therefore, make sure that you *proactively* troubleshoot your project, initiative, or intervention before implementing it. Simply ask yourself and your management team: "Are there any demotivators in the organizational context or in our project design that might undermine its effectiveness?"

REFERENCES

Levering, R. (1988) *A Great Place to Work.* New York: Random House.

Spitzer, Dean. (1995) *SuperMotivation: A Blueprint for Energizing Your Organization from Top to Bottom.* New York: AMACOM Books.

Sprouse, M. (1992) *Sabotage in the American Workplace.* San Francisco: Pressure Drop Press.

HOW TO BUILD A QUALITY-DRIVEN ENVIRONMENT

Phil Ventresca and Tom Flynn

Phil Ventresca *is president of Advanced Management Services, Inc. (968 Washington St., Stoughton, MA 02072, 617-344-1103, 73662, 3326@compuserve), a business consultancy specializing in total quality and project management.* **Tom Flynn** *is an AMS project consultant as well as president of T.A. Flynn & Associates. Phil and Tom are adjunct faculty members at Boston University Center for Management Development and Roger Williams University Center for Professional Development. They were also contributors to* **The 1996 McGraw-Hill Team and Organization Development Sourcebook.**

This guide presents a multidimensional look at the topics of quality and customer satisfaction. It introduces tools and techniques that contribute to enhancing employee competencies, participation, productivity, and overall effectiveness. Optimum levels of performance can be achieved if the corporate culture is focused on serving the internal and external customer rendering a standard of continuous improvement and quality. This guide introduces a three-dimensional model that sets the stage for strategic, organizational, and tactical implementation of a corporate culture that is committed to excellence. This model can be applied at any level, allowing professionals the flexibility to control their immediate environment and to build data that are necessary to sell ideas and communicate effectively through a cross-functional matrix.

Organizations are transforming from stovepipe hierarchies to customer focused enterprises that are built on cross-functional communications and shortened business processes. The Advanced Management Services, Inc. High Performance Quality™ (HPQ) model illustrates this three-dimensional framework.

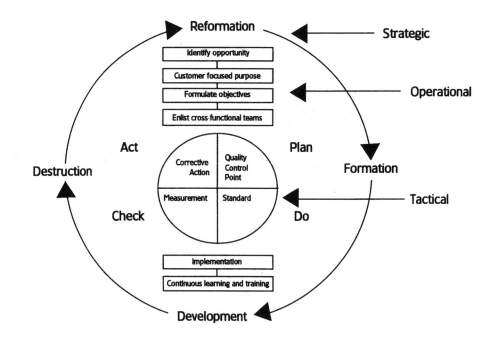

In order to accomplish true customer focus and satisfaction, a paradigm shift must occur.

Prepare for Change, Conflict, and Transformation

Creating a customer-driven quality environment involves both people and process. The first step in this task is to understand the dynamics of the people involved.

Innovation

Understanding that each and every individual within an organization has a purpose and is in some way connected to the success and satisfaction of its ultimate customer is the first step toward building a customer focused quality-driven environment. Internal and external customers must be treated equally. This is not an easy task. It takes time, commitment, and perseverance. Each individual must become a champion of that effort. Change will not occur until a critical mass has been established. When a critical mass begins to focus on the customer, excellence becomes a by-product.

Customer satisfaction is imperative for long-term business survival. Quality and continuous improvement philosophies are instrumental in achieving total customer satisfaction.

A paradigm is a model of how something is done. The old paradigm is quality control inspection of products and services after they are produced or implemented; this is inspected-in quality. The new paradigm is to design quality into the process so that products and services are error-free; this is referred to as designed-in quality.

The following model shows that the majority of individuals limit their thinking ability by perceiving boundaries around them.

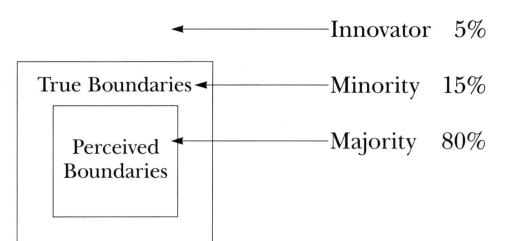

Change, Empowerment, and Improvement

In order to initiate a forward movement to improve customer satisfaction, it is necessary to identify the tired structures. "Out with the old, in with the new," may be a saying whose time has come. To achieve an improvement in the final results of work, an obvious change in the current methodology has to take place. However, change merely for the sake of change is not an effective course of action.

To create breakthrough improvement and customer delight, managers must reach beyond the comfort zone. Comfort is what happens to change when the energy is gone. In the initial stages of any type of change, one witnesses the energy inherent when something is dismantled, or in most cases, blown apart. This energy is most often labeled as chaos, yet it is energy at work just the same.

A functional imagination can utilize this energy as a springboard to propel a team forward. A leader's courage and ability to foresee the lifeline of this energy cycle will determine levels of motivation and inspiration.

Managing effectively in an environment of change requires a willingness to reinterpret the everyday methods of operation. "Kaizen" is a fundamental Japanese societal concept to view change as a constant flux of opportunities. Kaizen combines the possibilities to improve quality, productivity, and customer service.

Kaizen is a word that means small improvements. If managers set a tone of receptivity to new ideas, it will foster innovation through empowerment and the team will constantly search for excellence.

A proactive person plans for change to create resistance and discomfort. By creating, supporting, and maintaining a continuous environment of open communication, you can ensure that those most adversely affected by the reaction to change are validated and included rather than being distanced. An effective system of open communication provides the support to get through roadblocks brought on by change. The choice to recognize rather than avoid creates an opportunity that ensures inclusion, cohesion, and commitment (also known as buy-in). Buy-in is essential for the development and success of a results-driven environment.

As individuals our programming plays a large part in our ability to interact with others and situations. Education will help reduce the reactionary impulse to respond to our automatic thinking grid. If a new idea or concept fits between our programming lines it is common sense; when it does not fit between the lines it is rejected. This occurrence contributes to communication breakdowns and lack of innovation and growth.

Automatic Thinking Model

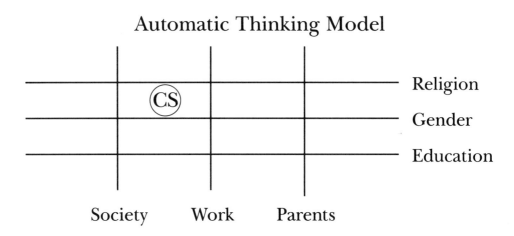

Downward Aimed Service

To serve effectively is to disappear. While industry's attention has been drawn to the necessity of top to bottom support for total customer satisfaction, who the customer actually is has been overlooked. Traditionally, the ultimate customer is defined as the end user or end recipient of a product.

In today's changing business environment we are required to do more with less, increasing productivity and quality with fewer resources.

The key to accomplishing this is to rethink who our customers are and classify them as any beneficiary of our work. This will allow each individual we contact a fair chance at achieving a personal level of quality. In this mindset, the word customer shifts to create a larger umbrella inclusive of organizations, fellow workers, citizens, end users, and anyone who may benefit from our service.

Downward aimed service is a cultural transformation. Those who have labored between the ranks of middle management and the front line are no strangers to downward aimed service. It is more widely recognized as having the support of higher-ups. This support, when aimed downward toward those closest to the actual work or end product, provides an environment that is conducive to success. Unfortunately for most businesses, the flow of downward service appears to have been interrupted. This interruption occurs when someone along the chain of top to bottom is focusing service on the top to yield them greater results (usually personal).

In a linear process, there is obvious diametric opposition when one function of the process looks up, while the balance of the functions focus downward. This interruption allows for adversarial role positions to spawn. These adversarial attitudes widen the gap, and the process repeats itself. This type of environment makes doing more with less virtually impossible. More companies are willing to acknowledge these gaps and fill them with a continuous flow of downward aimed service. A business structure based on downward aimed service creates an environment in which failure is virtually impossible.

The Importance of Teams

Managers can affect results by utilizing structure. Teams are an effective component. Why use teams?

✓ Team members deepen their understanding of their own work.

✓ Commitment and motivation are boosted.

✓ Better decisions can be made because the team has more complete knowledge about the process.

Team leaders must avoid the reverse responsibility syndrome. No one has to be a hero. Hold the team members individually and collectively accountable. Set up guidelines for the team's commitment to one another.

Team's Commitment to One Another

1. *(Example): Respect new ideas and don't criticize*

2.

3.

4.

5.

6.

This framework should be a guiding light for the team throughout its life cycle.

If a team wants to improve the results of a meeting, it must define and improve the meeting process.

Meeting Management

It is imperative to listen to both the voice of the customer and the voice of the process. If your customers and primary vendors are represented at team meetings, they share the buy-in. Management of a task is easier when you have an agreement on need with all parties responsible for completion. Utilize the following steps to ensure productive meetings:

✓ Set agenda against objectives.

✓ Work through the agenda items.

✓ Plan next steps and next meeting agenda.

✓ Recap the meeting.

As a team member, you are empowered to make creative contributions to the focused effort.

Team Tools and Techniques

There are several tools and techniques to generate innovative ideas within the team and foster decision making. Brainstorming is one of the most effective idea-generating tools. Follow the steps below to manage a brainstorming session.

Brainstorming

Generates a large number of ideas through team interaction.

Steps:

1. Set objective.
2. Call out ideas in turn around group.
3. Pass when an idea does not come quickly to mind.
4. Keep going, even when ideas slow.
5. Record ideas on a flip chart.
6. Build and expand on existing ideas.
7. Clarify thoughts and eliminate duplicates.

Fishbone Diagram

Teams that are empowered to work on improvement-based projects or are searching for root causes may find this tool helpful. It methodically provides the answer to the general question, What could be contributing to this problem? Once the general cause is identified, begin asking why. By continuously investigating the why for each cause, the root cause may be more concisely identified.

The true root cause of a problem is not always the obvious option. If you only react to symptoms of a problem, you will need to continually modify your process. Resolution of the root cause, once identified, could provide a permanent fix for a series of annoying problems.

The traditional construction of the fishbone involves identifying the effect, or symptom, on the right side of the diagram. The primary cause categories are identified through group brainstorming.

Identify the four major factors affecting your particular process problem. In most cases, Method, Personnel, Materials, and Machinery will apply and can be adapted to your specific situation. More bones can be added to specifically identify a particular process or service.

Here is a sample fishbone diagram:

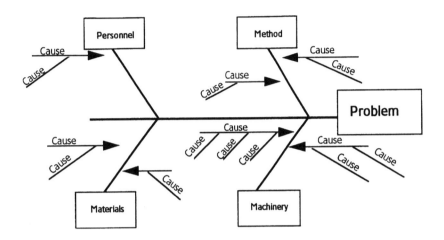

Force Field Analysis

This tool does not illustrate a solution merely through the values. You should use it in the team environment to arrive at areas of consensus based on the team's objectives. It is also a foundation for negotiation.

Objective:

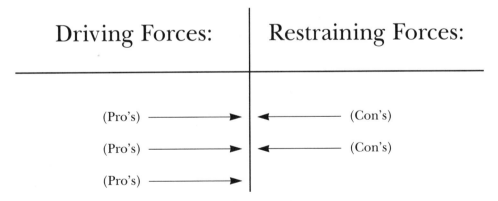

Flow Chart

Another tool that can be beneficial in making decisions and helping to map out strategy is the flow chart. A flow chart can be used to visualize a process, or look closer at an individual task. It can help managers find more efficient methods within an individual task that could improve efficiency throughout the process.

Considered one of the simplest tools, the flow chart can be as basic or technically intricate as the process it's used to illustrate. Each type of process step is traditionally identified on the chart by a standardized geometric shape. A flow chart illustrates a process from start to finish, and should include every step in between.

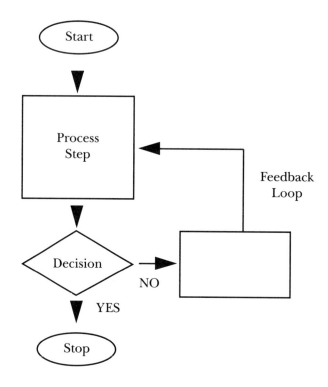

Once the team is in place and given the proper tools to work with, it is time to examine what can be done on the process side to enhance quality and customer satisfaction.

Learn to Identify, Plan, and Measure Against Customer
Requirements and Embed Quality

On the process side, customer satisfaction can be illustrated by a simple model. This model is built on the principles of Quality Function Deployment (QFD), a methodology involving a set of matrices. These matrices help determine exactly what the customer wants. The elements that are critical to customer satisfaction are called "whats" and "hows." Identifying "whats" and "hows" will allow you to generate tangible results around customer requirements.

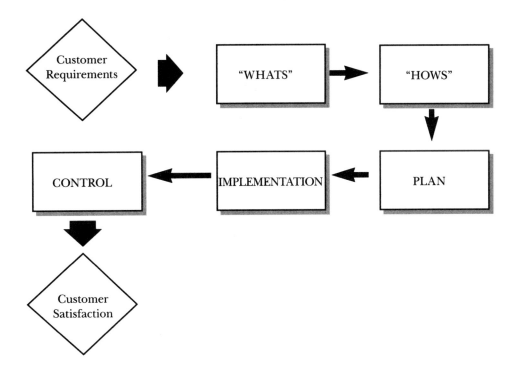

"Whats"

A "what" is simply what the customer wants—the individual characteristics of the product, service, or problem. Individuals on a team develop "whats" by brainstorming with the customer. The most effective way to do this is by focus group.

For example, suppose a software developer wanted to develop a user-friendly instruction manual for its new product. They would facilitate a customer focus group meeting and ask the question: "What are the important elements in a software program user manual?"

The following five items could be deemed important:

✓ Good illustrations
✓ Availability on-line
✓ Written in simple language
✓ Spiral bound
✓ Easy to use index

Next, the team asks the customers to rank these items in their order of importance. This is often the most difficult task for the customer. A statement like the following can be used: "If we can only accomplish one of these items for you, which should it be?" Keep asking the question until all of the items have been ranked. Rank the items on a scale of 1 to 5, with 5 being the most important. In the above example, the rankings were as follow:

"Whats"	Importance Ratio
Good illustrations	4
Availability on-line	2
Written in simple language	5
Spiral bound format	1
Easy to use index	3

Scale: 1 = low, 2 = medium, 3 = somewhat, 4 = high, 5 = very high

Pareto Analysis

This tool can be used to illustrate priorities. The first and highest bar traditionally indicates the number one priority. The left side of the graph represents the unit of comparison.

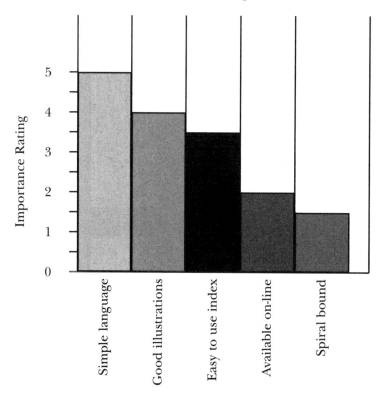

Now that the "whats" have been determined and prioritized, the next step is to translate them into a project overview statement with the customer. A Project Overview Statement (POS) represents the daily track over which your team will travel. Developing this statement puts boundaries around the project. This is our understanding of what our client, and our company, has chartered us to accomplish. The statement tells us where we are going and what it is going to be like when we get there.

To begin, clearly state what the product or service is that we are developing or improving. Be specific and make sure all team members agree.

What are the important _____ of _____?

When in doubt about the word to insert into the first blank, qualities usually work well. Others are characteristics, elements, and features. In the second blank, insert a noun naming the product or service. Then add an adjective to make the objective statement specific. For example, compare the three statements below:

✓ What are the important qualities of an instruction manual?

✓ What are the important qualities of a software instruction manual?

✓ What are the important qualities of a user-friendly software instruction manual?

Generate a POS that follows the above framework.

The first statement asks you to define the qualities of an instruction manual without reference to type; you may think of an appliance manual. Adding the adjective software in the second statement points them directly to the manual addressing a specific product. The addition of the adjectives in the third statement further restricts the customers' image of the manual. They will now be thinking about qualities needed for a software manual to be successful worldwide.

This process is critical and you should include the customer. Everyone can benefit, creating a win-win situation.

"Hows"

Virtually any idea that can help solve a problem or contribute to the creation of a new idea is a "how." "Hows" consist of processes and methods. This part of the customer satisfaction process uses the collective knowledge of your company. The team will take the "whats" and assign "hows." The team should begin by asking:

What are some of the ways we can help accomplish the list of "whats"?

"Whats"	Importance Ratio	"Hows"
Simple language	5	Write manual with 7th-grade-level English. Run Flesch-Kincaid grade level and reading ease tests to verify
Good illustrations	4	Print actual screens from program; supplement with easy to understand graphics
Easy to use index	3	List all potential subjects alphabetically
Available on-line	2	Have the user manual available to users by pressing "Help" key
Spiral bound	1	Change binder

After completing this exercise, evaluate the importance ratio of each item. The team can assess the likelihood of completing each task and weigh it against customer expectations. The team should also consider the effect on the budget, etc. and confirm that this is a feasible project based on the objectives.

If the team decides that the project is not feasible, a pushback strategy may be necessary. Utilizing the data generated in the assessment, work teams can generate better presentations to management and customers supporting the case for pushback.

Customer Focused Quality Control Chart

A quality control chart illustrates predetermined standards and allows for immediate feedback and corrective action. This method will render a foundation on which to build collective and individual performance assessments. It allows for true empowerment. By utilizing the data created by this exercise, the team can measure quality based on the conditions of satisfaction and begin to formulate the work breakdown structure.

Quality Control Point	Importance Ratio	Standard	Measurement Evaluation	Corrective Action
Good illustrations	4	Print actual screens from program; supplement with easy to understand graphics		
Availability on-line	2	Have the user manual available to users by pressing "Help" key		
Written in simple language	5	Write manual with 7th-grade-level English. Run Flesch-Kincaid grade level and reading ease tests to verify		
Spiral bound format	1	Change binder		
Easy to use index	3	List all potential subjects alphabetically		

Once the elements of people and process are in place and functioning, there will be no limit to the success and total customer satisfaction achieved through this process.

HOW TO BEAT THE NEWLY APPOINTED LEADER DILEMMA

31

Ed Betof and Raymond Harrison

Edward H. Betof, *Ed.D. is senior vice president of MCAssociates (Mellon Bank Center, 1735 Market Street, 43rd Floor, Philadelphia, PA 19103, 215-563-7800), a consulting firm specializing in organizational change and leadership development. Ed is an adjunct faculty member of the Center of Creative Leadership and the Human Resource Planning Society and the lead author of* **Just Promoted! Surviving and Thriving in Your First Twelve Months as a Manager** *(McGraw-Hill). Ed is the primary developer of MCAssociates' Newly Appointed Leader Coaching Service. He was also a contributor to* **The 1996 McGraw-Hill Team and Organization Development Sourcebook** *and* **The 1996 McGraw-Hill Training and Performance Sourcebook. Raymond Harrison** *is executive vice president and regional director, MCAssociates (Five Independence Way, Princeton, NJ 08540, 609-520-0900). He is past president of the Pennsylvania Psychological Association's Industrial/Organizational Division. For ten years, Ray was on the faculty of the University of Pennsylvania and is the author of numerous articles in the field of psychology.*

Assuming a new leadership role is an increasingly hazardous challenge. Current research indicates that approximately 40% of newly appointed managers and executives are either terminated, prove to be disappointing, or choose to leave the position of their own accord. The newly appointed leader dilemma in today's organizations is very real, as the expectations for results are as high or higher than they have ever been, but organizations' patience for results is at its lowest. This guide describes the reasons for this phenomenon and presents 15 concrete steps that leaders can take to address the new leader dilemma.

Introduction

Pat has been named President and Chief Executive Officer of a major consumer division of U.S. Financial Corporation. Business is changing faster than ever before, as are the expectations for greatly improved business results. The Chairman and the Board are committed to major changes in the way the business is managed. The industry is more competitive than it ever has been, and there have been numerous acquisitions and mergers over the past decade. The pace of these mega-deals

255

has accelerated in the past 5 years and has literally transformed the banking and financial services industry. This evolution in the marketplace continues to bring about dramatic changes, resulting in a need to become a faster, more flexible, and agile business.

Pat's challenges are daunting. Pat replaces a very well-liked C.E.O. who ran the business in a friendly, benevolent, even paternalistic way. However, market share has eroded. Shareholders have been disappointed and vocal.

The Board has acted by retiring Pat's predecessor two years earlier than he desired. The Consumer Division needs to be transformed. It lags behind the four other divisions of U.S. Financial Corporation in earnings and in its commitment to the cultural values that have driven the change, growth, and development of the other divisions. The employees are nervous. The industry has experienced well-publicized downsizings.

Pat is the first woman to be named President and Chief Executive Officer and member of the U.S.F.C. Executive Committee. The Board has made it clear that it wants a 7% rise in earnings within 12 months and another 10% the following year. Nothing else will be satisfactory. There is also a strong belief within the Board that there are significant cost reductions to be realized and that information services and the administrative infrastructure are woefully behind the competition. An important perception at the Board level is that of a fat, slow, and underproducing division as compared to other U.S.F.C. businesses as well as regional competition.

Pat has been brought into U.S.F.C. from a key competitor where she was Executive Vice President for Marketing and Customer Relations and had developed a well-earned reputation for results. Pat has received a very strong endorsement from both the Chairman and a majority of Board members. However, four highly influential board members preferred Joe Taggart, the current C.F.O, for Pat's new job. Joe had campaigned hard for the position and is bitterly disappointed that he was not selected.

Pat is expected to hit the road running. No honeymoon or grace period—just land and do what needs to be done to achieve the results expected of her.

Pat is experiencing **The Newly Appointed Leader Dilemma** so prevalent in today's organizations. It is the executive's blessing and curse of the mid-1990s. Great opportunities exist for large potential rewards yet there is little, if any, time allotted to learn the job. The message seems to be: Get in, make the necessary changes, and quickly demonstrate results. It is a type of organizational Darwinism in which only the fastest and strongest survive. However, based on recent interviews and polling of over one thousand executives, approximately **40%** of newly appointed leaders prove to be disappointing, are terminated, or leave the job voluntarily within 12 to 18 months of their initial appointment.

There appear to be a number of reasons why the Newly Appointed Leader Dilemma is a greater problem than it has ever been before. These include, but are not limited to the following:

✓ A recent review of literature indicates that **50% to 75% of change efforts fail to meet all their intended objectives**—usually because of human factors. *Most newly appointed leaders initiate some form of major change process.*

✓ *The Wall Street Journal* reported in 1994 that **"Many new executives are being discharged with stunning speed.** Not long ago employers gave the newly hired at least a year to prove themselves. But in a recent American Management Association survey, nearly 22% of the employers questioned said that in the past two years, they had fired a professional or manager after less than three months."** Lifetime employment is out. Corporations continue to lower staffing levels and any thought about permanent employment with employees at any level is a memory. It is a buyer's market with many displaced and highly mobile executives anxious to fill key executive roles, even for short periods of time.

✓ **Accountability is a prime organizational value and an active pressure point in today's organizations.** There appear to be at least three primary reasons for this. Shareholders are much more demanding. The quality movement has established metrics as an organizational expectation and performance management practices are improving. Fifty-five percent of available stock is now held by blocks such as institutions who can exert significant pressure, including voting pressure, on boards. In turn, boards have become more demanding of their C.E.O.'s, with higher results expected over shorter periods of time. The cycle continues when the C.E.O. pushes down on his/her executives. Scorecards of results are more and more apparent. Visible accountability commonly exists down to the individual contributor and team level which are tied to critical measurements of success much higher in the organization.

✓ **More pay is "at risk"** than ever before. New compensation systems have been devised that put executives under the gun for quick and measurable results. The days of high levels of guaranteed compensation that is not tied to measurable results are rapidly disappearing.

✓ **Today's society is highly litigious.** On the advice of counsel and experienced human resource executives, companies increasingly will cut their losses quickly if they determine an executive is not working out. The argument presented is that it can be legally easier and cleaner if an executive is released before a long employment history develops.

✓ **A higher than expected rate of repatriated executives leave.** Recent indications are that between 40% and 60% of repatriated executives leave their companies within a year of assuming a position upon their return to the U.S. Reasons for this high rate include companies not doing an effective job in managing these difficult career transitions, the increased value that executives with global experience have in the marketplace, and the targeting of such executives by retained search firms.

Frequently Cited Factors that Derail Newly Appointed
Managers/Executives

✓ Confusion over the Appointment Charter which should include key expectations, agreements, and ways of working to support the immediate manager and others to whom one is accountable

✓ Failure to identify stakeholders and build key partnerships

✓ Lack of time to learn the job

✓ Failure to mesh with the existing culture or conversely to build the type of culture that is needed

✓ Differences with other key individuals in the organization

✓ Failure to achieve the necessary balance between work and family life

✓ Overuse of or over-reliance on existing professional or managerial strengths

✓ Problems with previously untested skills or flaws

Recommendations for Dealing with the Newly Appointed
Leader Dilemma

The situations that newly appointed leaders face in contemporary society are extraordinary. While executive challenges can be stimulating, and even exhilarating for some individuals, they are vexing for others. Managed well, these challenges can lead to high levels of career success. For others, the same challenges can turn into a career derailing experience.

Here are 15 suggestions that increase the likelihood of success and minimize the career derailing factors for newly appointed leaders.

1. **Confirm Your Appointment Charter**
   These are the explicit agreements that should be negotiated with one's immediate manager and others with whom there are accountable relationships. Examples of the approximately dozen areas to be confirmed are reporting relationships, primary accountabilities, limits of decision-making authority, and ways the immediate manager wishes to be supported.

2. **Conduct a Comprehensive Stakeholder Analysis in Order to Build Effective Partnership**

Closely examine the full range of key working relationships that must be established, enhanced, or repaired. These can be relationships that are within or outside the immediate organization or company and frequently include customers. Areas of needed attention should be identified and action steps put in place in order to ensure that strong partnerships exist.

3. **Accelerate Your Job Learning Process including Skills, Knowledge, and Culture**

Research conducted at Harvard University in the 1980s demonstrated that it usually takes executives about two and one-half years to fully learn a complex management job. Few executives today have that amount of time available to them. There is evidence that the first eighty percent of that learning process can be accelerated considerably. Executives should access some of the learning options available to upper-level managers that have been developed in recent years. These options build on existing learning strengths and styles, but also address learning gaps and underdeveloped capabilities. Highly trained consultants and university-based executive education programs are good sources of support in this area.

4. **Build Strong First Impressions**

First impressions are made in a matter of seconds. Be careful of the verbal and nonverbal messages you send. Watch your pronouns. Use "we's and our's" vs. "I's and me's" and mean it. Reach out and be inclusive of others.

5. **Establish a Clear Communications Strategy**

How and what one communicates is a vital factor in executive success. Communications reflect much about the executive and what he or she stands for. The executive should prepare or at least review the announcement of his/her appointment. Every action that the executive plans or implements has communication implications that should be well considered. Key "message bits" should be carefully selected. Communications experts are frequently available in larger organizations. Others can be accessed on a need-to-know basis on the outside.

6. **Deal Effectively with Unsuccessful Candidates for Your Position**

The newly appointed executive should meet with unsuccessful candidates individually and as early as possible. Their expertise can be of great value if you can gain their support and commitment. If they will not be considered for an important role or continued employment, they should be told so privately and managed very professionally. Career transition services should be made available if an executive is being released.

7. **Create Empowering Relationships and a Learning Culture**
The ability of executives to help others feel important and part of the action is an essential leadership skill. Empowering others to feel *able, valuable, and responsible* will go a long way to building a high-performing and learning-based work culture.

8. **Design Your Vision and Mission with Involvement of Others**
Vision is the defining of what kind of business and organization we wish to become (future). Mission is the definition of what type of business and organization we are in (present). The executive should involve members of his/her team and others in the organization in the defining and confirming of both.

9. **Create a 12-Month Roadmap to Achieve Your Key Business and Functional Goals**
One of the factors that should be identified in the Appointment Charter are the two or three most important accomplishments that should be achieved during the executive's first year. A plan should be established by month or quarter to ensure that these accomplishments are achieved. This "Roadmap" should be re-visited at least once a week.

10. **Diagnose and Assess Your Organization's Health and Effectiveness**
Some executives get so busy focusing on results that they neglect to examine what is and isn't working well in their organizations. Work processes, quality of employees, and teamwork are examples of areas to examine. This can be done alone or preferably by involving others in the organization. Professionals who are well trained in the field of organizational development can also assist in the diagnostic process.

11. **Select, Build, and Train Your High-Performing Leadership Team**
Leaders are able to accomplish work by choosing the right people for important responsibilities, who are trained well and who work together effectively. This rarely happens by accident. Effective leaders are deliberate about surrounding themselves with others who are dedicated to the mission and vision of the organization and who are skilled at achieving desired results.

12. **Implement Necessary Change Processes**
Today's world operates in fast forward. Contemporary leaders have to be skilled as change masters with an ability to involve and excite others in the process of rapid, often transformational, change.

13. **Decide What Key Initiatives Must Be Taken and with Whom**
There is always more to do than there are available resources. Executives must choose from a host of possible initiatives including those involving business results, superiors, peers, direct reports, multiple functions, external stakeholders, personal development actions, and work/family balance issues.

14. Seek Out and Obtain as Much Help, Assistance, and Coaching as You Can Get

Assuming a new leadership role is hard and hazardous work. Seek the counsel of trusted advisors. Involve those in your organization whose opinions and perspectives can complement yours. Consider utilizing a professional with expertise and experience in making successful leadership transitions.

15. Give Full Consideration to the Cultural Issues and Power Base You Will Need to Accomplish Your Objectives

This is especially true if your objectives will challenge basic cultural assumptions of the organization. Building your power base is not necessarily a Machiavellian activity. It is merely a concession to the reality that in every organization there are competing interests and to get things done, power must be exercised in an appropriate way. If issues of timing, stakeholder commitment, use of formal and informal structures, and interpersonal commitment are fully considered, the outcome is likely to be a more successful one.

Conclusion

Nothing succeeds like success. If a newly appointed leader can achieve some early successes, he or she is likely to win greater confidence and support from the organization. That will give the executive increased leverage to focus on even more ambitious goals. By using the 15 suggestions detailed in this guide, leaders can take action to make sure that they stay on top of the challenges faced by executives in today's organizations.

HOW TO CREATE A HIGH PARTICIPATION WORKFORCE

32

Tom Devane

Thomas J. Devane *is president of Premier Integration Enterprises (317 Lookout View Court, Golden, CO 80401, 303-279-1099, tdevane@usa.net). Tom specializes in organizational development, Total Quality Management, fast cycle time, and activity-based costing. He is an author and international speaker on the topics of combining technical and human elements of large-scale change for knowledge work organizations. Tom is also a contributor to* **20 Active Training Programs,** *vol. III (Pfeiffer, in press).*

This guide is a discussion of how "high participation" workforces accelerate organizational change. The author has seen a wide variety of successful and not-so-successful change efforts. Learning from those experiences caused the author to combine the "best practices" from a variety of technical-based and people-based change efforts.

Change. Most organizations realize it's necessary. Many are trying to do it. Very few are doing it well. A McKinsey & Co. study in 1990 reported that 70% of all Total Quality Management programs did not yield the targeted financial benefits. Michael Hammer and CSC Index have reported that over 70% of all reengineering efforts fail. A 1993 study revealed that 60% of self-directed work teams disbanded within a year and returned to a hierarchical structure. And in 1993 an American Management Association study revealed that 65% of reengineering projects failed to yield any operating improvements that affected the bottom line.

So what gives? Why the low success rate of America's most popular change initiatives? The truth is, the tools and techniques of all of those initiatives can make, and have made, valuable contributions to improving organizational performance. The issue isn't that they're wrong—the issue is that they're incomplete. Each will have limited sustainable results without the following:

✓ A revised set of foundation assumptions about how to optimize organizational performance, and

✓ A change in the way that we implement organizational change.

Author Rita Mae Brown describes insanity as "doing the same thing over and over and expecting different results." We need to find a way to break past that pesky 60% to 70% failure rate for most change initiatives. This guide presents an alternative. It describes a proven approach to organizational change that combines the technical aspects of change (e.g., process workflows and technology) with the human aspects of change (e.g., organizational culture and patterns of communication).

Each of the previously described improvement philosophies has contributed to our body of knowledge about how to make organizations better. Business reengineering helped us to change our focus from functional departments to processes. It also introduced the concept of using information technology as a creative force, instead of using it only in a supporting role.

Total Quality Management brought us increased worker involvement and a rich set of tools and concepts that could be applied by most people in the organization to solve complex problems. And self-directed work teams showed us the power that could be unleashed by giving people increased control over their day-to-day destinies.

But many of these technical-based and human-based change initiatives are missing one important element. Ironically, it was this element that was determined to be the most significant predictor of organizational change success based on a recent statistical study of 131 North American companies studied from 1961 to 1991.

That element was *the level of personal worker responsibility*. Quite simply, high levels of personal responsibility were closely associated with successful change efforts, and low levels were associated with failures.

From a common sense perspective, it doesn't seem to be a great "aha" that increased responsibility leads to personal actions to improve a problem situation. Or, conversely, that the lack of responsibility leads to the opposite situation. (For example, how many times have you volunteered to fix a dripping faucet in your hotel room, or washed a rental car on the way to the airport?) Quite interestingly, the responsibility revelation for us in the business world resides in the discovery that our organizational structures actually systematically remove responsibility from workers at each level of the organization.

But wait a minute. Are we saying that people in organizations today aren't held responsible for their actions? Not at all. What we're pointing out is that responsibility for truly important work decisions, such as work redesign and control and coordination of day-to-day work, often resides at a level above where the work actually gets done. In many cases, redesign responsibilities don't even reside one or two levels above where the work gets done. Today quite often for many organizations design responsibility resides in a small, select reengineering group who launch their designs of a representative few on an unsuspecting, nonparticipating many in the organization.

By failing to specifically address the redistribution of "typical management tasks," each of the previously mentioned practices actually tends to decrease the amount of personal responsibility in organizations. As a recent presidential candidate might put it, in these organizations we hear a "giant sucking sound as the power rapidly moves from the bottom of the organization to the top."

In a 1993 interview, noted business strategist Peter Drucker talked about the danger of the "empowerment" concept. "It is not a great step forward," he noted, "to take power out at the top and put it in at the bottom. It's still power. To build achieving organizations, you must replace power with responsibility."

But merely knowing this concept of localized responsibility will get you nothing. The $64,000 question is, "How do we change organizations to generate high levels of personal responsibility?" Experience has shown that to achieve higher levels of organizational performance through more personal responsibility, *we need to increase the participation of workers at all levels in the areas of work redesign and self-management.* To reflect the increased levels of involvement at all levels of the organization we call these organizations "High Participation Workforces."

On the surface, the approach described here may look somewhat similar to existing approaches because it combines "best in class" elements from many diverse change philosophies. But at its deep foundation level, this approach differs dramatically from typical change programs. Upon close examination of this approach, many would label it as radical, and assert that it is too revolutionary for their organization. As you read on, you need to decide its applicability for your organization.

This approach has been proven to accomplish two important objectives for American organizations:

✓ Improve organizational performance, and

✓ Accelerate the change process.

Exceptional companies in the private sector that are using these techniques include Hewlett-Packard, MCI, DuPont, Syntex, and Levi Strauss. Groundbreaking progressive government organizations that have benefited from this approach include the U.S. Forest Service, the U.S. Court System, and the states of Michigan, Colorado, and Nebraska.

To provide a rapid overview of the principles and processes associated with this high participation approach, this guide is organized by commonly asked questions about high participation workforces. They are:

1. What is a "High Participation Workforce?"

2. Why would my organization want to be one?

3. What paradigm shifts are required?
4. What are the key principles?
5. What's the process for implementing one?
6. What are the key enabling factors?
7. What does the organizational structure look like?
8. Is a high participation environment right for us?
9. What decisions do we need to make before embarking on this strategy?

What Is a "High Participation Workforce"?

Simply put, a high participation workforce is one in which all employees participate in key organizational decisions and activities. This includes organizational change issues as well as day-to-day operating decisions. This type of environment provides for more rapid responses and self-correcting adaptive actions than traditional organizational environments. While high employee participation is a primary feature of an improved work environment, it is by far not the only one. From this point on we will refer to our high performing target work environment as a Model 2 environment, as contrasted to the traditional Model 1 work environment. (See Figure 32.1.)

The Model 1 bureaucratic form served U.S. companies well for years. It was particularly popular after World War II when worldwide economic and U.S. business conditions were well-served by such a structure.

This bureaucratic form of structure (Model 1) takes a somewhat mechanistic view of organizations, and tends to perform well under those same conditions under which a machine would perform well. Specifically,

✓ in a stable environment where the products and services produced will always be the right ones,

✓ when there is a straightforward task to perform,

✓ when one wishes to produce exactly the same product time and time again, and

✓ when the human "machine" parts are compliant and behave as they have been designed to behave.

Traditional bureaucratic structures tend to be less effective in turbulent environments, industries affected by rapid technological change, markets of quickly shifting customer demands, periods of increasing complexity in products and external interfaces, and in workforces with increasing worker demands for participation.

Incorrectly matching a bureaucratic structure to a turbulent environment causes a number of problems such as: few incentives

Traditional versus High Participation Workforces		
Workplace Characteristic	**Model 1 (Traditional)**	**Model 2 (High Participation)**
Key Design and Operational Decisions	Made by representative few.	Participation by all people affected.
Basic Operating Unit	Individual worker.	Team, Work group.
Optimization Rule	Make me & the boss look good.	Make the work group look good.
Coordination & Control of Work	Performed at one level above the level where work is performed.	Performed at the same level where the work is performed.
Responsibility	Own task.	Group tasks.
Communications	Selectively passed downward on a "need to know" basis. Flows upward after filters are applied to protect the message bearer.	High degree of information sharing, both upwards and downwards.
Individual Skills	Specialized.	Jack of all trades where possible.
Meets human psychological criteria for high performance	Not specifically designed into work structure; any match is coincidental.	Automatically addressed because designed in to work structure.
Work Roles	Fixed.	Interchangeable.
Continual Improvement	Special event, project basis.	Part of the everyday work.
Strutural Design Encourages ...	Competition (among individuals, groups) and functional specialization.	Collaboration and cross-functional learning.

Figure 32.1.

exist for innovation, diminished ability to detect and correct errors, increased dependency on superiors and "the system," decreased personal responsibility, and poor communication patterns among multilevel and cross-functional groups.

These are the specific problems that we address with a high participation workforce. The Model 2 approach tends to view organizations as living organisms, rather than as machines (the primary metaphor for Model 1 environments). Organizational designs using Model 2 recognize the importance of the human aspects of change, such as motivation and desire for autonomy, and the criticality of interrelationships among people and organizational units.

Many people think, "Oh, yeah, the 'self-managing team' concept of the 1980s." But with the Model 2 concept we go far beyond the self-managing teams of years ago. Not only are these work groups self-managing, but they are also self-designing. They design their own workflows, design their own organizational structure, and design their own patterns of communication among themselves and other work groups.

Why Would My Organization Want to Be One?

High Participation Workforces typically exhibit a number of advantages over their traditional bureaucratic counterparts:

✓ they are quicker to react to outside crises and opportunities

✓ they tend to have lower operating costs

✓ they are able to detect and correct internal errors more quickly

✓ the people in the organization share a common, articulated set of values

✓ there is a higher likelihood of innovation

✓ the people in the organization enjoy a higher degree of satisfaction at work

✓ authentic communication is practiced more often

✓ information technology tends to be more quickly implemented, and more fully utilized.

These advantages are a direct result of the work environment known as a Model 2 Environment.

What Paradigm Shifts Are Required?

Effective change doesn't come cheaply. To become a high performing Model 2 environment a group must begin to make several key paradigm shifts. The good news with this approach is that when it is done well, management doesn't need to completely drop one paradigm for the entire organization and immediately replace it with an entirely new one. Often all that's required is movement along a continuum from left to right (see Figure 32.2).

Self-management. In a Model 2 environment, control and coordination of work resides within the work group performing the work, not at the level above that group in the hierarchy. So does this mean that work groups get to do whatever they want? Absolutely not. But

Paradigm Continuum Shifts		
Manager control	⇒	Self-management
Imposed design	⇒	Self-design
Distrust employees	⇒	Trust employees
Set strategy	⇒	Define purpose
Organizational control	⇒	Organizational stimuli
Organizational boxes in concrete	⇒	Fluid, adaptive units
Dependency	⇒	Interdependency

Figure 32.2.

a primary difference from today's Model 1 environment is that work groups are "managed" by guidelines, boundaries, and shared organizational values and purpose—not by management overrides.

Self-design. The days of hiring an outside expert who imposes a design structure on the organization are gone, at least as we move from left to right for this continuum item. In a true, functioning Model 2 environment work groups are self-organizing, self-regulating units that organize around desired outcomes.

So does this mean that people break into small groups and design whatever kind of organization they feel like? Of course not. Based on customer requirements and organizational strategy, there are certain "minimum critical specifications" provided to the design groups. These are a small number of design guidelines and parameters that establish boundary conditions for the redesign group.

Trust employees. This is not merely a platitude admonishing us to give our fellow man the benefit of the doubt. This goes deep to the core of how our organizations are now designed, and how we need to change those founding assumptions and resultant structures.

Most organizations today are built on the assumptions made by the now infamous Frederick Taylor, the father of scientific management. He thought that basically workers would seek every opportunity to slack off that they could find. He believed that all responsibility for the organization of work should rest with the manager, not the individual worker. And he believed that control of people and work was best achieved by iteratively decomposing work into its smallest, most idiot-proof unit of performance.

Our assumptions determine our values. Our values guide the rules and structures we build, which in turn determine the way we behave. The Taylor rules for organizational design reflect the assumption that basically workers are untrustworthy. When we begin to trust workers more, we will not only behave differently toward them on a day-to-day basis, but we will redesign our work structures to take advantage of full human potential. Increasing this trust factor is mandatory, particularly when one considers the implications for virtual organizations that span wide geographic distances. Does this mean we should leave the safe open every night when we leave the building? Not at all. Unconditional, unchecked trust is not the answer. We do, however, need to select areas and monitor the results of increased trust levels as we diffuse new high performance concepts through the organization.

Define purpose. As mentioned in Chris Bartlett's HBR article in Nov-Dec 94, " today's world-class organizations are moving beyond strategy, structure, and systems to a framework built on purpose, process and people." Many employees today don't just want to work for a company. They want to belong to an organization. Because of longer hours many people seek more of a "community-type" environment at work. If we want people to perform at their best, we need to provide them with an opportunity to emotionally attach themselves to what the organization stands for. A Model 2 organization gives them the opportunity to emphasize both strategy and purpose.

In addition, though we have known for years that intrinsic motivation tends to elicit higher performance than extrinsic motivation, most reward systems are still based on the extrinsic variety. A well-defined purpose in a Model 2 organization gives us an opportunity to tap into people's intrinsic motivation factors, and initiate a move away from carrots and sticks.

Organizational stimuli. Mandates and other attempts to directly control people seem to have limited effectiveness. In keeping with our analogy of an organization and a living organism, it makes sense to think in terms of management introducing stimuli and impulses into the environment, and not having them try to directly control components of a complex interconnected social system.

Fluid, adaptive units. One reason many organizations are reluctant to redesign is the implied semi-permanency of the design. They envision going from one set of concretized organizational boxes in the hierarchy to another, that will last perhaps another two years. In a Model 2 environment the new organization is much more fluid. Because it is designed by the workers who perform the work, it can be redesigned by them at a moment's notice to quickly adapt to changing conditions.

Interdependency. To achieve high levels of organizational and individual performance, dependency must be eliminated. This dependency issue, in fact, is why many reengineering efforts fail. In many of these failures the entire organization was depending on a representative group to redesign for a larger group of people. In systems thinking terms, they have shifted the burden to a small design group instead of recognizing that they all must play a role in creating their new future.

Why is it that many workers in an "empowered" organization feel they have no power? In many cases it's because management continues to assume responsibility for many decisions and control of day-to-day operational work. This creates a vicious circle: management makes all the critical decisions, then employees feel "the system will take care of me, I don't have any real power anyway," then management sees that employees aren't assuming responsibility and takes more away, then the employees feel less power, and so on ...

The good news is that movement along these continuums needn't be as painful as an organization might think. Changes can be addressed in small movements along the continuum, with an appropriate analysis of how effective the movement was. What you need to do is start. As author Richard Pascale once said, "Often it's a lot easier to act ourselves into a new way of thinking than it is to think ourselves into a new way of acting."

What Are the Key Principles?

There are five high leverage principles that govern the migration to, and operation of, a Model 2 environment.

Redundancy of Skills within People, Not Redundancy of People

Redundancy of skill sets is necessary in any organization to ensure uninterrupted customer service in the case of unexpected events. There are two ways to incorporate this necessary redundancy into the design of an organization.

The first way is to have more than one person who can do the same work. For example, under this approach you might have three customer order takers and two financial analysts who do the credit checking for customer orders. Because of this redundancy, if one of these people got hit by a truck, the order entry and credit functions would not come to a screeching halt. This "people redundancy" approach is the one most often selected in a Model 1 environment. The battle cry of this approach can be summarized as, "One person, one skill!"

The second way to address the skills redundancy issue is to have people trained in more than one skill. Often fewer people in total are needed to perform the daily work because the organization doesn't have to balance peak and trough workloads for multiple functions. For example, if we combine the customer order taker positions and the credit checking functions in the previous example (let's call it the order entry process) we may only require three people instead of the original five. This would be possible because each of the three people would be trained in customer order taking and credit checking. The battle cry of this approach is, "One person, multiple skills!"

But, a cynical person might ask, "What if I don't want the charge nurse stepping in for the neurosurgeon just as he opens my cranium?" There are, of course, many situations where it is not feasible to multiskill all individuals. In such cases it is important that the team be as multiskilled as they need to be to achieve the desired outcome (without needing to go outside the team).

Focus on Entire Work Systems

A work system has technical elements and people elements. Both must be addressed to have a successful change effort. Unfortunately many organizations only address one element, or they make the decision to address these elements sequentially. Big mistake.

In a Model 2 change effort, we simultaneously address technical and people issues. These two subsystems are inseparable, and need to be addressed that way. For example, you would not want to implement a new e-mail system (a technical element) but have executives keep all important information in desk drawers and private memos (culture and communication practices, people elements).

William Bridges, a noted psychologist and consultant to many corporations, has asserted that, "Today's organization is rapidly being transformed from a structure built out of jobs into a field of work needing to be done. Jobs are artificial units superimposed on this field." If an organization is to move successfully to a Model 2 environment, they must discard old notions of "one-person-one-job," and begin to think in terms of entire work systems.

People Don't Resist Change, They
Resist Being Changed

We used to think that people automatically resist change. Now we know that is not necessarily true. If people have input into the change, they are very likely to accept the change. In fact, since they have partial ownership in the change, they will most likely go out of their way to fix any fouled up results.

The processes to get to a Model 2 organization use a series of large-group participation sessions to involve all people in the design of changes for their immediate work area. This increases the likelihood of both logical and emotional buy-in at the individual level. This makes the psychological transitioning process to a new environment much easier for all the individuals involved.

When You Change the Structural Relationships Between People,
They Will Change the Way They Communicate and the Way
They Behave Toward Each Other

Changing the structural relationships of people, tasks, and supervision in the organization can have a dramatic effect on organizational performance.

The simple act of changing from a boss-to-subordinate relationship to a peer-to-peer relationship can totally change the character of communications in the organization. For one thing, it eliminates a

perceptual political filter that many often use to second-guess political motives in boss-to-subordinate conversations. It also encourages
people to behave more collaboratively.

With Minimal Guidance, People Can Create Their Own,
Extremely Effective, Organizational Structure

People tend to work better in structures that they themselves create.
Does this mean that people in today's structure should just stop work
and redesign a new organizational structure when the feeling moves
them? Not at all. There are some minimal critical specifications, the
results of an external environment scan, and some brief instructions
on work group design that need to be provided before letting a
group redesign itself. But with this minimal input, yes, they are ready
to design the workflow and organizational structure for which they
will take ownership!

What's the Process for Implementing One?

The process for implementing a Model 2 work environment will vary
for each organization. This is because this process recognizes that
complex social and technical systems can rarely be addressed in a linear fashion. This approach is principle-based, not task-based. At the
center of this model is a work group continuously designing and
managing its work. (See Figure 32.3.)

ORGANIZATIONAL CHANGE IN A MODEL 2 ENVIRONMENT

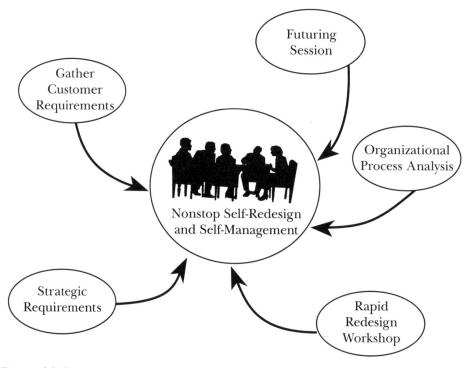

Figure 32.3.

As mentioned previously, the concept of a work group designing and managing its own work is central to increasing personal levels of responsibility and enhancing organizational performance.

While many models of organizational change depict linear, sequential tasks to be executed, this model does not. Our premise is that you can't address complex nonlinear systems with linear processes. As long as we keep in mind the core principle (people designing and managing their own work), an organization may select any of the elements around the circle as a starting point.

The point is simple: The conditions in your organization will determine your sequence of implementation. A "standard sequence" does not exist in any methodology cookbook. Your organization decides where to start, and how to sequence the remaining activities surrounding the "Nonstop self-redesign and self-management" center.

There is great variety in how organizations begin their migration to a Model 2 environment. In one telecommunications company they decided to start with a real-time futuring session. A federal agency began differently by immediately starting several rapid redesign workshops across the country. In yet another strategy, a billion-dollar high-tech assembly company began by gathering customer requirements, feeding those into an organizational process analysis, and then redesigned their work groups within a period of six weeks.

The bottom line is this: Your organization needs to decide how best to move from a Model 1 to a Model 2 environment. The sequence is all very situation-dependent. Factors people typically examine when deciding upon a sequence include: competitive threats, general market conditions, customer satisfaction ratings, pain associated with a particular business process, projected technological advances, impending regulation, understanding of existing business process contributions, and energy levels for change within the organization.

There are four primary processes that help organizations move from a Model 1 environment to a Model 2 environment. In keeping with the spirit of high participation, each of these is conducted with a group of 10 to 35 people. These four processes are: market/customer requirements gathering, real-time futuring, organizational process analysis, and rapid redesign workshops. Each of these is explained in greater detail in the remainder of this section.

Market/Customer Requirements Gathering. First, the organization needs to determine what does the customer, and even more broadly, what does the market want that the organization could provide. In the past, it's been a common mistake to only ask your customer base what they want, and what directions they think the industry might be taking. As a hypothetical example, if you ask your large computer mainframe customers what they think will be the future of computing, they are most likely to resoundingly answer, "Mainframes!" If you were to base your strategy on that, you could be in trouble …

One of the more useful systematic ways of collecting this information is a technique called Quality Function Deployment. If an organization is unfamiliar with this, they may opt for another method of collecting market requirements. While many organizations start their change process with this activity, many use existing market data.

Real-Time Futuring Session. In this session the organization articulates its desirable future and develops action plans that describe how to get there from the current reality. This session differs from traditional planning sessions in several ways. First, it is not a problem-solving focus. In their strategic planning efforts, many organizations first develop a list of problems, then prioritize these problems, and then develop action plans to address them. This process is usually very time-consuming, energy-consuming, and quite often depressing. The result is usually that the action plans do not get done because the large number of problems seems so overwhelming. We typically framed these planning sessions with the two questions "What's the problem?" and "How do we fix it?" Now we replace those framing questions with the questions "What's possible?" and "Who cares?" These generate higher energy and better results.

This Real-Time Futuring Session is a drastic departure from traditional planning approaches. After examining the history of how organizations arrived where they are and what current reality is, the organizations develop a vision of what they want the future to be. They then develop action plans to reach that vision. The focus is on getting to the future, not on leaving the past. We have noted that it is considerably more effective to pull people into the future than it is to push them out of the past.

Another important distinction is that all key members of the "system" are in the room to interactively challenge assumptions and gain a shared understanding. Usually this process has 20 to 30 people off-site for a two-and-a-half-day period. This process is often called a Search Conference. For a more detailed description of Search Conferences please refer to "Search Conferences: A Management Briefing" by Tom Devane.

Organizational Process Analysis. Another critical input in a Model 2 environment is an understanding of the organization's business processes—at a high level. In this group session, approximately 10 to 30 people conduct a high level "As Is" process analysis. Then, often the group uses previously collected data from the Market/Customer Requirements Gathering activity and other strategic inputs to develop a list of the top 5 to 12 business processes in the organization.

These arc the high level "To Be" processes that will serve as a foundation for the later redesign efforts. If there is time, it is often helpful to graphically show and name the interfaces among these key processes. Some organizations take the opportunity to map these key processes to key customer and market requirements that may have been identified previously.

Rapid Redesign Workshops. These workshops are critical to helping build personal commitment to organizational excellence. In these sessions, work groups design their own work, including structures, process flows, and new patterns of communication for the work group.

Sometimes these sessions are the first step in a Model 2 journey, sometimes they are the last. This type of redesign differs from traditional redesign efforts in several respects.

First, the entire work group who will be executing the work are the ones who will be designing the work. For this reason sometimes these design sessions are called "Participative Design Sessions." These design sessions do not use a handful of representatives to design the work for a larger group—all who are involved redesign the work. For work groups over 35 people, multiple design sessions are used and their results may then be integrated in a town meeting if necessary.

Second, the group is not only responsible for designing their new process workflow, they are responsible for designing their work group structure and patterns of communication within their group and among other groups. Experience has shown that with minimal instruction and facilitation from the outside a work group does an excellent job of design—far better than if an external or internal design had been imposed on them.

The third key difference from traditional redesign efforts is in the possession of knowledge of key redesign principles. In a traditional Model 1 environment, specifics of redesign principles and their processes are in the heads of a few people. In a Model 2 environment, all people in the organization are taught the principles for designing high performing, adaptive work structures and the processes needed to produce those structures. This widespread knowledge is key because it supports a nonstop change environment in which work groups and teams continually redesign themselves as external conditions change.

This rapid, continuous self-redesign capability provided by Rapid Redesign Workshops is the foundation for highly adaptive organizations. For a more detailed discussion of Rapid Redesign Workshops, please refer to "Participative Design" by Bob Rehm, or "Rapid Redesign Workshops: A Management Briefing" by Tom Devane.

While there are many contributing factors to the successful transition to a high performing Model 2 environment, we have found that the following seven have particularly high leverage. While each of these factors need not be present everywhere in the organization at the start of the effort, it is very helpful if they are present in the first work group that embarks upon a new design.

Availability of information. In the new organizational world it is critical that employees have access to information formerly held only by their superiors. As has been cited in many studies before, *Harvard Business Review* again reported in May, 1995 that "given the same information as their supervisors, those in middle and front-line positions usually reach the same conclusion as their bosses. More important, this arrangement allows front-line managers to fix problems at their low level instead of sending variance reports up the hierarchy and then waiting for top-down judgments." Advances in information technology have made it easier to share information than it was just ten years ago, and effective organizations are now designing processes to distribute information quickly to all who need it.

Effective environmental scan. All bets are off that a Model 2 organization will succeed if there is no effective information gathering about the "world outside the organization." It is essential that periodically there is a scan of the market, specific customers, industry forces, trends, "best practices," and the competition.

Commitment to learning. We're not talking about the type of learning many people do in college to get reasonable grades to graduate and get a good job. We're talking about something that will improve the overall performance of the business.

I believe that three definitions, when considered together, accurately reflect the type of learning that we are looking for in a business environment. Peter Senge states that learning is "expanding the ability to produce the results we truly want." Chris Argyris defines learning as "the ability to detect and correct errors." And quite an interesting nonbusiness definition of learning comes from Jean Piaget who asserts that learning is "a new way of organizing reality." Model 2 organizations must make a commitment to each of these learning types at every level, or they will perform no better than their hierarchical command-and-control counterparts.

Safe environment for learning and mistakes. As somewhat of a corollary to the commitment to learning, Model 2 organizations must provide a time and space in which it's okay to make mistakes. One way to do this is to allow people to make mistakes on the job without blowing their heads off. It's been said that the Motorola culture "celebrates noble failures."

But for many organizations this is far too risky a strategy. Instead, they opt for "practice fields." The concept is similar to that for a sports team: practice the techniques you need in a non-fatal environment, get good at them, and then bring them with you to the real game. Organizations that subscribe to this philosophy often set up "learning labs," in which people practice new skills in role plays, computerized "microworld" simulations, and alternative business scenarios.

A shift in top management's role. Under Model 1, top management tends to focus on developing strategy, and designing organizations and systems that facilitate a hierarchical review of results and subsequent use of hierarchical corrective mechanisms. Under Model 2, top management's key role is to create an environment in which managers and employees monitor and correct errors themselves.

While strategy development is still a part of senior management's job, it tends to be shared more, and it tends to be ongoing throughout the year instead of just once a year as in a Model 1 environment. Typically aspects of bureaucratic hierarchical management tend to disappear as it is demonstrated that they are less effective.

While this description is the ideal situation, it is unrealistic to expect that a Model 1 senior manager leaves the office on a Wednesday night and returns Thursday morning excited to abandon all vestiges of the hierarchy by Thursday lunch. For many organizations, this migration process works best when it is done gradually and systematically, and its results are monitored.

Systemic thinking. One problem that organizations face as they try to change is the problem of fragmentation. Systemic, or systems, thinking encourages us to look at the system-wide impacts of our actions. The concept, recently popularized by Peter Senge, has a number of useful principles and hard tools for organizations making the move to a Model 2 organization.

One important systems thinking principle that we use in this approach is the principle of leverage. Senge points out that "the bottom line of systems thinking is leverage—seeing where actions and changes in structure can lead to significant, enduring improvement." Experience has shown us that worker involvement—in both work design and self-management—is a very significant leverage point in helping organizations reach higher levels of performance.

Experience has also demonstrated that creating peer-to-peer working relationships is an extremely high leverage point. This leads to much richer business solutions and more truly collaborative efforts than traditional superior-to-subordinate relationships.

Mark Paitch defines systems thinking as "the art and science of linking structure and behavior." Structure, as used in this context, consists of the key variables in a system of interest, and their interrelationships.

For example, process workflow, an organizational structure, the reward system, trust levels, and training policies could all be considered elements of a "structure." Managing the interrelationships of these elements during a transition period is just as important as, if not more important than, managing each of these elements as an independent variable. When we refer to behavior in a systems thinking sense, we mean directly observable events that can be plotted over time, such as stock price, invoice errors, or employee morale.

Because an organization is a combination of complex technical and social systems, it is important that change agents take a systems view of problems and opportunities, rather than a component view, as they move toward a Model 2 organization.

Individual responsibility. In a Model 2 organization people must have the mindset that they, themselves, are contributing factors to problems in the organization. As Dr. Deming and Dr. Juran in the total quality movement have pointed out, the structure of the business and its existing rules and procedures are major parts of any organization's problems, as well as its opportunities. But we can't just throw up our hands and blame the structure. In a Model 2 organization everyone must also take on a high level of personal responsibility for contributing to improved overall organizational performance. For this to happen management must allow employees to develop new work structures and become more self-managed.

Bob Rehm, one of the leaders in participative design techniques, has stated that "the most effective leverage point for systemic change is relocation of responsibility." By giving workers more responsibility we tap into an often neglected aspect of effective organizational change—intrinsic motivation. If we ever hope to tap into the energies and ideas present in every worker, we need to combine extrinsically-based motivation techniques with those that generate intrinsic motivation by creating conditions that increase personal responsibility.

The four group processes mentioned earlier that help migrate to a Model 2 environment do precisely that.

What Does the Organizational Structure Look Like?

In a Model 2 environment, the organizational structure matches the desired business outcomes with the skills, interests, and knowledge of people in the organization. There are a wide variety of options, such as modified hierarchy, network organization, process organization, process organization with a "home room location" for skill set maintenance, or a product-based organization.

We also see a lot of temporary work groups, fluidly forming and dissolving. They set up governing practices as needed, and operate under what Warren Bennis of Stanford calls an "adhocracy," to stress the temporary, purposeful nature of the structure.

One major difference in a Model 2 environment is that managers no longer manage people. They manage work groups and results. It's a common mistake to proudly announce that, "Last year our manager to staff ratio was 1:8. This year, under Model 2, the ratio is 1:50." A more accurate description would be to say that this year one manager manages 5 self-directed teams of 10 people each. In a Model 2 environment, the managed unit is no longer people, but work groups and results. This is a subtle but extremely important distinction. Work groups and teams are replacing functional departments and managers as the high leverage, basic performing units of the organization.

This mindset shift has some dramatic implications for training, information distribution, and reward systems in the future. For example, many Model 2 organizations institute a combination of pay for skill and pay for performance compensation strategies after the structures and business processes are redesigned. This mindset shift helps reinforce the new values of continual learning, team performance, and increased personal responsibility.

Is a Model 2 Environment Right for Our Organization?

That is for you and members of your organization to decide. As mentioned previously, world-class organizations in both the private and public sectors are migrating to a Model 2 environment to enhance performance and reduce costs.

The performance improvement possibilities of a Model 2 environment are great, but Model 2 environments are not for everyone. Ultimately the decision is up to the members of the organization after they understand the implications for the organization.

What Decisions Do We Need to Make Before Embarking on This Strategy?

There are three key questions an organization should ask itself before embarking on any large-scale change effort. The combination of answers will help determine two things. First, it will help determine if the organization should be in a Model 1 or Model 2 environment. Second, the combination of answers will help plan the migration effectively. Organizations, particularly at the senior management level, need to be very honest when answering the following three questions.

Who will participate in the change effort? Possible options are: a representative sample of people from the affected areas, a floating team of corporate change experts, or everyone who will be affected.

Generally speaking, the more people management will allow to participate in the change, the more ready the organization is for a Model 2 environment.

How will the new work groups be managed? Possible answers include: actively managed by the level above them in the organization, in a laissez-faire mode (much work is delegated, but nothing is followed up on), or the teams will be self-managed with boundaries and guidelines.

In general, increased levels of self-management in the new environment indicate a greater preference for a Model 2 environment.

What will the resulting organizational structure look like? Possible answers include: like the status quo, not like the status quo but some other predetermined form, status quo with minor variations, or the new structure will be truly emergent based on the results of the Search Conference and work group designs.

Generally speaking, the more senior management is willing to let the design emerge based on strategic input and some boundaries, the greater the chances the organization has as a Model 2 operating environment.

The Model 2 environment has provided improved performance for many organizations. In addition, the process tends to be completed in less than half the time of a traditional change effort, and with a greater degree of employee buy-in. In 1992 a study of 96 high involvement organizations found that approximately three-fourths outperformed their industries on a variety of measures. Hard performance data from a larger subset of that sample revealed that the high involvement organizations outperformed their industries on return on sales by an average of 532 percent and on return on investment by 388 percent.

Creating a Model 2 environment requires a substantial commitment to change, and should be carefully evaluated by any organization considering it. Though the benefits are great, an organization must decide if it is ready to implement the new paradigms required for Model 2 success. Without the necessary changes in assumption sets and change methods, Model 2 performance is simply not possible. But with the necessary paradigm changes, performance can be extraordinary.

REFERENCES

Argyris, C. and Schon, D. (1978) *Organizational Learning: A Theory of Action Perspective.* Reading: Addison-Wesley.

Argyris, Chris. (1982) *Reasoning, Learning, and Action.* San Francisco: Jossey-Bass.

Bartlett, C.A., and Ghoshal, S. "Changing the Role of Top Management: Beyond Strategy to Purpose." *Harvard Business Review,* Nov-Dec 1994, pp. 79-88.

Bartlett, C. A., and Ghoshal, S. "Changing the Role of Top Management: Beyond Systems to People." *Harvard Business Review,* May-Jun 1995, pp. 132-142.

Bennis, Warren. (1990) *Why Leaders Can't Lead.* San Francisco: Jossey-Bass.

Block, Peter. (1993) *Stewardship.* San Francisco: Berrett-Koehler.

Bridges, William. "The End of the Job." *Fortune,* Vol. 130, September, 1994.

Checkland, Peter. (1981) *Systems Thinking, Systems Practice.* New York: John Wiley.

Covey, Stephen R. (1990) *Principle-Centered Leadership.* New York: Simon & Schuster.

Devane, T., Slater, J., and Hume, S. "Organizational Prototyping: Embarking on Organizational Transformation." Society for Information Management National Competition (2nd place), 1994.

Devane, Thomas. "Rapid Redesign Workshops: A Management Briefing." 1995.

Devane, Thomas. "Search Conferences: A Management Briefing." 1994.

Emery, Merrelyn. (1993) *Participative Design for Participative Democracy.* Canberra: Australian National University.

Goldstein, Jeffrey. (1994) *The Unshackled Organization.* Portland: Productivity Press.

Hammer, Michael. (1993) *Reengineering the Corporation.* New York: HarperBusiness.

Kotter, J. P., and Heskett, J. L. (1992) *Corporate Culture and Performance.* New York: The Free Press.

Ledford, G. E., Jr., Cummings, T. G., and Wright, R. W. "The Design and Effectiveness of High-Involvement Organization." Working Paper, Center for Effective Organizations, University of Southern California at Los Angeles, 1992.

Manz, C. C., and Sims, H. P. (1993) *Business Without Bosses.* New York: John Wiley & Sons.

Morgan, Gareth. (1986) *Images of Organizations.* Newbury Park: Sage Publications.

Morgan, Gareth. "Rethinking Corporate Strategy: A Cybernetic Perspective." *Human Relations,* Vol. 36, 1983, pp. 345-360.

Oakley, E., and Krug, D. (1992) *Enlightened Leadership.* Denver: Stone Tree Publishing.

Pascale, Richard. (1990) *Managing On the Edge.* New York: Touchstone.

Semler, Ricardo. (1993) *Maverick: The Success Story Behind the World's Most Unusual Workplace.* New York: Tableturn.

Senge, Peter. (1990) *The Fifth Discipline.* New York: Doubleday/Currency.

Senge, Peter, et al. (1990) *The Fifth Discipline Fieldbook.* New York: Doubleday/Currency.

Stata, Ray. "Organizational Learning—The Key to Management Innovation." *Sloan Management Review,* Spring, 1989, pp. 63-64.

Trist, Eric. "The Evolution of Sociotechnical Systems as a Conceptual Framework and as an Action Research Program." *Perspectives on Organization Design and Behavior,* New York: John Wiley, 1982, pp. 19-75.

Weisbord, Marvin. (1992) *Discovering Common Ground.* San Francisco: Berrett-Koehler.

Weisbord, Marvin. (1987) *Productive Workplaces.* San Francisco: Jossey-Bass.

HOW TO DOWNSIZE WITH TOTAL QUALITY MANAGEMENT

33

Joycelyn Stabler and Peggy Sullivan

Joycelyn (Lyn) D. Stabler *is a management consultant at Group Performance Processes (147 St. Charles Street, Bay St. Louis, MS 39520, 601-467-0358, jstabler@falcon.st.usm.edu), specializing in organizational dynamics. Lyn provides consultation and educational services to help members of organizations understand, manage, and enjoy change. Lyn examined the layoff process as an insider when she volunteered to be laid off in 1992.* **Peggy S. Sullivan,** *Ph.D. is a management consultant at Quality Process Consulting (2402 Nashville Avenue, New Orleans, LA 70115, 504-865-8447), focusing on quality processes and designing and implementing TQM or CQI programs. Peggy was a member of a downsizing team of a large aerospace company, and gained quite another perspective when she herself was laid off during a major downsizing. These experiences, along with her work in TQM, led her to write these articles with Lyn Stabler.*

The 1990s have seen a rush by many large organizations to implement the methods and techniques of Total Quality Management (TQM). TQM is a management philosophy that defines quality based on customer needs and provides techniques to involve employees in the continuous improvement of their work processes. This improvement in efficiency often arrives at a time when economic conditions demand that companies shrink the overall size of the workforce. This guide demonstrates that, when a workforce reduction is needed, the philosophy and methods of TQM can be applied to the layoff process just as they are applied to improve operational processes.

TQM principles can help a company accomplish the transition from one organizational configuration to another. A layoff process grounded in TQM principles uses open communication with customers, systems thinking, process analysis, and maximum employee involvement along with data-based decision making to enable the company to redefine operating structures and improve processes. The result is a company that not only improves financially, but also becomes more capable of delivering quality products and/or services to its customers.

Although familiar approaches such as across-the-board cuts are a tempting response to distribute the pain of having to lay off employees, they rarely produce the fundamental changes that are needed. If the philosophy and methods of TQM are desirable before and after the layoff period, the organization that uses those same methods in the process itself will be most successful. TQM can help management and employees plan and execute layoffs using a process that leads to an improved, as well as smaller, organization. The accompanying flow chart (see Figure 33.1) diagrams the process and indicates the organizational level responsible for leading each activity.

Step 1: Design, Plan, and Schedule the Downsizing Process

As soon as workforce reductions are known to be necessary, key executives must define the overall process by which the needed reduction will be accomplished. In order to maximize involvement throughout the organization, it becomes critically important to plan ahead and schedule time for the appropriate groups to identify requirements, conduct analyses, reach consensus, and make recommendations. An understanding of the entire event as a process helps key executives maintain focus and alignment throughout the tumultuous period ahead. This understanding enables leaders to communicate openly to the rest of the organization about roles, responsibilities, and involvement in decision making.

Executive management, with leadership from the CEO, conducts the analysis to identify company customers and prioritize their requirements. Much is lost if this exercise is delegated to another level. Key processes necessary to support requirements surface next and become the focus for all subsequent decision making throughout the layoff process. The focus is on designing a new organizational configuration based on supporting these core processes.

The importance of scheduling key executives to devote effort to this analysis cannot be overemphasized. Concurrent with this analysis, the rest of the organization will be constructing a description of the current "as is" condition. All of this takes time. Time tables outlining milestones and due dates will determine the depth of detail possible. The intensive effort required by this approach is certainly preferable to the severe apathy, lethargy, complaining, and backbiting so common in organizations during periods of workforce reduction.

Step 2: Announce the Layoff and the Method by Which It Will Be Accomplished

Once the downsizing process has been planned, waste no time in informing the employees that it will occur. The workers are told in detail why the company has chosen to reduce the workforce, the

How to Lay Off Employees Without Laying Off TQM

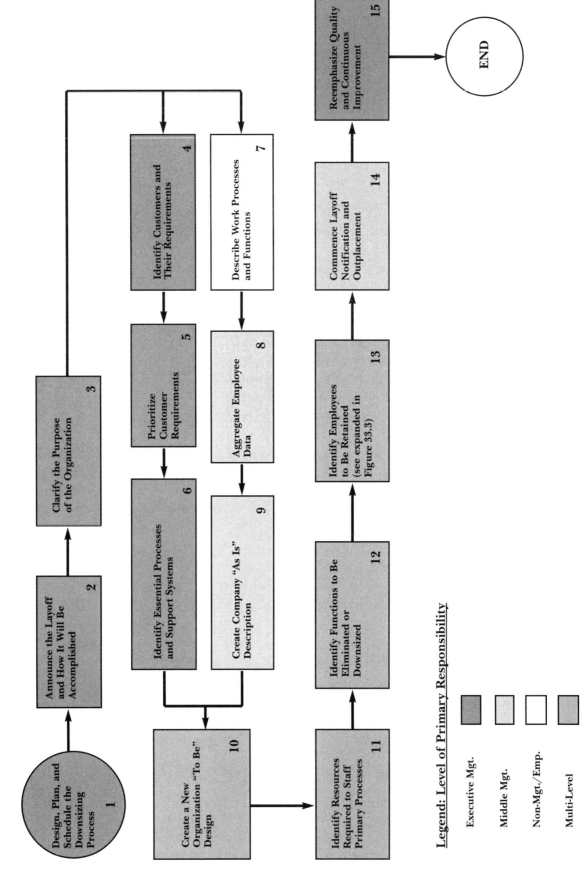

Figure 33.1.

method by which it will be accomplished, their roles and responsibilities, and the expected timetable. A rumor hot-line to keep communication lines open up and down the chain of command will facilitate information flow and help avoid vacuums. Expect a frenzy of activity and emotion or "dead calm" as the organization lurches into survival mode. At regular intervals (e.g., weekly staff meetings), update the workers on the progress of the effort and gather feedback as to their reactions and concerns.

Step 3: Communicate the Purpose of the Organization

Dr. Deming's first of 14 points for quality management says, "Create constancy of purpose." Communicating the continuing purpose of the organization orients its systems toward the future and in the direction of a successful new configuration. Since this new configuration is rarely known to organizational leaders at the onset of downsizing, the danger exists that reducing the workforce will become the de facto purpose of the organization. Too often, companies become so totally consumed with downsizing that ongoing business suffers. This dangerous tendency is overcome by emphasizing a purpose that runs through and beyond eliminating jobs.

Constancy of purpose requires that there be faith in a future. When employees are consumed with worry about workforce reduction, it is hard to believe in the company's future and work toward improving quality and productivity. Employees become lethargic, apathetic, and preoccupied with questions about their security. Improvement teams question management's support for their projects; weekly meetings become worry sessions and members seek reassurance. Planning efforts and implementation of new processes slow down or stop as questions are raised about the ultimate need for these improvements "after we're restructured." Continuing reinforcement of the company's purpose directs attention and activity and encourages employees to be confident enough about the existence of a future to stay emotionally engaged in creating it.

Step 4: Identify External Customers and Their Requirements

When downsizing is required, managers often focus on eliminating individuals without analyzing requirements for the processes they carry out. Identification of primary customers and their requirements indicates which processes are essential from the customers' point of view. Unfortunately this is often a difficult task because the customers may be vague about expectations and indeed not totally knowledgeable about their needs. Nevertheless, articulating requirements is useful in any circumstance and absolutely essential for downsizing. Brainstorming and formal customer surveys are two tools that are frequently used at this stage of the process.

Step 5: Prioritize External Customer Requirements

It is not uncommon to identify hundreds of requirements that delineate the way customers currently expect business to be done. After requirements are identified, meetings with the customers to prioritize critical requirements are conducted. Company leaders and customer representatives agree on the relative importance of various criteria and rate each of the identified requirements. Discussion of the results leads to consensus on the ranking of criticality and establishes mutually agreed on priorities. The priority requirements will guide downsizing decisions. That is, the most critical requirements must receive continued support while less critical requirements are candidates for reduction or elimination. Consider priority requirements from each external customer group to ensure a balanced approach that addresses the needs of each constituency. Quality Function Deployment (QFD) can provide a useful approach to surface the priorities and connect customer requirements with valued attributes and operational processes.

Step 6: Identify Essential Processes and Support Systems

With customer requirements prioritized, the processes driving the organization's success are more easily identified. The quality of products/services generated by these core processes, defined in terms of the customers' requirements, will be pursued relentlessly throughout the downsizing period. Many subprocesses may support an activity needed to satisfy a primary customer requirement. Construction of a Process Decomposition diagram (see Figure 33.2) can help depict various levels of detail and show which subprocesses are really needed. Level C processes are usually good candidates for simplification and consolidation as they may be redundant and overlapping across functional departments.

The results of this process analysis will be compared to data about the current organization and used to construct a new organizational structure that supports critical requirements using a smaller workforce. For example, Figure 33.2 shows cost reporting, R&D, and test activities within the Quality Assurance department. Such activities usually occur in other functional departments as well and could be consolidated. Likewise, functional responsibility for production-related inspection might be moved to Manufacturing. These decisions must be made in light of what processes are really needed to support key customer requirements. At this step in the analysis, identify those that are essential and simply note where redundancy and overlap exist.

Step 7: Describe Current Work Processes and Functions

All employees write descriptions of their job responsibilities and the processes that they participate in or support. Using a standardized format is advisable to promote a consistent level of detail. The

Process Decomposition

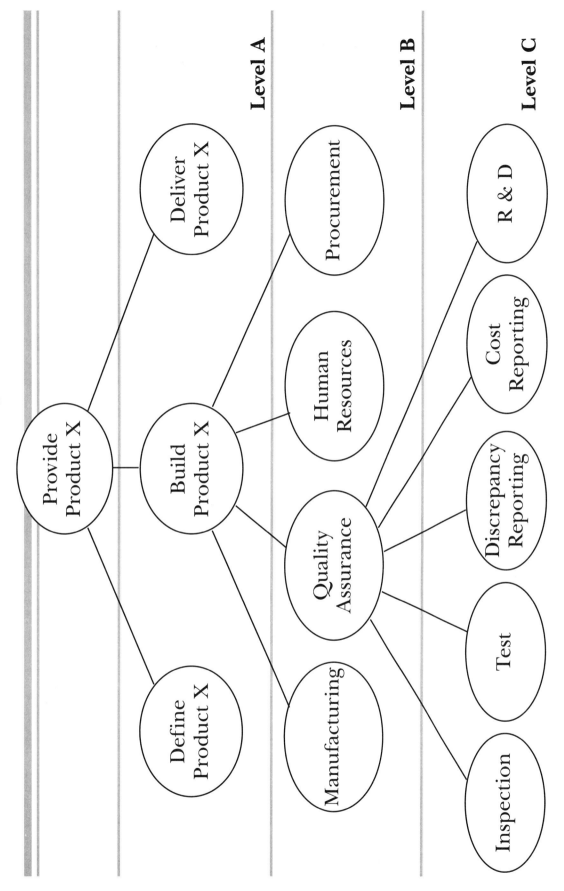

Level A

Level B

Level C

Figure 33.2.

description should include a listing of task assignments, internal customers, and any external customer requirements that dictate that the activity be performed. These descriptions are forwarded to middle management.

Expect a strong reaction to this activity from the organization. Most employees will initially be suspicious about the purpose of this data. It is important to convince employees that accurate data is critical for comparison to the process analysis and to reassure them that redundant job functions are not automatic grounds for dismissal. Here again, understanding the overall layoff process will help people see how the data will be used and how the decisions will be made. Employees whose current job responsibilities are redundant or unnecessary must not be afraid to say so.

Step 8: Aggregate Employee Data

Middle management receives the functional descriptions from those employees who report to them and aggregates the information in a manner that accurately describes how their department or division of the company is currently working (i.e., what is being done and why). This description must include department mission or purpose, cross-functional customer-supplier relationships, and independent functional responsibilities. Use of a standardized format is recommended for easier comparisons from one department to another.

Step 9: Create Company "As Is" Description

Representatives from various functional areas of the company convene and construct an overall "As Is" understanding and written documentation of the company, based on employee-generated data. Flow charts will be especially useful to display the data. The level of detail depicted will usually depend on the amount of time available. Resist allowing level of detail to become a stumbling block. Detail will often differ from one department to another due to the way job responsibilities are currently assigned. Do not be discouraged by the apparent complexity of the information submitted. The objective is to review it for understanding, and gain a general perception of how things are currently being done. Computer software, available for mapping customer requirements to operational processes, is helpful to elicit similar levels of detail.

Additional detail and/or clarification can be provided by multidisciplinary process improvement teams already working to examine and improve systems. Do not miss the opportunity to draw upon the expertise of any employees currently involved in continuous improvement activities; they are your internal experts. These teams have usually studied current operations in depth and are giving considerable thought and creative attention to defining new ways of doing business.

Step 10: Create a New Organization "To Be" Design

Executive management meets with the mid-management cross-functional team to compare the existing organization "As Is" with prioritized customer requirements and primary processes to establish the new organization design. Drawing upon the data generated earlier, the team identifies essential and nonredundant processes, subprocesses, and support systems. The management team must prepare a complete proposal for a "new way" of doing business. Sometimes referred to as a "green field" approach, the organization is built from the ground up as if it were a new operation. A new Process Decomposition diagram showing core processes, subprocesses, and support processes is a good way to communicate the new design without drawing a traditional organization chart. The Process Decomposition diagram will focus attention immediately on the necessary processes, not on who has the functional responsibility for managing them.

Step 11: Identify Resources Required to Staff Primary Processes

The management team determines what resources (personnel, skills, and equipment) will be needed to operate key processes. These resource requirements are matched to existing operations and personnel. Concentrate on defining resources needed to support the new organizational structure. The temptation will be strong to justify maintaining existing empires. By concentrating the analysis on identifying essential resources to support operations for a "new company," the discussion stays focused on defining the new configuration, not protecting the old one. The objective is to add detail to the key customer requirements and process analysis completed earlier. The new organization becomes more and more concrete as this proposal for a new way of operating takes shape.

Step 12: Identify Functions to Be Eliminated or Downsized

Compare the new configuration with the "As Is" description to highlight redundant, unnecessary, and overstaffed functions. These functions represent groups of employees whose job classifications will be drastically changed or eliminated. These jobs are either no longer needed by the company or the numbers of employees devoted to these assignments can be significantly reduced. For example, functions devoted to collecting mass inspection data, engineering functions duplicated in various departments, and redundant planning functions might surface as candidates for elimination or reduction. With this step in mind from the outset, all data generated for the "As Is" description and the "green field" description will be as similar as possible (i.e., similar levels of detail, terminology, and format).

The tough decisions about who to keep and who to let go can best be made by distributing the decision-making burden throughout the organization. Involve all affected employees in this process. Figure 33.3 diagrams the procedure whereby personnel who are currently employed in functions targeted for elimination or downsizing can contribute by identifying criteria for continued employment and generating self-evaluation data.

13a: Downsize or Eliminate Function?

If the activity is being downsized, proceed to notify affected employees and involve them in contributing a much needed perspective to the decision-making process. If the decision is to eliminate the activity, identify personnel currently responsible for performing the activity and consider them relative to the total layoff pool for potential transfer to other areas of the company.

13b: State the Intention to Downsize Support for a Process and Involve Affected Employees

Announce to the affected people that support for a particular process will be reduced. Tell the employees the amount or percentage by which the affected area will be cut and explain how the workers will participate. Be truthful with employees about the potential for losing their jobs and trust people to respond in a mature manner.

Employee groups are being involved in order to generate data for consideration by management. Making informed, data-based decisions is preferable to the traditional approach in which management makes such decisions in isolation. Employees who participate in the decision-making process will gain insight and understanding as they provide their unique perspective. Asking them to contribute to the decision-making process demonstrates trust. The likely response will be respect and mutual appreciation for the difficulties in making the hard choices.

13c: Define Criteria for Continued Employment

Affected employee groups meet, and using TQM tools such as brainstorming, Pareto analysis, criteria matrix, and consensus, each group identifies criteria for continued employment. For example, a group of quality inspectors might identify length of service, job knowledge, and attendance as meaningful criteria. The help of a trained facilitator is useful as employees may or may not be accustomed to group decision making.

These data alone do not determine the decisions. Managers make the decisions using this data to provide additional insight and information.

Step 13 Expanded: Identify Employees to Be Retained

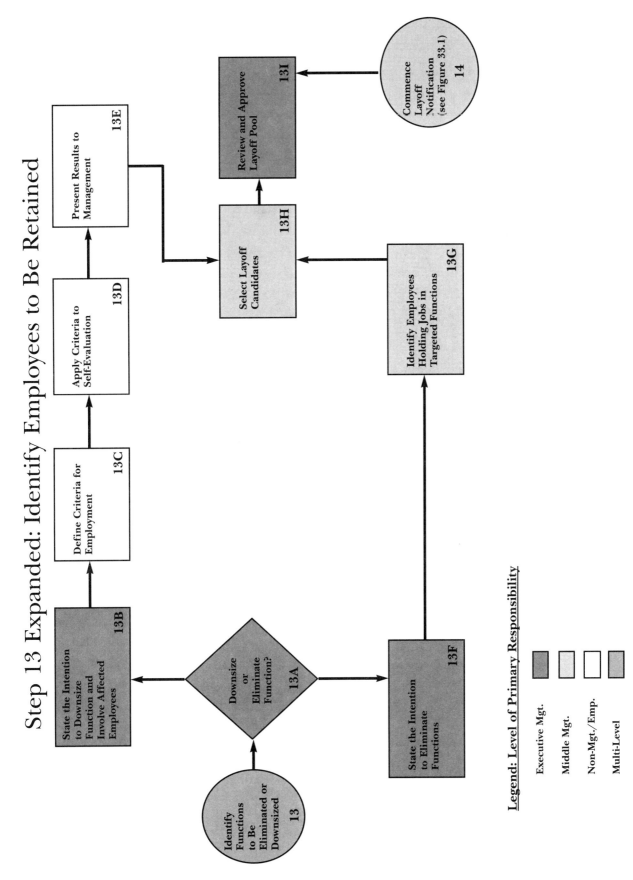

Legend: Level of Primary Responsibility

Executive Mgt.

Middle Mgt.

Non-Mgt./Emp.

Multi-Level

Figure 33.3.

13d: Apply Criteria to Self-Evaluation

Affected employees may be asked to rate themselves against the identified criteria. This step adds personal perspective to the data generated. Each individual at risk assesses his/her chances of being laid off and the results of this self-evaluation are given to the manager. Although the validity of the ratings may be open to question, most employees will have a good idea of their real standing. It will be obvious to some that they are candidates for pink slips. They may draw some comfort from knowing that the decisions are being made rationally, fairly, and with their participation.

13e: Present Results to Management

The group presents the results and individual evaluations to its immediate management. The data is used by management as input for consideration, not to rank the group of employees. At this point management can communicate any legal restrictions, company policy, or any other known influences on the final decision that the employees may not have considered. This frank exchange will clear up many misconceptions, provide further insight into the real-life complexity of such a decision, and reassure workers that the company does not make these decisions arbitrarily or in isolation.

13f: State Intentions to Eliminate Functions or Processes

Announce to the affected employees that a particular function or process will be eliminated and that the chances are good that they will either be laid off or transferred to another part of the company. It should be emphasized that the layoffs are based on the decision to eliminate support for specific requirements, not arbitrary elimination of people in response to headcount reduction.

13g: Identify Employees Holding Jobs in Targeted Functions or Processes

Area managers identify employees who currently hold positions targeted to be eliminated and forward the list to the management team. At this point, seniority, skill mix, and affirmative action plans will influence the possibility for transferring some employees to other areas of the company. Employees whose job responsibilities include functions that will be eliminated and others that will be downsized or retained will need to be considered carefully. New job descriptions will be created as the organizational structure shifts. Some ambiguity is to be expected. Open communication, reassurance, and honest confrontation will help employees deal with the ambiguity and allow the company to weather this difficult period with minimum impact on ongoing operations.

13h: Select Layoff Candidates

Area management identifies the specific employees to be laid off in their department. It remains the responsibility of managers to make the decisions about who to keep in their department and most employees will gratefully let them do it. No one relishes making decisions that hurt people and disrupt their lives. With the insight gained from their own deliberations, employees may even be more supportive of their managers knowing that they are under the stress of this unpleasant responsibility. Some companies allow work teams to decide which members to lay off. The existing decision-making hierarchy and the degree of trust present between employees and management will determine whether this latter option is feasible.

13i: Review and Approve Layoff Pool

A layoff pool created from the lists generated at the mid-management level is reviewed and finalized by the executive management team. At this level, their perspectives about the possibility of transfer to other departments or divisions, needed skill mix, political considerations, and other impacts on the final choice for layoff can be added to the manager's and the work group's input.

Step 14: Commence Layoff Notification and Outplacement

The way the layoff notifications and outplacement are treated will send strong messages to employees who stay with the organization. Managers faced with the unpleasant task of informing people of their termination will benefit from training and/or coaching to help them understand the most effective, gentle way to give notification. The climate of openness created thus far will make the job easier, but neither the recipient nor the messenger is fully prepared for the impact of this news. To the extent that analyses have been complete and aboveboard all along, the news at this stage will be perceived as less shocking and arbitrary.

Step 15: Reemphasize Quality and Continuous Improvement

Quality and continuous improvement have been embraced by all in the company during a most difficult transition and are now ensured a firm hold in the culture of the newly reorganized company. Companies that have undergone significant changes will anchor themselves with a shared vision that includes quality and continuous improvement in all aspects of the operation. The values, philosophy, and tools of total quality management combined with the dedicated effort of the organization's members have allowed the company to survive and will continue to ensure its success in the future.

Layoffs with TQM seem to be an oxymoron. The two should have nothing to do with each other. In an ideal world, they would not. In reality, sometimes a company has to reduce its workforce. When it does, the company can maximize intended results, protect the emerging TQM culture, and show respect for employees by continuing to follow the basic tenets of Total Quality Management. The key principles of TQM are essential to create the workplace of the future. The fact that they also minimize the pain for employees, customers, and stockholders during a stressful time is an added bonus.

HOW TO **34** T YOUR MEETINGS WITH BRAINWALKING

Bryan Mattimore

Bryan W. Mattimore *is president of The Mattimore Group (One Landmark Square, Stamford, CT 06901, 203-359-1801), an innovation training and creative problem-solving consulting firm. He is the author of the book* **99% Inspiration: Tips, Tales & Techniques to Liberate Your Business Creativity** *(AMACOM, 1994), as well as contributing editor to* **SUCCESS Magazine.** *Bryan facilitates over 100 ideation sessions per year and is a popular keynote speaker. He was also a contributor to* **The 1996 McGraw-Hill Team and Organization Development Sourcebook.**

This first-person account of a consultant who facilitates ideation sessions for a wide array of clients describes how to stimulate brainstorming in a unique way. He also explains several reasons for adopting this unusual approach.

I facilitate over 100 ideation sessions per year. And no two sessions are ever the same. One day I might be facilitating a new product development session for Neutrogena. The next, trying to imaginatively position Old El Paso Salsa. And the next, helping AT&T develop customer loyalty programs. Content, as you might imagine, always varies in such sessions. But, frankly, so does process. Designing a new product naming session is very different from, say, designing a strategic planning session. Facilitating a creative cost cutting session is worlds apart from running a new product development session.

And yet, I'm going to propose, based on some hard-won experience, that there is a *single best technique* to begin meetings with, regardless of the task or desired outcome.

And that one technique is the newly-invented *brainwalking*™ (a trademark of the Mattimore Group) which evolved out of work with its close cousin, *brainwriting.*

What Is Brainwriting?

Let's take a look at brainwriting first. As its name implies, it is a writing exercise and, as it turns out, a very simple writing exercise at that. It's kind of a writing volleyball exercise where participants write down ideas and then rotate their papers among other participants to build on their original idea.

To facilitate the brainwriting technique, the meeting leader simply asks each participant to take out a blank 8.5" × 11" sheet of paper and write down one idea (related to the task at hand) at the top of that paper. Then the leader asks each participant to pass the paper (usually clockwise) to a neighbor. The person receiving the paper then reads his neighbor's idea and either a) tries to build on/evolve in some way the idea he/she has just read, or b) uses the neighbor's idea to stimulate an entirely new idea. In either case, he/she writes down an idea on his neighbor's sheet, just below the idea he has just read. Papers continue to be passed (usually four to five times) until each paper has four to five ideas on it (all, of course, written by different people). The sheets are then passed back to their original owner (his or her handwriting will be at the top) so that each participant can see how his or her idea was built on by co-participants. Each participant is then asked to pick the one or two best ideas from his sheet, and share them with the group as a whole for further discussion/building.

Incredibly simple, right? A technique that's both easy to learn and easy to facilitate.

And yet, don't let the simplicity of this technique fool you. Every single time I start my sessions with this technique, I am truly amazed at the results, both in terms of raw ideas/output, as well as the power it has to transform a group of diverse individuals, with their own potentially selfish agendas, into a cohesive, peak-performing, idea-generating team.

Why is brainwriting such a powerful way to start a meeting? Let me share with you several of my ideas, theories, and/or explanations.

The Benefits of Brainwriting

Diverse Thought Streams

In a typical brainstorming session, one person will throw out an idea, another will build on it, and yet another person will build on that build. Ideas are used to spark other ideas. The problem is that as a group goes down certain avenues, or "streams of thought," it may be difficult to get back to new, "usefully naive" points of view. The group may be beginning to know too much. It may have gone down a path that it cannot get back from.

One of the wonderful things about brainwriting is that if there are, say, eleven people in a meeting, the group finds itself going down eleven different thought streams at once. Each person's starting point is a starting point for the group as a whole. If you're looking for new ideas, what better place than to start at the beginning. *Everyone's* beginning, that is.

Extroverting the Introverts

In any group, you typically have a mixture of extroverts and introverts. Not surprisingly, in any meeting, it's the extroverts we hear from most. It is, however, often the case that introverts have some of the most interesting, occasionally profound ideas—and, paradoxically, from whom we are likely to hear the least. Introverts are often simply afraid to speak up and let their ideas be known. Brainwriting gets around this problem by having everyone, introverts and extroverts alike, "voice" their ideas in a form that is nonthreatening to an introverted personality—by simply writing it down.

Silencing the Problem Child

The process that allows introverts to communicate their ideas in a nonthreatening way, by writing them down, also has the advantage of effectively silencing any participant who has a tendency to monopolize—or worse yet—torpedo the productivity and effectiveness of the meeting. Like everyone else, they're just writing down ideas. Everyone gets equal time in brainwriting.

Let Democracy Reign

The president is in the meeting. And so is a junior account executive. Whose idea is more important? In an ideal world, you'd like to think that it's not *who* had the idea—but the inherent value of the *idea itself* that will determine its ultimate worth to a company or organization. We all know that this is, however, a naive point of view. Brainwriting, while not anonymous, is pretty close to it. The president's ideas get passed around just like everyone else's—and in the process come to be seen as no more or less important than anyone else's.

Encouraging "Idea Piggybacking"

One way to measure the effectiveness of any meeting is to study the amount of "idea piggybacking" that occurs: that is, the time spent by participants building on each other's ideas to get more and better new ideas. This, after all, is the main reason to have a meeting in the first place, isn't it: to share and build on each other's ideas (otherwise, why not just handle "it" in a memo?)? Because idea piggybacking or building is the essential activity in every pass of the papers, brainwriting is both encouraging and giving participants practice in what they should be doing in all their meetings anyway—trying to a) make other people's good ideas even better, or b) use other people's thoughts to stimulate their own thinking toward entirely new and original ideas.

Crystallized Ideas

We've all been in sessions where someone just rambles on and on, seemingly endlessly. We begin to wonder if the person even has a point, much less whether we'll ever get to hear it in this millennium. Simply by having to write ideas down, brainwriting promotes a level of "idea crystallization" or "headlining" that you simply don't get when people are verbalizing their ideas. Writing forces focus, and ultimately brevity.

Making Room for New Ideas

People often come into meetings with ideas. You want to get these ideas out as early as you can for two reasons. For one, people feel that their idea is "the best idea," and are often hard to convince otherwise. The reality is, though, that even the best idea can often benefit from the building/input of other people. Brainwriting encourages making good ideas great, and great ideas even better.

The other reason for getting "old ideas" out quickly is that you want to make room for entirely new ideas. It's as if you have to empty the glass before you can fill it up again. Unfortunately, participants will too often wait for the "perfect time" to present their idea. As such, throughout the meeting, they are focused on themselves and their idea, rather than trying to build on others' ideas, or even come up with new ideas of their own. Brainwriting makes room for the as-yet-to-be-discovered ideas that will often come later in a meeting.

Championing Participant Expertise

Brainwriting champions the intelligence, savvy, and expertise of the participants themselves. Because each participant is assumed to have come into the meeting with an idea worthy of writing down, it sets a nice tone for the meeting. The participants are the experts, not the meeting leader.

Incredibly Prolific

Let's say you have ten people in a meeting. And you do five rounds of brainwriting. In less than fifteen minutes you'll have 50 ideas (five passes times ten people equals fifty). In a conventional meeting, how many ideas might you have in fifteen minutes? Five? Ten? Obviously, brainwriting can be an incredibly efficient way to get a lot of ideas out very, very quickly.

What Is Brainwalking?

I hope you agree that, after reading the above points, it is hard to imagine a better technique than brainwriting with which to start most meetings. And yet, in my opinion, brainwalking, while still a close cousin of brainwriting, also has some powerful and important benefits beyond the classic brainwriting technique.

Brainwalking evolved out of ideation sessions I did for the Warner-Lambert company. The assignment, in session one, was to generate some innovative marketing ideas for their Trident brand of gum. I started the meeting with the *brainwriting* exercise—and it worked beautifully, even better than I had expected.

A week later, I was asked to facilitate a similar session for Warner-Lambert, only this time for their Dentyne brand of gum. The problem was that many of the people who had been in the Trident session would also be in the Dentyne session. I had to figure out a way to "change the act," so that people would continue to be excited about the process, and not feel that we were simply doing the "same old thing." And yet, because brainwriting is such a powerful way to start a meeting (for all the reasons above), I still wanted to use it. A difficult problem, to say the least.

I solved this dilemma by moving the *people* instead of the *papers*. I taped large sheets of flip chart paper on the walls around the room. Then, I gave everyone a colored marker and asked them to find a sheet on the wall and write down an idea at the top of the sheet. Next, I had them physically move/rotate (clockwise) to their neighbor's paper and add an idea much as they might do in a typical brainwriting exercise. After five rotations I had them rotate back to their original sheet and pick the idea that they liked best to discuss with the group as a whole.

The Added Benefits of Brainwalking

Pretty straightforward. Brainwalking is, at its essence, seemingly the same technique as brainwriting. And yet to my surprise, I found at least six very powerful and profoundly important differences between brainwriting and brainwalking.

Physical Movement Is Energizing

The sheer act of getting people up and moving significantly increases the energy in the room—especially when brainwalking is the first exercise of the day. And more energy means that if need be, participants can more easily rotate more often without getting tired of or bored with the process.

Aren't We Creative

Another important benefit of brainwalking is that it is incredibly reinforcing for the group as a whole to see all of its ideas posted around the room. In only a few short minutes of brainwalking, there can be literally a hundred ideas or more on the flip chart papers. Success can often feed on itself in a meeting like this. As one client once said to me, "I feel like if we went home now we'd be successful. Look what we've done in the first 20 minutes of our session."

Shared Purpose

Seeing all the ideas emerge simultaneously around the room, created by everyone in the room, creates a wonderful sense of shared purpose, identity, and team building. And this shared identity makes it that much easier to facilitate the rest of the session.

Continued Building

We have also found that participants want to see what everyone else has written. Consequently, we'll often see participants "walking the walls" during breaks looking for new and interesting ideas. Many times entirely new ideas will be triggered by this walking the walls exercise.

Emerging Themes

Another advantage of having the ideas posted around the room, both for the participants and the facilitator, is that it is relatively easy to begin to group and then identify key emerging themes and/or patterns.

Where Have We Been, Where Are We Going?

Finally, having the ideas posted around the room gives the facilitator a very good idea both of where the group is "coming from" and where it might be headed. In this way, the facilitator, if need be, can either lead the group into a different strategic direction or facilitate "deeper" to help the group develop certain specific kinds/classes of ideas.

One final thought. By using markers and flip chart paper in the brainwalking exercise, participants find themselves literally writing the ideas bigger than they ever could with just a pencil and paper at their tables. And after all, isn't coming up with "bigger ideas" what a meeting is all about?!

HOW TO PUT ORGANIZATIONAL LEARNING INTO PRACTICE

35

Thomas Bertels

Thomas Bertels *is the manager of the customer center at a German subsidiary of Cooper Industries. Thomas has published a book on organizational learning and dozens of articles and essays on change management and organizational behavior. He can be contacted about managing change and organizational learning issues at Ulrich-Jakobi-Wall 1a, 59494 Soest, Germany, +49-292-115-726, tb@knipp.de.*

Changing where you work into a Learning Organization has a great deal of theoretical support, but how do you actually do it? Read this practical guide to discover how you can embed change management into your organization's daily operations and make strategic learning a lasting reality.

The concept of a Learning Organization has become increasingly prominent over the last few years. The concept has evolved into a management theory based on the insight that a fast changing business environment requires organizations to change quickly as well, and that the only sustainable competitive business advantage is the organization's ability to learn. Organizational learning can be defined as the continuous testing of experience and mental models, and the transformation of that experience into knowledge. This knowledge is accessible to the whole organization, and is applied within the business to create results.

What many organizational change activities lack is a strategic focus, a clear commitment to create lasting results. Ideas on organizational learning have until now mostly been utilized to achieve short-term results and to solve current problems. Typically they have failed to have any lasting impact on the organization's output in measurable terms.

A lack of focus and commitment is the reason that many organizations cannot unleash the real potential of organizational learning. Successful organizational learning is characterized by setting a strategic direction, choosing the areas of learning, committing to these areas, and realizing the vision through constant effort.

The ability to create values and market alignment is basic to the development of competitive strength.

Strategic learning supports the process of acquiring these competencies by providing an agenda for change that aims to develop these skills. Cultural characteristics are extremely well protected against imitation. Strategic learning aims to support the development of these strengths by pursuing a future-directed agenda to enhance the core competencies of the organization. (See Figure 35.1.)

Key Features of the Strategic Learning Approach

The key features of the strategic learning approach are:

✓ It helps to achieve short- *and* long-term success.

✓ It embeds change into the organizational structure and daily operations.

✓ It is focused on key areas.

✓ It produces tangible results.

✓ It is directed to realize the companies' vision of its future.

Because managing existing business requires skills other than inventing future markets and developing new opportunities, the strategic learning approach focuses on developing an agenda for change in order to ensure both short- and long-term success. Strategic learning embeds change into the organizational structure, thereby avoiding the "not invented here" syndrome. It unleashes the experience and creativity of the organization's members by including everyone into the approach and by integrating the ideas and instruments into the organizational reality. It helps people to reinvent their jobs and their tasks by offering instruments to guide their energy. Because strategic learning concentrates on key areas, it can help to achieve tangible results on the essential topics for the organization. Without concentration or focus the organization is lost in the complexity of the marketplace, and in the stream of technologies and social changes. Strategic learning is about conscious decision making and direction.

The only reason for change is the need for results and the only place where tangible results can be generated is the organizational reality. Strategic learning is focused on implementation in the organization. Due to the fact that successful change needs to have direction, and because the future is the best guide for an organization to avoid reactiveness and to create future markets, strategic learning is oriented toward realizing the organization's vision of its future. Without commitment to a long-term change strategy initiatives have little chance to be successful. Learning is an investment as well as a decision toward future markets and needed competencies but it is the only way to be able to compete in future markets.

Strategic Learning Improves Long-Range Competitive Strength

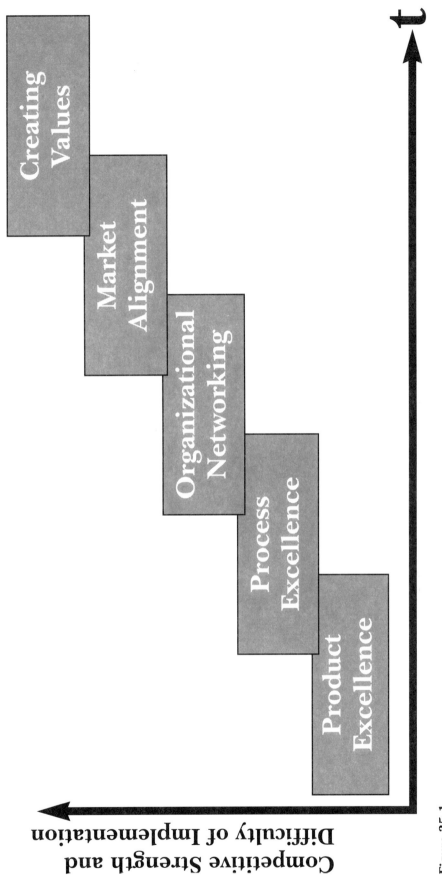

Figure 35.1.

The development of a long-range strategy for organizational change is based on an assessment of the present markets and competencies and the anticipated future conditions. The goal is to create an understanding of the future's opportunities based on the present skill and experiences of the organization.

The result of this process is the learning agenda, a map to direct organizational learning and a commitment toward creating the organization's future by activity (see Figure 35.1). This agenda comprises competence areas and levels that must be developed to be able to sustain the organization's survival and development. It is necessary to analyze the corporation's present situation for this development to occur.

Possible questions to create a picture of the present situation could be:

✓ Who are our customers?

✓ Who are our customers' customers?

✓ What challenges do our customers and their clients face?

✓ What changes are going on in the market?

✓ What kind of communication is significant under present conditions?

✓ Where do competitive pressures result from?

The present condition is reflected by the organization's existing competencies. These skills should be examined in terms of leadership, culture, customer, and process skills and result in answers to the questions:

✓ What are our competencies (positive as well as negative)?

✓ What competence does the market currently require and pay for?

✓ Where do we lack competence?

The analysis of the mismatch of present market condition and organizational competencies would at this point result in a reactive repair program.

To develop a proactive organization prepared to respond to future changes, the same scheme is applied to future markets and competencies. The results of both assessments can be mapped in the competence portfolio (see Figure 35.3) that indicates the necessary competencies and skills to develop and nurture.

Realizing the Strategic Learning—Instruments and Tools

Strategic learning offers a well-known set of instruments and practices to implement the learning agenda. These tools are grouped into the main areas for organizational renewal (see Figure 35.4).

Developing a Learning Agenda

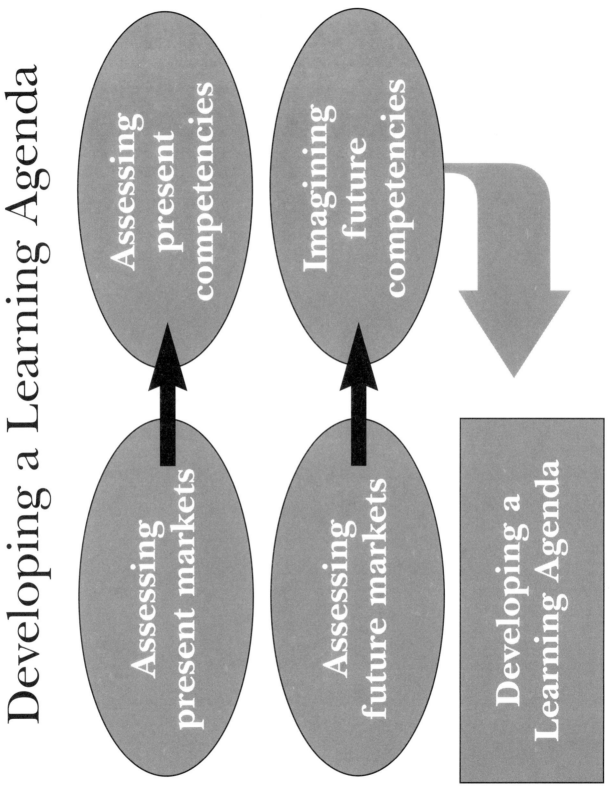

Figure 35.2.

Competence Portfolio

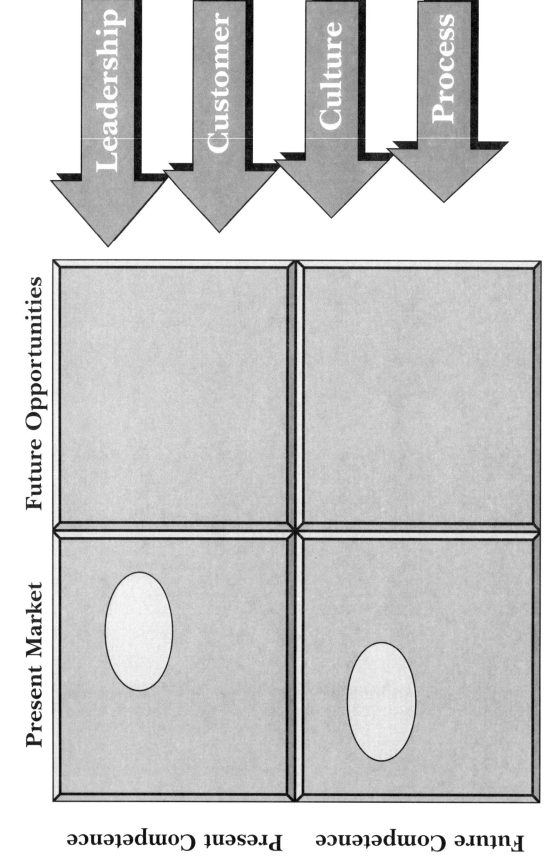

Figure 35.3.

Strategic learning uses existing instruments to achieve the desired change. *Methods and instruments are always means to an end.* Strategic learning applies these ideas to achieve measurable results.

Central to the application of these instruments is that they become an integral part of daily operations. This represents the perspective of strategic learning that fundamental organizational change is hard to achieve unless the necessary change efforts are part of the organization's structures and processes.

A. *Leadership.* Leadership is about creating an organization that performs at higher levels. The Strategic Learning approach supports the organization's leaders by utilizing Coaching, Visioning, and Strategic Discussions to help the management redesign their mental maps of the organization to support the process of creating and developing core competencies.

✓ **Coaching** is a useful tool to help leaders redesign basic beliefs about the company's business and competencies and to support change agents. The coaching process supports management to recreate their organizational picture by providing an opportunity to revise and recreate basic assumptions about the organization's purpose, the individual role of the manager, and the required new behavior and skills to match with the requirements of the learning agenda. These basic beliefs have an emotional foundation because they are a part of a manager's self-view. Therefore coaching provides an environment to test new behavior and ideas in order to prepare for a new organizational reality.

✓ **Visioning** is the process of discovering the organization's destiny: the deep purpose that expresses the organization's reason for existence. The process of developing a vision and a strategic intent is central for the ability to learn strategically. The vision sets the direction for the future orientation of the entire organization. The learning agenda is directed toward realizing the vision. The process of designing and communicating the vision is a powerful instrument to approach the hearts of people, a necessary ingredient for successful learning. The process of visioning helps to discover organizational beliefs and stimulates lateral thinking.

✓ **Strategic Discussions** utilize the fact that without language knowledge cannot flow from person to person within a company. On the high value-added boundaries of knowledge creation, the ability to "make" new language—and rapidly diffuse it through a company—is a strategic advantage. The organizational world, in this sense of evolving meaning and concepts, is brought forth in language and in conversations. Language and knowledge go hand in hand. If the currency of business operations is money, the currency of knowledge development

Realizing the Learning Agenda

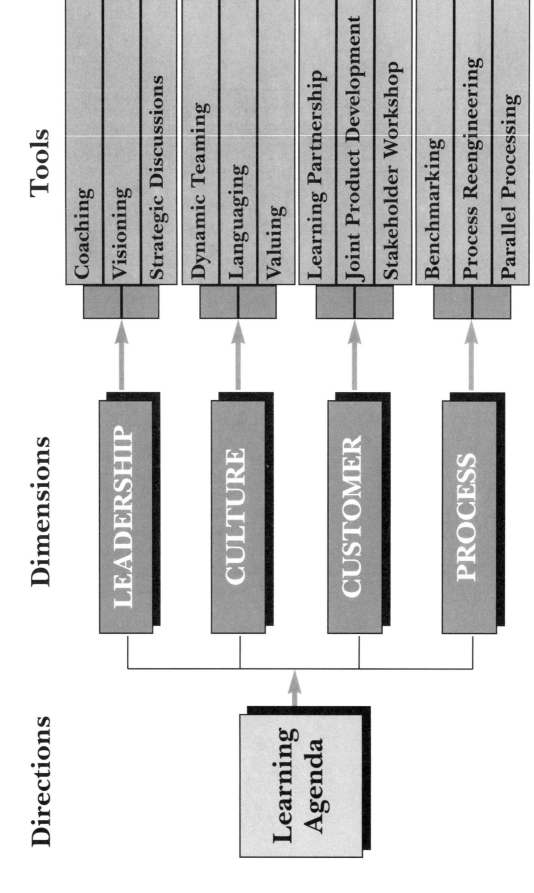

Figure 35.4.

is language. Operational conversations are oriented toward the survival of the company, the day-to-day operation of the business. Strategic discussions are oriented toward the advancement of the company, toward the creation of the future. Strategic discussions are also about the creation and acquisition of resources for the future, and how these resources should be allocated. In short, strategic discussions are the cradle of a company's strategy.

B. *Culture.* Incorporating a culture of learning within the organization reinforces these principles daily. Dynamic Teaming, Languaging, and Valuing are three aspects of an organization's culture in which strategic learning is reinforced.

✓ **Dynamic Teaming** is more than creating another team structure. The challenge is not to build teams but to manage the process of dynamic teaming, to best match the given strengths to create a team best prepared to realize existing business opportunities. Dynamic teaming provides individuals, groups, and companies the opportunity to recognize the abilities and aspirations of others and to support the process of enhancing these skills. The process focuses on supporting individuals and groups to realize the other's strengths and goals and to develop the skills to match these competencies to serve concrete market opportunities. Dynamic Teaming implies managing "coopurrence," the art of active cooperation with competitors to develop basic entrepreneurial skills.

✓ **Languaging** is the art of utilizing communication and discussion to realize the learning agenda. Language is our distinctive way of being human and humanly active. When we speak, we act in a very special way and when we speak effectively, we have a profound impact on the world. Consequently, the approach of strategic learning supports the belief that attaining mastery in the art of speaking and listening is probably one of the most important skills to possess when facilitating organizational change. Beliefs and basic assumptions are encoded in language, and a shift in languaging supports the recreation of organizational values.

✓ **Valuing** is about committing, about setting limits to organizational activity as well as providing areas for individual action and growth. The process of creating and establishing new values empowers organizational members and helps to shift decisions to the lowest possible level in order to increase speed and applied knowledge. Managing values is an essential task for executives in the knowledge era to empower employees and increase the organization's speed of response. Values guide behavior and help to overcome functional mentalities when they are held in common throughout the whole organization.

C. *Customer.* Involving the customer in the change process is an integral part of strategic learning. An organization's ability to serve its customers is the only reason for its existence. To ensure a customer-directed change approach, strategic learning integrates the customer into the organizational reality. Learning with and from customers is one of the sources of organizational renewal. Strategic learning applies such techniques and instruments as Learning Partnerships, Joint Product Development, and Stakeholder Workshops to ensure that the learning effort is directed toward increasing customer focus.

✓ **Learning Partnerships** are means to increase awareness toward customer expectations and standards. Learning Partnerships support revision of the corporate self-image, realization of customers' perspectives, and the development of competencies according to market requirements. Learning Partnerships help to refocus such functions as accounting and production toward a customer-oriented perspective. These partnerships mirror organizational performance and are intended to create awareness of the real reason for organizational existence: customers.

✓ **Joint Product Development** extends the idea of integrating customer views another step and helps to decrease the time between customers' requirements and organizational response. Joint approaches help to match the organization best to their client's needs and affect organizational behavior in advance. To meet customers' requirements the organization has to realize its competencies and apply these competencies to solve customer problems or demands.

✓ **Stakeholder Workshops** offer great opportunities. The organization can learn about the abilities and goals of their external stakeholders and can therefore direct their learning to make best use of this connectivity. By exchanging information and ideas the participants can make best use of the capabilities of their partners (see Figure 35.5). As organizations flatten and become more virtual they increase the focus on key competencies and therefore reduce the amount of internal value creation.

This process creates a growing dependence on suppliers. Learning along with customers helps to ensure that the company's learning is aligned to the market. By embedding customers' customers, the corporation connects itself to the challenges of the future. Such workshops are a holistic approach to add value at a meta-level.

D. *Process.* Processes shape organizations. Core business processes influence organizational success in terms of costs, quality, customer orientation, and culture. The management of processes is an important aspect of Strategic Learning in order to develop process competence. The approach applies Benchmarking,

Workshops with Stakeholders

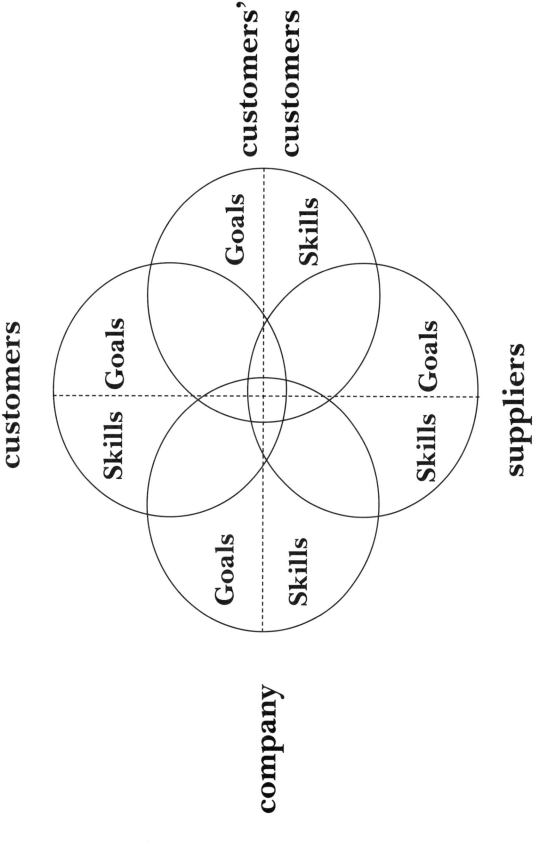

customers

customers' customers

suppliers

company

Figure 35.5.

Process Reengineering, and Parallel Processing to improve organizational efficiency, to develop skills for mastering of tomorrow's processes, and to achieve measurable results.

✓ **Benchmarking,** often characterized as SIS ("steal ideas shamelessly"), can be much more than imitating patterns of success. The real potential to be realized by a strategic learning organization is that it allows buy-in to fresh views that have proven to be successful. Benchmarking avoids the "not invented here" syndrome associated with external interventions because it is a process of learning from the very best in that specific field. Successful benchmarking needs to be much more than simply imitating the best approach—the innovative potential to be unleashed lies in adapting the process model to the organization. Process design improves organizational effectiveness as the organization accepts the process and adapts to it. Initiating successful benchmarking requires the involvement of the process owners and the empowerment of them to achieve results.

✓ **Process Reengineering,** understood as the art of reshaping the business process to fit the real purpose, can achieve powerful results in terms of creating lean structures and processes with a maximum of efficiency. Once again, the real potential to be released depends on the involvement of the process owners. The critical processes to be mastered according to the learning agenda are redesigned by re-orienting the process toward the required output and reducing process-inherent complexity and time consumption. To embed process reengineering into the daily operations allows the organization to follow a path of renewal that shifts organizational processes toward serving its inherent purpose—and nothing else.

✓ **Parallel Processing** can help to establish a new way of working and cooperating, allowing organizations to deliver faster and better output by applying new technologies. Besides the advantages in terms of technology and speed, the main potential lies in preparing people to work parallel to each other, thereby increasing the need for successful cooperation. Enabling people to work parallel changes the patterns of communication and the way processes are carried out significantly. Traditional sequential thinking will not be a successful mode of behavior within a parallel process: Working in a virtual team, for example, requires open communication and information sharing. Being able to work in parallel changes the way the organization operates and interacts and offers opportunities to revolutionize processes and achieve outstanding results.

HOW TO FORM SUCCESSFUL TEAMS USING TEAM TASK AGREEMENTS

36

Deborah Hopen and Laura Gregg

Deborah Hopen *has over twenty years of experience in total quality management (6400 Southcenter Boulevard, Tukwila, WA 98188, 206-241-1464, deb-hopen@aol.com). She has served as a senior executive with Fortune and Inc 500 companies and was the 1995-96 President of the American Society for Quality Control. Her consulting clients include Disney University, Weyerhaeuser, Microsoft, the city of Tacoma, and the state of Washington.*
Laura Gregg *owns Wizard Textware (15600 NE 8th Street, Suite B1-167, Bellevue, WA 98008, 206-641-5951, wizeljay@aol.com). She specializes in the instructional design of quality training. Her current interest is in the application of American archetype research to team formation and development.*

This guide describes how you can form stronger work teams within your organization. The information is based on the results of recent research about American cultural forces and how they affect team design and performance.

Introduction

In American organizations, the search for quality through team-based processes has had mixed results. Attempts to replicate the Japanese model have not been particularly successful, and despite the occasional business press reports of a high-performing team, many articles raise doubts about the effectiveness of teams.

Recent cultural archetype research may provide insight into why American teams organized for quality improvement don't work the way organizations expect. Americans have a distinctive view of the concepts of quality and improvement in general, and of team participation in particular.

In the book *The Stuff Americans Are Made Of* (Hammond, Morrison, 1996), the authors outline several cultural forces that define us as Americans. Related archetype studies on quality and teams in America have linked these forces to the nature and function of teams in the American workplace. The preliminary results offer useful guidance for creating effective teams.

A successful American team formation strategy:

✓ emphasizes clarity from the beginning about mission, goals, and authority as they relate to the organization's desired business results

✓ explicitly aligns individual team members' needs for personal achievement through work on a team with the organization's needs for team effectiveness

✓ accepts and exploits the American "bias for action," which requires less focus on planning and more focus on immediate results and opportunities for improvisation

✓ allows mistakes and encourages learning from them for potential breakthroughs

The process and agreements described here are designed to harness American cultural forces in the service of organizational needs for effective teams.

The Process

Team results can fall short of expectations for a lot of reasons, but many of these poor outcomes result from a failure to make explicit agreements about the team's mission, goals, roles, and authority. Sponsoring managers, team members, supervisors, and all other stakeholders in the organization should have the same understanding about what the team is supposed to do, why it is doing it, and what resources it will need to succeed.

An effective way to do this is through a Team Task Agreement for the team, which includes individual Team Member/Supervisor Contracts for each team member. Following is a process for developing these agreements followed by descriptions of the agreements themselves.

Step 1. Sponsoring Manager Prepares Preliminary Information

The sponsoring manager should start by preparing a preliminary statement of the team's purpose, the intended process, and any known constraints. It's better if this information isn't overly detailed and doesn't contain too many constraints because that may limit the team's ability to create an environment that best fits team members' capabilities and styles.

Step 2. Team Meets to Review the Manager's Input.

The preliminary information is presented to the team in a meeting away from the sponsoring manager, during which the team begins the first draft of a Team Task Agreement. Often, the team will have many questions about the purpose of the team and processes to be used. Even when sponsoring managers devote significant effort to defining these issues in advance, most teams raise additional questions. Sometimes these questions stem from specific needs of team members to better understand their roles and responsibilities, but it is equally common for the questions to reflect unease about overall organizational issues, including a fear of hidden agendas.

This initial team discussion provides an opportunity to air concerns that may need to be organized and clarified before being presented to the sponsoring manager. If this step isn't taken, team members sometimes unwittingly bombard the sponsoring manager with questions and create unnecessary tension. The team should limit its questions to the essential issues that will get it off to a good start. There will be many opportunities to delve into other issues during the team's work process.

Step 3. Team Leader and Coach/Facilitator Meet with the Manager.

The team leader (and coach or facilitator) visits the sponsoring manager to review the draft Team Task Agreement and explain the rationale behind each proposal. In this meeting, the sponsoring manager can test planned feedback and decisions. If possible, the leader should present the information while the coach helps clarify the discussion when asked for input. The coach can also help the sponsoring manager build a trusting relationship with the team by making sure proper authority is assigned based on team members' experience.

Step 4. Manager Meets with the Team.

Now the sponsoring manager and the team can prepare the final working version of the Team Task Agreement. Once they have agreed on the overall time requirements for the project, the manager can effectively oversee the preparation of the individual Team Member/Supervisor Contracts for each team member.

Don't Waste Project Time

The team does not have to let valuable time pass waiting for the finalized agreements. Rely on the American bias for action and willingness to learn from mistakes to carry the team through the formation period. Just make sure the power and authority issues are resolved before the team invests significant time in data analysis or solution generation. Data collection, including discussions with the customers, generally can begin while the agreement negotiations are in progress. The following describes the parts of the Team Task Agreement and the Team Member/Supervisor Contract.

Before the team begins its work, the team and the sponsoring manager should develop a detailed team task agreement that reflects the way they really want to operate. The task agreement includes the mutually arrived at answers to a set of questions about mission, goals, roles, and responsibilities. The resulting document (which can and should be revised as the team proceeds through a project) is the primary tool for resolving conflict and keeping teams on track and on task.

Part 1. Mission or Problem Statement

Why was the team formed? What are the business goals? What are the customer concerns? What is the team's specific assignment, role, or function? What need, system, or problem is to be addressed? What is the scope? Where are the boundaries? What is the history of earlier similar projects? What are the potential barriers the team should know about?

There are three main areas that need to be clarified at this point:

1. The sponsoring manager and the team must share a clear understanding of the project's purpose. This may involve process improvement, cost savings or avoidance, cycle time reduction, or many other outcomes. The key is to be specific about the intended purpose and to work together until the sponsoring manager and all team members share the same view.

2. The team's mission should support the overall organizational goals. If a strategic plan exists, the project should support its objectives. Fundamentally, projects that are aligned with broader organizational goals are more likely to be appreciated, recognized, and rewarded appropriately. They are also more likely to obtain the needed time, priority, and resources.

3. Nothing is more frustrating or able to derail a team than boundary conflicts. It's essential to avoid having two teams working on overlapping projects. It's fine to have multiple teams working on different parts of a bigger problem if the boundaries between the teams are differentiated clearly.

Part 2. Target Results

How will the team and sponsoring manager know that the team has completed its task?

The best measurement systems are:

✓ Built from existing systems whenever possible. It's always helpful to have a history of data available as a baseline.

✓ Checked to make sure that data collection and analysis aren't too cumbersome.

✓ Reliable—data collected is accurate and precise.

✓ Focused on the key results that need to be improved.

Measurement is a recurring theme in quality improvement. It's also a topic that creates concern for many team members because they worry that they'll be held accountable if they're measured, and often they're unsure what constitutes an appropriate measurement system.

The team and manager may have difficulty reaching consensus on reasonable targets for the performance indicators (that contain enough stretch to represent significant improvement, but not an unattainable level). The manager and the team should check with customers to determine the best ways to measure and define improvement levels. This takes away much of the debate on how much improvement is needed to be significant.

Part 3. Time Allotted and Completion Date

How much time should team members be expected to spend on the task? What is the expected deadline?

Teams that meet less than two hours per week tend to have problems maintaining energy for the task. Likewise, teams that meet for too long and pull members away from regular duties (even when care has been taken to rearrange priorities and reassign tasks) create tension that undermines progress.

In addition to time spent in team meetings, team members need to allocate time for outside assignments. It's best to assume that each team member will spend at least two hours on outside assignments every week. This time needs to be included in the overall team plan so that priority conflicts are less likely to occur.

Once the team members determine their weekly time investment, a rough estimate of total time required can be made. This helps team members set expectations—for themselves, associates, and supervisors. The individual Team Member/Supervisor Contracts specifically define how much time team members will spend on team meetings and team-related activities.

Problem-solving teams should last 12 or fewer weeks under most circumstances. If the team predicts a longer timeline, the manager should reduce the project scope to a more manageable level.

Part 4. Individual Goals

If the team focuses only on organizational goals, team members may feel that their individualism is jeopardized. A conscious effort must be made to ensure that every team member has a chance to concurrently achieve her individual goals as the organizational goal is pursued. By building on each team member's unique capabilities, you can determine what contributions she expects to make and what opportunities for growth need to be created.

Once again, the key is to have a clearly defined process for measuring progress and taking corrective action. You may want to incorporate this process into your norms so that the team remembers that good performance must occur on two levels simultaneously—the organization's and the team members'.

Some team members may be uncomfortable with sharing their individual goals. This is particularly true if candor has been discouraged in their past team experiences.

Sometimes team members believe that stating their needs will be viewed as a selfish behavior by other team members. Quite often, careful wording can be used to reduce this perception.

If a team member seems to be holding back desired outcomes, a separate one-on-one meeting might help the team member to develop a statement of personal goals that can be shared with the team.

Part 5. Frequency of Reporting

On the surface, the decision about how frequently to report may seem fairly arbitrary. Be aware, however, that the frequency of communication depends greatly on the trust level between the sponsoring manager and the team.

Teams that have less experienced members or sponsoring managers should plan on more regular progress reports. More experienced teams can report less frequently.

Report timing can be based on the calendar or milestones. Short written progress summaries are useful for frequent reporting schedules. More formal presentations work best for milestone summaries or lengthier calendar intervals.

Team members may complain about reporting, particularly if the sponsoring manager requires frequent summaries. Reporting, however, is a two-way process. In addition to providing a progress summary to the sponsoring manager, the report also gives the team an opportunity to describe issues and barriers and request the sponsoring manager's help.

Teams should be encouraged to take advantage of the sponsoring manager's willingness to "clear the decks" for them. It is unacceptable to blame poor team results on lack of outside support if the team has not communicated its needs to the sponsoring manager.

Part 6. Power and Authority

How much authority does the team have? The following table is one way to define the boundaries of a team's authority. Check the boxes that apply to your team's situation.

Team power and authority	Team decides	Team recommends and sponsoring manager approves	Sponsoring manager decides
Spending daily operational funds up to $_____	❑	❑	❑
Spending special project funds up to $_____	❑	❑	❑
Obtaining support from internal resources	❑	❑	❑
Increasing employee workload temporarily during the project	❑	❑	❑
Increasing employee workload permanently as a result of the project	❑	❑	❑

Operational funds include costs related to trials, waste, and overtime. Generally, teams should have some authority to affect operations without further approval. For engineering problems, the authority level may be thousands of dollars. For most other problems, $100 to $500 is sufficient.

Special project funds include costs related to team treats (food and other celebratory items), supplies, and outside consultants. Obviously, these costs can vary greatly depending on resources the team is authorized to use. Every team should be given at least $200 for incidentals.

Team members and sponsoring managers may be cavalier about setting these limits. They *should* be thoughtful about expected costs and the manager should empower the team appropriately.

The most common source of temporary workload increases for quality improvement teams involves added inspection and testing. It's important to remember that defective products or services should be detected and removed until they can be eliminated. This means that auditing, sorting, and rework may be required while the team develops a better system for delivering the product or service to the customer.

Giving broad authority to the team in the area of temporary workload increases sends a sign to the entire organization that the sponsoring manager is willing to suffer short-term cost increases to satisfy customers. It also shows the team has the sponsoring manager's confidence that improvement will occur rapidly.

Permanent workload increases are quite rare. The team should be encouraged to pursue many options before recommending permanent workload increases. Situations involving human safety and health, environmental protection, or regulatory compliance are generally the source of these costly changes.

Most sponsoring managers will retain authority for approving permanent workload increases. Teams often will be relieved to have management support for these decisions.

Part 7. Outside and Other Resources

What other resources may the team use without further approval?

It's good for the team to recognize that outside resources aid the quality improvement process. Even though the team may have lots of information about the project and many possible solutions, there are others in the organization who have an interest in the outcomes. By involving these internal resources early in the process, the team improves its data collection, analysis, and change management processes.

External resources usually include customers, suppliers, and consultants. Teams that don't check with customers often develop solutions that do little to improve satisfaction; therefore, almost every team should be authorized to contact customers.

Suppliers can come from within and outside the organization. If the solution includes changes to supplier requirements, the team should work directly with the suppliers to resolve any issues. Sometimes, the sponsoring manager may want to have the team include a non-team member, such as an employee from the purchasing department, in conversations with external suppliers.

Generally, the sponsoring manager will want to approve requests for consultants unless the consultant is on retainer to the organization.

Team Member/Supervisor Contract

The Team Member/Supervisor Contract will help team members and their supervisors anticipate and prepare for potential conflicts between the regular work and the team project. The contract also addresses an archetype-related requirement that individual team members not be penalized for participating on a team.

The sponsoring manager should meet with each team member's supervisor. Expectations should be set for the supervisor to work with the team member to reassign duties to clear time for the project.

This liaison with team member supervisors is one of the sponsoring manager's most important roles; it provides an opportunity for the manager to better understand the team's work environment and eliminate potential barriers. During this discussion, the organization's commitment to the project should be made clear.

Like the Team Task Agreement, The Team Member/Supervisor Contract can be revised as the work of the team proceeds, but drafting an agreement from the beginning demonstrates commitment by the organization to the individual's participation on the team.

Warnings

✓ The contracts must be reviewed regularly to update them as conditions change *and* to check that there is compliance with the terms. If both parties do not abide by the terms of the contract, it can create permanent distrust and undermine the effectiveness not only of the team member, but of the team as a whole.

✓ Team members can be their own worst enemies. They are often reluctant to hand off routine duties for fear that someone else will perform better or permanently absorb their favorite tasks. Sometimes after they have transferred the duties, they interfere from the sidelines.

✓ The contract terms must be communicated to anyone who is affected by them; otherwise, the team member and supervisor will be constantly subject to questions and demands for explanations about the changed duty arrangements.

Part 1. Time Allotted

How much time will this team member be expected to spend on the task?

The team member and supervisor should agree on an estimate of how much time the team member will spend per week in team meetings and how much time per week working on team tasks outside meetings. This estimate will have to be an overall average for the duration of the project, because the actual time spent per week in meetings and outside activities will vary.

Part 2. How Regular Duties Will Be Covered

Who will do the team members' regular work while they are doing the team's work?

Each team member and supervisor should also determine how the team member's current duties will be reassigned. This discussion should include developing a training plan for other employees who are temporarily assuming work. This area is almost always a concern for team members. All too often, however, they abdicate responsibility for resolving time and priority conflicts. There is much "we/them talk" during this stage. Many team members are unaccustomed to handing off duties. Overload often is blamed on nameless outsiders. Supervisors and team members must work together to ensure that both regular work and the project are completed successfully.

The following form can be used to specify and document how a team member's regular work will be handled while he or she is devoting time to the team-related tasks.

Duties	Transfer	Delay	Discontinue
1.	To: _____[Name]_____ Training needed? ❏ yes ❏ no If yes, training completion date: _____	To Date: _____	
2.	To: _____[Name]_____ Training needed? ❏ yes ❏ no If yes, training completion date: _____	To Date: _____	
3.	To: _____[Name]_____ Training needed? ❏ yes ❏ no If yes, training completion date: _____	To Date: _____	

REFERENCES

Hammond, Joshua, and James Morrison. 1996. *The Stuff Americans Are Made Of*. New York: Macmillan.

For more information about American archetype research, contact the American Society for Quality Control, P.O. Box 3005, Milwaukee, WI 53201-3005, 414-272-8575.

HOW TO BE A CUSTOMER ADVOCATE

37

Jane Seiling

Jane G. Seiling *is the founder of the Business Performance Group (1916 Allentown Road, Suite 211, Lima, OH 45805, 419-222-2000, jseiling@aol.com), a consulting firm specializing in organizational change, membership and leadership training, and customer advocacy responsibilities in organizations. Jane is the author of* **A Handbook of Team Techniques** *and will publish a book focusing on advocacy in 1997.*

"No, customers are not always right." So says the author in this guide, which presents a refreshingly new approach to providing positive customer service. Her call for Customer Advocacy challenges employees to positively connect with the customer through a process of partnering. This guide may be just what your organization needs to update its view of appropriate levels of service to its most important clients—its customers.

Customer service is the key to success for organizations in every industry. Front-line employees performing in the "emotional labor" role are seen as "the company" by customers, and, as such, bear heavy responsibility to positively represent their organization to customers under good and bad circumstances.

It follows that employees are consciously or unconsciously delivering to the customer messages of concern or unconcern and support or nonsupport regarding customer welfare and satisfaction. This conscious or unconscious, positive or negative service delivery and the employee's response to the customer delivers messages that impact the customer's desire to continue to be a customer of the employee's organization.

In a nutshell, the employee performs as a representative of the organization with every service gesture. The customers watch as the service is being performed and even participate as partners in the process through their own behavior. In the best of worlds, the employee must identify with the customer, positively connect to the customer, and become committed to serving the customer—while performing in the best interest of the employer.

Positive identification or connection with the customer creates an atmosphere of advocacy between the customer and the employee. The customer now sees the employee as a liaison of the company.

Customer Advocacy as an Employee Responsibility

The role of the Customer Advocate is to:

✓ represent the company positively to both internal and external customers;

✓ represent the customer to the company; and

✓ facilitate recovery of the concerned customer to satisfied (or, at minimum, neutral) in the event of a service problem.

Successful Customer Advocates are employees who:

✓ are in contact with an organization's customers—they enjoy the role and demonstrate the feelings of enjoyment of the role to the customer;

✓ care about their organization's success;

✓ are proud of the organization they work for;

✓ are "energized" by the opportunity to serve organizational customers;

✓ care about the welfare of their organization's customers;

✓ know that satisfied customers mean job security for themselves;

✓ are willing to positively represent their organization to the customer;

✓ actively represent the customer's needs to the organization;

✓ are willing and able to make appropriate decisions on the spot to meet the needs of the customer; and

✓ are trained to make decisions that are appropriate.

Customer Advocates are in a "customer influencing" responsibility. No matter how much potential to succeed an organization has, no matter how good the product is (if there is a product), it is the influencing skills of the employees delivering services that determines the level of success of the organization.

Influencing the customer requires Advocates to positively connect with the customer through a process of partnering with the customer. Partnering suggests there are responsibilities for both persons in the accomplishment of a transaction of service. Those responsibilities include:

Customer Responsibilities	Advocate Responsibilities
To be respectful	To be respectful
Request politely	Respond positively
Communicate concerns	Answer with knowledge
Participate with patience	Provide active evidence of service being provided
Share expectations	Meet expectations within reason
Communicate problems (in an appropriate way)	Facilitate recovery (appropriately)

Employees are seen as "the company" in the eyes of customers. As a result, at a minimum customers expect for the employee to be positive about their company and the performance of their peers. There are three automatic employee influencing activities that place the responsibility of being a positive Advocate with individual employees:

1. Employees cannot *not* communicate their feelings and perceptions of the customer—employees, in every phase of their work, are stewards of their organization and must accept responsibility for being so.

2. An employee cannot *not* influence customers regarding the service being provided and the organization the employee is representing.

3. Employees cannot *not* evaluate their own organization through the eyes of the customer. Therefore, the service provided to the customer and the positive actions of advocacy demonstrated toward the organization by the employee starts a cycle that begins with the employee and resonates back and forth between the customer and employee resulting in a partnership of positive or negative advocacy for the organization. Good service performance, as perceived by the customer, results in a positive Cycle of Advocacy:

   ✓ The employee gives good service;

   ✓ the customer responds positively;

   ✓ the employee gives more good service; and

   ✓ the customer again assesses the service, resulting in a partnership of positive advocacy for the organization.

Positive service and advocacy of the organization to the customer results in the customer being an Advocate of the represented organization.

Yeah, right. This is not only unrealistic, it is the basis for solidifying the negativity of employees who are located in the role of being in constant contact with customers—and are left out there hanging, with no perceived empathy or support from their organization when something goes wrong. The message may be: "You must have done something wrong to cause this." No, customers are not always right. There are three levels of chaotic customer behavior:

Customer is Nasty	Neutral	Dream Customer is a Positive Advocate
/ _____ /		_____ /

NASTY Customer	DREAM Customer
C hallenges everything	C ooperate as best they can
H ostile to service provider	H onest and forthright
A ssumes the wrong things	A ware of limitations
O bnoxious and obstructive	O pen and responsive
S ecretive and self-serving	S elective of products/services

These acronyms are built around CHAOS—something that is happening whether the customer is a nasty or a dream customer. CHAOS is characteristic of the environment that happens when you are directly serving customers. Unpredictability is predictable. This is the reason why direct customer contact is an "emotional labor" concern.

Every day the employee dealing with customers is faced with:

Inconsiderate Customers: These customers forget that the person serving them has rights also and deserves respect for the good service that is given. (Good service should trigger consideration from the customer.)

Crisis Customers: Customers who always have unrealistic expectations of performance of the provider—everything is an emergency, and it is often an emergency created by the customer.

Nitpicker Customers: These customers are never satisfied. There will always be something that is not exactly right. In the end, they will go somewhere else to find the perfect provider of the service or product they need—and they will always be looking for the next provider.

Entitled Customers: The entitled customers are those who believe that "customer" means that all demands they make are reasonable and possible. These customers heard someone say that "the customer is always right" and took it as a badge of entitlement.

So, how does the employee survive with so many nasty, unrealistic customers out there?

First and foremost: Always assume that the customer is a DREAM customer and is willingly going to partner with you in meeting needs.

Second, create a game plan that you automatically flip to if things start to go badly. If recovery has to happen (after something big or little has gone awry), be the best Advocate you can be:

> Be Pleasant
> Be Credible
> Be an Expert in Your Area
> Be Empathetic
> Be Customer-Oriented

Communicating the above game plan to the customer requires:

✓ A positive attitude
   Must be believable, observable

✓ Visible demonstrations of credibility
   Seen as an expert in what they do

✓ Vocal support of the customer/company
   Words of support, pride, fun

✓ Verbal responsibility
   Knowing what to say when

✓ Realistic expectations of the customer and the company
   Being willing to explain "why"
   Checking to see if "it's ok" with the customer
   Understanding that the company has limitations

Third, at all times attempt to connect with the customer in a friendly way.

The Connecting Process

> An appropriate greeting;
> Listening for concerns;
> Discovering needs;
> Advocating a solution;
> Handling objections;
> Recognizing/addressing barriers;
> Reaching tolerance/acceptance;
> Emphasizing *connections*;
> Reinforcing/advocating the solution (and any
>   other participant(s) that are involved);
> Following up to ensure outcome.

It is vital that the employee sees Customer Advocacy as a bottom line issue and accepts personal responsibility for Advocacy as a tool for the success of the organization—and, ultimately, the employee's own success. Customer Advocacy must become a part of the organization—built into the fiber and culture as an "expectation" that is promoted and articulated by all members and all levels of the company.

What is expected, happens. As employees, we are the catalysts for the success of our organizations, our teams, and ourselves. We set the tone. We support. We influence. We inform. We initiate. We respond. We are the reason it happens. The responsibility starts here.

What Has Been Learned

✓ The customer sees every employee as "the company";

✓ Every employee must serve as a Customer Advocate for the company;

✓ As a Customer Advocate the employee represents the customer to the company and the company to the customer;

✓ Customer Advocacy is a customer influencing responsibility;

✓ Customer Advocacy is a bottom line issue;

✓ Successful Customer Advocacy requires the Advocate to connect with the customer; and

✓ It's a tough job ... but every employee has to do it, because ...

What we do,

how we act,

what we praise, and

what we ridicule,

all convey our messages of encouragement
or our wish for failure of
our customers,
our coworkers, and
our employer.

HOW TO RUN AN EFFECTIVE TELECONFERENCE

38

Patricia Philips

Patricia Philips *is the president of Philips Consulting, Inc. (514 Radnor Ave., Pine Beach, NJ 08741, 908-505-0689, Patricia.Philips@ASTD.Noli.com.), a training and development company that provides training, developmental, and administrative services to small and medium-sized companies. Pat, a former corporate trainer, has over twenty years of experience writing and presenting technical and management programs. She is a member of the New Jersey Association of Women Business Owners, the Society of Insurance Trainers and Educators, and a Board Member of the Central Jersey Chapter of ASTD.*

Looking for a way to save on airfares and hotel bills? Here is a cost-effective option for gathering together geographically dispersed team members without anyone having to leave their home city. By simply traveling to the nearest conference room with a speakerphone, your team can take part in effective team meetings. Read this guide to learn more about how to make teleconferencing really work.

At the heart of any team is the team meeting where goals are set, conflicts resolved, problems solved, and decisions made. These meetings pose a challenge when team members are geographically dispersed. Teleconferencing provides a way for teams to conduct their business in an efficient, productive, and cost-effective manner.

The success of any team meeting is based on preparation. This is especially true when the team is joining together through the phone lines, as a teleconference requires more planning than a face-to-face interaction to be successful. An ill-planned meeting affects the team's overall functioning, for if the team meeting is of poor quality, then the team's functioning is of poor quality as well.

Participants take on certain roles during meetings in order to handle tasks such as leadership, note-keeping, and process observation. These roles are especially important during teleconferencing. A lack of face-to-face interaction means that participants need to be reminded to use active listening techniques, encourage participation from those who are silent, and follow the stated agenda. These responsibilities and more are described in detail on the following pages, and are organized under the following role titles: Leader, Recorder, Gatekeeper, and Participant. A checklist included at the end of this guide will help all who participate in teleconferences make their meetings more effective and productive.

Leader

The leader or facilitator is usually, though not always, the person who has called the meeting. It is the leader's responsibility to plan the agenda, handle logistics, manage meeting processes, and conduct follow-up activities. While these responsibilities are important for face-to-face interactions, they are crucial to teleconferencing.

Planning

During the planning stage the leader or facilitator needs to determine the purpose and the objective of the teleconference. Here are questions to ask yourself before the meeting takes place:

1. What needs to be achieved? What is the objective?
2. Is a teleconference necessary to accomplish the objective?
3. What would happen if there wasn't a teleconference?
4. Who should participate in the teleconference if the objective is to be accomplished?
5. When should the teleconference be held?
6. How long does the teleconference need to be?
7. Is there any pre-teleconference work that needs to be done by me or any of the participants in order to accomplish the objective?
8. What process will accomplish the objective (e.g., brainstorming, problem-solving model, or focus group)?

Logistics

Once the above questions have been answered, you can proceed with the logistics of setting up the teleconference. The logistics include the development of the agenda, determining the date and time of the conference call, locating a room with a speakerphone, distributing the agenda, confirming attendance and phone numbers, and making arrangements with the phone company.

Publish a meeting agenda that includes all of the following information: the date and time, the objective, a tentative list of participants, any specific information needed, the process to be used to accomplish the objective, and the time frames involved. The agenda should be accompanied by a cover note requesting confirmation of attendance, notification of any specific role the participant is expected to play, the phone number to be used for the teleconference, and the names of any additional participants or observers who may be attending from that location. Distribute the agenda to the participants at least a week before the scheduled teleconference. This allows the participants time to schedule the meeting and locate a conference room and phone.

It is helpful for you to conduct the teleconference in a room with a speakerphone. The speakerphone allows you to have your hands free to take notes without having to cradle the phone on your shoulder. The leader has a great deal of responsibility during the call and you need to be assured that you will have privacy and be free of distractions.

Once you have received attendance confirmation from the participants, it is time to schedule the teleconference with the local phone company. The teleconference operator will want to know:

✓ Your name.

✓ Phone number where you can be reached and the teleconference phone number.

✓ The phone number to which the teleconference call will be billed.

✓ The date and time for the teleconference.

✓ The parties to be called, their locations, and their phone numbers.

Management

Arrive at the conference room about fifteen minutes before the call is scheduled on the day of the teleconference. The operator will often call to check in with you a few minutes before the scheduled start time. Ask the operator to take a roll call so that you can determine if all the participants are on-line, check for any substitute participants, and discover if there are any unannounced "observers."

As the leader you will be providing most of the control for the management of the teleconference (in addition to a designated gatekeeper). At the beginning of the call greet all the participants and introduce the recorder, gatekeeper, and any observers. Referring to the written agenda, briefly describe the objective and the process of the teleconference.

During the actual discussion you will need to use active listening techniques such as paraphrasing, asking clarifying questions, and summarizing. Some people are uncomfortable with speakerphones and teleconferences. It is easy for such people to hide and not participate. Encourage participation by specifically asking these silent members for their ideas and opinions. This is particularly important if agreement is needed on an issue.

Handling Conflicts

One of the most difficult activities for a leader is the management of conflicts. Heated discussions are difficult during a face-to-face interaction and can be overwhelming during a teleconference. If conflict should arise, you will need to take a firm stand and control the situation quickly. Nothing can destroy a teleconference faster than two (or more) people shouting at each other over the phone.

The first thing you need to determine is if the conflict is related to the discussion at hand. If not, you will need to tell the individuals that the conflict is inappropriate and disruptive to the purpose of the meeting. Ask them to table it for later resolution.

If the conflict is relevant to the discussion, put a conflict resolution process into place as follows:

✓ Clarify and define the issue
✓ Identify positions
✓ Identify areas of agreement
✓ Identify possible solutions
✓ Choose a mutually agreeable solution

If the conflict can't be quickly and effectively resolved, either terminate the teleconference until such time as it is resolved or ask the individuals to agree to disagree for the moment, and move on.

Summarizing and Follow-Up

At the conclusion of the teleconference, summarize what has been accomplished, specify what needs to be done, identify who is going to take action within what time frame, and schedule the next teleconference (if appropriate). Before you terminate the meeting thank the participants for their time and participation and request that they provide you with feedback regarding the teleconference's effectiveness.

After the meeting is over, take a few minutes to evaluate the effectiveness of the teleconference from your own perspective. Note any areas that went particularly well and those that could stand some improvement. Use your personal evaluation and participant feedback when planning your next teleconference.

Be sure to follow up on action items identified during the meeting. Follow-up is needed as a general rule after any meeting, but is even more important when the participants are geographically dispersed. The first reminder to the participants will come in the minutes of the teleconference written by the recorder. After they have received the minutes, remind the participants of their action items intermittently, according to your time frame for completion, by phone or e-mail.

Recorder

A participant who is designated as the recorder relieves others from the need to take general notes and allows them to concentrate on the objective of the teleconference. The recorder is the memory of the participants and the leader. He provides an accurate account of the teleconference for all others in the form of minutes.

The recorder summarizes the teleconference using the agenda as a basis for the minutes. The minutes should include the time, date, participants, objectives, issues discussed, decisions made, problems identified or resolved, ideas, discussions that were tabled, and action assignments. The minutes of the teleconference should be written within forty-eight hours of the teleconference to ensure an accurate recounting. As time goes by, notes can lose their meaning even to the person who wrote them. The minutes should be distributed in the manner agreed upon by the team.

Gatekeeper

The gatekeeper is the process observer. This person is responsible for watching the interactions of the participants and helping them to keep communication channels open. Gatekeepers aren't always used in face-to-face interactions, because it is generally easier for the leader/facilitator to manage meetings that take place in person. In those situations, the participants and their nonverbal behaviors are visible to the facilitator. During a teleconference, however, all a leader has to use are the words being said and the associated tone of voice. A lack of participation isn't as easily noticed and the tone of voice may be missed.

A gatekeeper keeps track of participation levels. By using a participation log, she notes who isn't participating, who has dominated the discussion, and those that fall in between. The log is an excellent tool when you need team agreement on a particular issue.

The gatekeeper can also reinforce the facilitator when the conversation wanders or conflicts erupt.

Participants

Participants are the heart of the teleconference and have a responsibility for the accomplishment of its objectives. Participants have to schedule their availability for the teleconference and make arrangements for a place to take the call. It is helpful to take the phone call away from the work area to ensure quiet, privacy, and a minimum of distractions. Participants need to respond in a timely manner to the leader's requests for participation confirmation and a teleconference phone number so that she can make final arrangements.

Complete pre-teleconference work before the meeting begins. If other participants need the information or it would be helpful to have it before the meeting, distribute the information to each participant in time for them to read and digest the information.

On the day of the teleconference, arrive at the site about fifteen minutes before the scheduled call. Active listening skills are especially important in these phone meetings. Side conversations either with someone in the room or especially with someone on the call are very distracting and rude. Keep an open mind to ideas and opinions that are different from your own. Questions are useful for clarifying positions and ensuring understanding. Make a special note of action items that are your responsibility.

After the meeting is over, provide the leader with helpful feedback. Brief those that didn't attend the teleconference on its results. Review the minutes when you receive them to make sure they are accurate. And, most importantly, complete all action items on time.

Conclusion

A successful teleconference saves your organization the expense of bringing team members together in one physical location. Holding a team meeting over the phone, however, does require more planning and preparation than a face-to-face interaction. By establishing set roles and following the suggestions detailed in this guide, your teleconferences are well positioned to be both effective and productive. The following pages contain a checklist for the leader and reminder notes for the recorder, gatekeeper, and participants. Use these lists the next time you take part in a teleconference.

TELECONFERENCE CHECKLISTS

Leader/Facilitator

Before the teleconference:

- ❏ Define objectives of the meeting—*what is to be accomplished?*
  - ✓ What decision(s) is to be made?
  - ✓ What problem(s) is to be solved?
  - ✓ What discussion is to take place?
  - ✓ What information is to be relayed?
- ❏ Select participants—*who needs to be there to accomplish the objective?*
  - ✓ Identify those who will play particular roles such as recorder or gatekeeper
- ❏ Set a tentative date and time.
- ❏ Notify participants of the date and time and roles to be played.
  - ✓ Request teleconference phone number
  - ✓ Request confirmation of availability
- ❏ Make arrangements for use of conference room with speaker-phone.
- ❏ Receive confirmation and phone numbers from participants.
- ❏ Make arrangements with AT&T or local phone company for teleconference upon confirmation of availability of participants. Provide teleconference operator with the following information:
  - ✓ Your name
  - ✓ Phone number(s)—*work and teleconference number*
  - ✓ The billing phone number
  - ✓ Date of teleconference
  - ✓ Time of teleconference
  - ✓ Names of parties to be called
  - ✓ Locations of parties to be called
  - ✓ Phone numbers of parties to be called
- ❏ Prepare a detailed agenda complete with responsibilities and time frames.
- ❏ Distribute agenda, timing it for arrival three to five days before the teleconference.

During the teleconference:

❏ Arrive at the conference room about fifteen (15) minutes before the scheduled call.

❏ Have the conference operator take a roll call.

❏ Write down phone company reference number for use in case of problems.

❏ Greet participants.

❏ Introduce any nonparticipants ("observers") who may be listening.

❏ Briefly describe the objective of the meeting, referencing the agenda.

❏ Manage the discussion.

   ✓ Stick to agenda

   ✓ Use active listening techniques

   ✓ Encourage participation—ask silent members for opinions and ideas

   ✓ If agreement is necessary be sure to hear from everyone

   ✓ Resolve conflict

   ✓ Clarify actions to be taken

❏ Summarize results and actions to be taken.

❏ Schedule next teleconference if appropriate.

❏ Thank participants for their time and participation.

Following teleconference:

❏ Restore room and return equipment as needed.

❏ Evaluate meeting results in relationship to objectives and agenda.

❏ Follow up on action items.

Recorder

During the teleconference:

Take minutes and include:

   ✓ Participants taking part in teleconference and any "observers"

   ✓ Objective of the meeting

   ✓ Date and time of meeting

   ✓ Summary of issues discussed

✓ Make note of:

Decisions made

Problems identified/resolved

Ideas/problems/discussions tabled to a later meeting

Action assignments and responsible individuals

Following the teleconference:

Write minutes and distribute in the manner and time frame agreed upon.

Gatekeeper

During the teleconference:

Assist the teleconference leader/facilitator:

✓ Ensure agenda is being followed

✓ Manage use of time

✓ Control discussion

✓ Encourage participation

Have a list of participants and make "tick" marks indicating participation. *(See sample log at end of guide.)*

Specifically ask silent members for opinions and ideas.

If agreement is necessary be sure everyone is heard from.

Participant

Before the teleconference:

1. Respond in a timely manner to leader's/facilitator's request for confirmation of availability and phone number.

2. Make arrangements for use of a speakerphone and conference room if necessary.

3. Block out the time for the teleconference on your calendar.

4. Read the agenda and know the objective of the meeting.

5. Do any preliminary work as necessary.

6. Suggest other participants that may be needed.

7. Arrive at the conference room 15 minutes before the scheduled call.

During the teleconference:

8. Actively listen—don't interrupt.
9. Participate.
10. Be open-minded.
11. Stay on the agenda/subject.
12. Avoid side conversations both in the room and on the phone.
13. Ask questions to ensure understanding.
14. Take notes on your action items.

After the teleconference:

15. Evaluate the effectiveness of the teleconference in relationship to agenda and objectives.
16. Read the minutes of the teleconference.
17. Brief others as needed.
18. Do action items.

TELECONFERENCING PARTICIPATION LOG

Participant's Name:	Participation Log
Grady White	✓ ✓ ✓ ✓
George Smith	✓ ✓
Ima Sweety	✓
Elizabeth Muffin	

HOW TO CONDUCT A CULTURE AUDIT

39

Cathleen Smith Hutchison

Cathleen Smith Hutchison is *Managing Partner of Metamorphosis Consulting Group (P.O. Box 1147, Cedar Crest, NM 87008, 505-281-4496), a full-service human resources consulting firm specializing in managing corporate change. She is the coauthor of* **Instructor Competencies: The Standards,** *vol. I and vol. II and numerous professional articles. She is a past officer of the International Society for Performance Improvement at international and chapter levels and of the International Board of Standards for Training Performance and Instruction. Cathleen was a contributor to* **The 1996 McGraw-Hill Team and Organization Development Sourcebook.**

Every organization has its own culture: a set of practices, rituals, and myths that give a working environment a particular feel. The cultures of certain organizations such as IBM and Microsoft are well-documented and discussed. But what is the culture like at your organization? What does it feel like to work in your organization's environment? Read this guide on conducting a culture audit to discover just how much an organization's culture says about how it conducts its business.

As with the culture of a country, the culture of an organization is comprised of how and why people in the culture behave and act as they do. Understanding the culture of either a country or an organization allows the observer to understand the beliefs behind and underneath surface behaviors. Knowledge of an organization's culture may yield the ability to broadly predict reactions and behaviors in future situations.

Organizational culture has become a topic of increasing interest in the business press over the past 15 years. In the 1980s business authors began to study organizational cultures in earnest. They observed that organizations had differing cultures, some of which were strong, others that were not so strong. Organizations with strong cultures seemed to frequently be included in lists of "excellent companies." In the early 1990s some long-term research studies on the connection between corporate cultures and organizational performance were published, notably Kotter and Heskett's *Corporate Culture and Performance* (1992).

Managers and organizational developers now focus on designing cultures to support the organization's strategic plan and therefore enhance organizational performance and the bottom line. However, designing an effective and supportive, strategic culture and implementing it throughout an organization are two very different enterprises.

Definitions

Let's begin with definitions of commonly used terms:

✓ *Culture.* The simple definition of culture is "how we do things around here." Culture is the summation of the typical behavioral practices of a group, particularly those that become norms, values, and patterns within that group. Culture includes the assumptions people hold of how the world operates. The culture is the organization's unique combination of underlying values, beliefs, and principles that serve as a foundation for its management system as well as the practices and behaviors that both exemplify and reinforce those principles (Denison, 1990). We typically are used to thinking about cultures as they relate to countries and ethnic groups, and only more recently as they relate to organizations.

✓ *Audit.* An audit is an examination and verification of the accuracy of accounts and records. An audit can also be an evaluation of current conditions in order to improve appropriateness, safety, efficiency, or the like. (Random House Dictionary, 1987)

✓ *Culture Audit.* This is a method of assessing the values, beliefs, and behavioral practices in place within an organization and the manner in which an organization conducts its business on a day-to-day basis.

    Culture audits move beyond a true identification and description of the organization's culture. A culture audit is conducted in order to create improvement. It examines values and beliefs held by organizational groups in order to ensure the appropriateness for the strategy.

Objectives and Uses

There are several possible improvement-related objectives for conducting a culture audit.

✓ *To Establish a Baseline.* The culture audit can be the first step in identifying and understanding an organization's culture. It provides initial documentation of existing practices and behaviors occurring on a day-to-day basis. The culture audit can provide an accurate "picture" of the beliefs, values, and practices that currently exist within an organization as baseline data for any changes an organization may choose to make.

✓ *To Assess Alignment.* The picture provided by the audit can be compared to a defined, desired culture and/or to a strategic plan to determine the level of alignment in existence at the time of the audit. It can also be used to determine the level of alignment between various segments and subdivisions of an organization.

✓ *To Monitor Progress.* Periodic culture audits can monitor and assess the level of progress being made by an organization's efforts to develop a supportive and strategically aligned culture.

Process

The process for conducting a culture audit is made up of 18 steps, each ranging from simple to complex. Some of the steps, particularly those around the actual data collection and analysis, refer the facilitator to other resources to acquire more detailed information.

1. *Confirm That Culture Is What the Organization Should Assess.* There are several types of Organizational Assessment tactics. Be sure that the culture audit is appropriate for the organization's needs.

   ✓ Is the organization interested in what employees feel about one or more specific topics, issues, or initiatives? If so, it should conduct an attitude survey.

   ✓ Is the organization interested in how closely employees are adhering to its prescribed policies, procedures, and methods? If so, it should conduct an operational audit.

   ✓ Is the organization interested in assessing the behavioral practices, values, and belief systems in place within the organization? If so, it should conduct a culture audit.

   ✓ Is the organization interested in a comprehensive assessment of the alignment between behaviors and practices of employees and operational strategies? If so, it should conduct an organizational scan. (See Hutchison, 1996)

2. *Recognize the Consequences.* There are consequences to any data collection effort. People expect changes to occur when data is collected. By addressing cultural issues in a formal and management-sponsored audit, members of an organization will anticipate behavior changes, most likely on the part of managers. Additionally, management must recognize that the act of collecting data alters an organization in and of itself, particularly if the organization seldom collects this type of data. There may also be issues, either overt or covert, related to previous data-gathering activities.

3. *Determine the Scope.* The organization must decide how extensive the culture audit should be. Culture audits can encompass the entire organization or be limited to specific divisions, functions, management levels, and segments of the organization.

4. *Identify the Sample Population to Involve.* Except with small organizations, the culture audit will usually involve data collection from a sample of the total population being assessed. The organization must decide on the appropriate size and composition of the sample population in order to ensure that the data from the sample accurately reflects the entire population.

   ✓ Size—Tables are available in most behavioral research or statistical methods texts to determine the number of individuals necessary to provide statistically accurate information. As the size of the total population increases, the percentage required for the sample population decreases.

   ✓ Composition—A completely random sample can be selected from total employee lists, or a stratified random sample can be selected that mirrors the composition by subgroups within the population. A stratified random sample ensures that an accurate number of individuals from specific and targeted subgroups is selected. For example, the organization may wish to ensure that an adequate number of technicians and support services employees are selected, or they may wish to ensure adequate representation from each level of management and each division, function, and location across the organization.

5. *Choose Data Collection Efforts.* Data can be collected in a number of ways, singly or in combination. Focus groups and/or one-on-one interviews are strongly recommended because of the ability to follow up on information and gain greater detail and clarity from the individuals providing the information. The organization may also want to include a questionnaire or survey. Ideally a combination of focus groups, interviews, and rating scales would be used. There are a number of texts that list and describe a variety of available data collection techniques. (See Hutchison, 1994b)

6. *Select Questions.* Be sure that the questions selected address a broad range of topics and cover all aspects of the organization's culture. Some sample questions are listed below:

   ✓ What does the organization do best?

   ✓ What does the organization do least well? Where does the organization have the most opportunity for improvement?

   ✓ What do you like best about working here?

   ✓ What do you like least about working here?

   ✓ When you are talking with friends and neighbors, what makes you proud to be associated with this company?

   ✓ When you are talking with friends and neighbors, what makes you embarrassed to be associated with this company?

✓ What kinds of people and actions are rewarded in this company?

✓ What kinds of people and actions are punished in this company?

✓ How is information communicated in this company?

✓ How well does the formal communication system work?

✓ Where do you usually find out most company information?

✓ What is the strategy of the organization? How did you find out about the strategy?

✓ What details do you know about the strategy?

✓ How do decisions get made within this company?

✓ What kinds of decisions are made at various levels within the organization?

✓ On a scale of 1 to 10 with 1 being no politics at all and 10 being the most political organization ever, how political is this organization in comparison to others of which you are aware?

✓ How would you describe the politics in this organization?

✓ How well managed is this company?

✓ Who are the leaders in the company, regardless of title or position in the company?

✓ What kind of people become leaders in this organization? Why are they leaders?

✓ If this organization was a person, what adjectives would you use to describe it?

7. *Design the Focus Group/Interview.* Sequence the questions and activities that will be conducted so that they flow logically from one to another and increase the effective and efficient use of the time. A sample focus group design is listed below:

✓ Introduce self. Do not ask for participant names and explain that in order to ensure anonymity you will not be asking for names.

✓ Explain the purpose and process of the culture audit. Describe who the sponsors are, what they intend to do with the information, and who will receive feedback in what format.

✓ Ask for any participant comments or questions on the following:

strengths and weaknesses;

what is best and worst;

corporate pride;

reward and recognition;

communication;

decision making;

politics; and

management and leadership.

✓ List adjectives describing organization.

✓ Complete questionnaire/rating scale.

✓ Mark flip chart items for level of participant agreement with each item. (Ask each participant to take a marker and place a check mark next to every item listed with which they agree. Explain that in this way you will determine how much agreement there is on each item, or if outspoken participants have unique views.)

✓ Have participants vote on three most critical items mentioned. (Ask each participant to rank the top three items listed on all the flip chart pages.)

✓ Thank participants for their participation. Reinforce anonymity and remind them of the next steps in the process and the timings they will require.

8. *Design All Support Data Collection Efforts.* As with the focus groups and interviews, determine the questions that will be asked and the sequence that is most appropriate. Determine how they will integrate with the focus group and/or interviews. Determine the population size and composition for each.

9. *Pilot Test All Data Collection Efforts.* Conduct a pilot test of all data collection instruments and activities to ensure that they are understandable to the target populations and will elicit the type of information they are designed to elicit.

10. *Revise Data Collection Efforts as Needed.* Based on information obtained during the Pilot Tests, revise the data collection instruments and designs as needed.

11. *Determine the Relative Timing of All Data Collection Efforts.* Just as you sequenced the questions within each data collection instrument, sequence the data collection activities. You may choose to have some data collection activities occurring concurrently.

12. *Choose Who Will Collect Data.* Individuals doing the actual data collection, particularly in interviews or focus groups, must be perceived as neutral, trustworthy, and without power over the employees participating in the audit. Participants must feel totally confident in the anonymity of their remarks in order to provide candid and accurate information. This means that a "stranger" should collect the data in most cases. This can be an internal facilitator from a different part of the organization, newly hired internal facilitators, or it can be an external consultant. Small organizations may be forced to hire an external consultant or barter with another organization to exchange services.

13. *Train the Data Collectors.* Ensure that data collectors will not interject their feelings into the process and bias the results either favorably or unfavorably. Agree on the questions, explanations, and follow-up techniques that will be used in order to ensure consistency across facilitators. Clarify all instructions on how to ensure individual anonymity while identifying which segment of the organization is represented by the participant(s). If a questionnaire is to be read to participants, describe and practice the tone and stress of each question to ensure consistency of item interpretation by participants. Ensure that all facilitators understand which questions and areas have priority in case timing requires any activities to be deleted. Share expected timings for each section of the data collection effort.

14. *Schedule Focus Groups and Other Data Collection Efforts.* Arrange with participants and the organization's facilities groups to schedule appropriately sized and equipped conference/meeting rooms. Ensure that focus groups meet in rooms with flip charts and markers available. Consider providing beverages and snacks for participants in both focus groups and interviews. Remember to allow some time between interviews and focus groups so that the facilitator/interviewer has time to straighten the room, collect and organize flip chart pages or interview notes, and take a brief break.

15. *Collect Data.* Conduct the focus groups, interviews, and other data collection efforts as designed. Be sure to indicate on flip chart pages and interview notes which subgroup of the organization is represented. (See Hutchison, 1994b)

16. *Organize Data.* Group the information according to subgroup and content area and other logical groupings. There are many books and articles that describe data organization techniques. (See Hutchison, 1994c)

17. *Analyze Data.* Apply both qualitative and quantitative analysis techniques. Simple analysis techniques are probably sufficient, however if they are available, you can involve corporate statisticians. Be aware that advanced analysis techniques will probably not yield dramatically more learning or understanding of the information. There are many books and articles that describe data analysis techniques. (See Hutchison, 1994a)

18. *Report Data and Provide Feedback.* The report should be in narrative form, describing the process used, conclusions drawn, and providing anecdotal examples to justify the conclusions. Often, direct quotes from "credible sources" (e.g., a vice president or a manager in the marketing department) used to support major themes helps to break through normal resistance and denial that many executives and managers have when receiving the report.

The information, results, and conclusions are organized into themes and priorities based upon the importance of various issues to the organization and/or the prevalence and strength of the beliefs. Conclusions from any quantitative data should be compared and contrasted to the qualitative data. Significant variances within and between types of data should be pointed out and, where possible, explained.

Executives may wish to have the report delivered both in person and in writing. Many executives will want to be able to ask questions on specific points.

Management should receive their reports prior to feedback going out to participants, in case they choose to share information regarding their planned actions at the same time they are sharing the results. However, everyone should remember that participants are generally curious and will be anticipating feedback on the results. It is best to share information with them in a timely manner. Particularly in a low trust environment, a multitude of motivations and rationales will be ascribed to any perceived management delay.

Time Required

The time varies greatly with the size of the data collection effort. However, data collection efforts should allow one-and-a-half to two hours for each individual interview and two to three hours for each focus group.

Resources Required

One to two facilitators are needed for each focus group. Some facilitators are comfortable and skilled at both leading the questions and answers and also capturing the data on flip charts. Others work better if these two roles are divided between two facilitators.

Products

The output from the culture audit is a report that organizes, describes, and interprets both the qualitative and quantitative information and draws appropriate conclusions and makes appropriate recommendations for next steps. Conclusions should indicate the impact and implications that the results have for the future of the organization. Recommendations for next steps should include a menu of options to address issues that imply potential problems for the organization.

REFERENCES

Denison, Daniel R. 1990. *Corporate Culture and Organizational Effectiveness.* New York: John Wiley.

Hutchison, Cathleen Smith. 1994a. "Data Analysis Techniques." Unpublished concept paper available from Metamorphosis Consulting Group: Cedar Crest, New Mexico.

Hutchison, Cathleen Smith. 1994b. "Data Collection Techniques." Unpublished concept paper available from Metamorphosis Consulting Group: Cedar Crest, New Mexico.

Hutchison, Cathleen Smith. 1994c. "Data Organization Techniques." Unpublished concept paper available from Metamorphosis Consulting Group: Cedar Crest, New Mexico.

Hutchison, Cathleen Smith. 1997. "Four Organizational Assessment Tools." *1997 Team and Organization Development Sourcebook*. New York: McGraw-Hill.

Kotter, John P. and James L. Heskett. 1992. *Corporate Culture and Performance*. New York: The Free Press.

Random House Dictionary of the English Language. 1987. New York: Random House.

HOW TO IDENTIFY AND ANALYZE PROBLEMS IN YOUR ORGANIZATION*

40

G.M. (Bud) Benscoter

Bud Benscoter, *Ph.D. is the Manager for Performance Development, Information Systems Group, The Vanguard Group of Investment Companies (100 Vanguard Boulevard, A30, Malvern, PA 19355, 610-669-6647, bud_benscoter@vanguard.com). Bud has over thirty years of training, consulting, and management experience. He received his M.Ed. and Ph.D. in Instructional Systems from Penn State University, and teaches in the colleges of Education and Management at Penn State's Great Valley (PA) graduate campus.*

*How many times have you heard it said that one of the biggest challenges faced by American business is finding or developing people to solve problems effectively? A fact that's often ignored, though, is that problem **identification** and **analysis** are critical first steps to good problem **solving,** since successfully solving the wrong problem is worse than not addressing the real problems at all.*

*This how-to guide presents you with a format for identifying which problems to attack and how to analyze the impact they are having on your organization. The approach used is a six-step process called **PRIAM,** for **PR**oblem **I**dentification and **A**nalysis **M**odel. While the model can be used by an individual working alone, it is also very effective with intact working groups who sometimes find it difficult to sort out the "trivial many" from the "critical few" issues on their plates.*

By following this six-step process, you should discover that you're working on the problems that have the greatest impact on your business and that you're laying a foundation for selecting the appropriate solution that will yield measurable results. Happy hunting!!

The PRIAM Model

Figure 40.1 is a graphic representation of the model, which looks at four areas:

Note: A special thanks to James and Dana Gaines Robinson and to the late Thomas F. Gilbert for the inspiration their work provided in formulating the PRIAM approach.

354

✓ Impact on the business in terms of business metrics

✓ Impact on business processes

✓ Impact on worker performance

✓ Obstacles to top performance

Gap Analysis

A "Gap" is the difference between what IS happening and what SHOULD or COULD be happening.

For each of the impact areas, you'll be asked to think about the following:

✓ The "should" vision of the area of the model under investigation: What results should be happening that aren't?

The Model

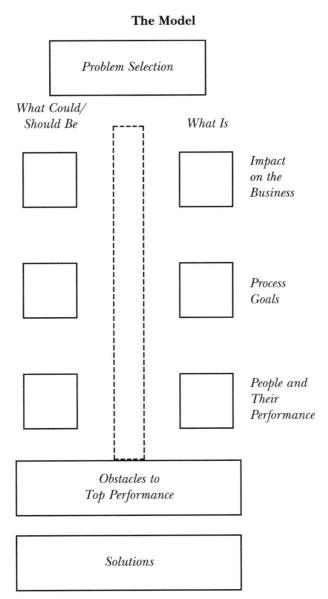

Figure 40.1.

✓ The "is" of the issue: In terms of results, what is actually happening? What adverse impact is it having on business results?

You should find the model to be useful for not only improving conditions that are currently deficient, but also those that meet your standards today but will need to improve to meet the challenges of tomorrow. You can enter the model at different places and move back and forth depending on where your analysis leads you.

Applying the PRIAM Model

Step #1: Select an Issue

The first step in the model is to identify an issue. Your group may want to brainstorm potential issues and list them on a board or flip chart. When selecting an issue or a problem from the list you've developed, consider how you can separate the "critical few" from the "trivial many." The questions listed under Step #1 get to the heart of what's causing "pain" in the organization, how the pain is measured, the benefits to solving the issue, and how "solvable" the problem is.

Step #2: Analyze the Issue in Terms of Impact on the Business

Look at the impact of your group's issue on the business (e.g., lost revenue, reduced productivity, cost overruns, turnover). Issues that have greater impact are likely to deserve attention. From there, describe what the situation should (or could) be if the issue were resolved to everyone's satisfaction.

Step #3: Analyze the Process Issue

Process seems to be everyone's focus since the advent of Business Process Reengineering. Recognize the impact that a poor process can have on our operations. To analyze the process issues, identify process goals, which are the gaps between desired and actual process results, and any "disconnects" (gaps) in the current process flow.

Step #4: Analyze the People and Their Performance

Describe what worker performance looks like now, then what it should or could look like if performance dramatically improved. Focus on performance and its outcomes as well as on behavior, attitudes, and morale.

Step #5: Analyze the Obstacles to Top Performance

More problems are caused by deficiencies in the work environment than by people in the workplace. The key to investigating problems within a process is measurement. A series of core questions in step #5 are designed to identify obstacles to top performance. The questions relate to what is expected of people on their jobs, whether they're receiving timely, appropriate, and relevant feedback on their performance, and any incentives or disincentives to perform that may exist in the workplace. For each question, answer "yes" or "no." The questions that you answer "no" to should be areas of opportunity for improvement.

Step #6: Select Solution Criteria

You now have the information you need to identify possible solutions to the issue you selected in Step #1. Before doing so, ask yourself what requirements (such as cost, practicality, or cultural impact) any final solution must meet.

STEP #1: SELECT AN ISSUE

✓ Is the issue causing pain in the organization?

✓ How do I know it's a "problem"?

✓ Who else sees this issue as a problem?

✓ How are business metrics impacted by this issue?

✓ What would happen if I did nothing about this issue?

✓ What will be the benefits to the company and/or the business unit if the issue is successfully addressed?

✓ Is the problem "leverageable"; i.e., can a significant improvement be made with a minimum of effort?

STEP #2: ANALYZE THE ISSUE IN TERMS OF IMPACT ON THE BUSINESS

Describe, in economic terms, the current situation:

Describe what the situation should (or could) be if the issue were resolved to everyone's satisfaction:

STEP #3: ANALYZE THE PROCESS ISSUE

✓ What are the goals of the process?

✓ If the goals are not being achieved, what is the gap between desired and actual process results?

✓ Can you "map" both the current and desired processes and identify the critical differences in terms of process efficiency, effectiveness, cost?

✓ Are there "disconnects" (gaps in process flow) in the current process?

✓ Is the process being managed cross-functionally?

STEP #4: ANALYZE THE PEOPLE AND THEIR PERFORMANCE

Describe what worker performance looks like now, then what it should or could look like if performance dramatically improved or changed. Try to focus on performance and its outcomes as well as on behavior, attitudes, and morale.

<u>Current Performance</u>

<u>Desired Performance</u>

STEP #5: ANALYZE THE OBSTACLES TO TOP PERFORMANCE

(Answer "yes" or "no" for each of the following questions. The ones you answer "no" to should be examined more closely.)

1. Are the goals and objectives of the work unit/process/job clear and well communicated to everyone?

2. Do people know what's expected of them in their jobs? For example, are there job descriptions that include job expectations and performance standards?

3. Do people receive relevant, timely, and appropriate feedback on their performance?

4. Do people have the tools and resources needed to achieve top performance?

5. Do people have good work processes?

6. Do people have relevant and effective incentives for doing their jobs?

7. Are incentives contingent on job performance?

8. Is good performance rewarded?

9. Is poor performance punished?

10. Do people have the necessary skills and knowledge to do their jobs?

11. Do people have the mental, emotional, physical, and psychological capacity to do their jobs?

12. If other obstacles were removed, would people want to do well in their jobs?

STEP #6: SELECT SOLUTION CRITERIA

What criteria must your proposed solution meet for it to be acceptable?

1.

2.

3.

4.

About the Editors

Mel Silberman, Ph.D. is President of Active Training (26 Linden Lane, Princeton, New Jersey 08540, 609-924-8157, mel@tigger.jvnc.net, http:\\www.activetraining.com). He is also Professor of Adult and Organizational Development at Temple University where he specializes in instructional design and team building.

He is the author of

Active Training (Lexington Books, 1990)
101 Ways to Make Training Active (Pfeiffer & Co., 1995)
Active Learning (Allyn & Bacon, 1996)

He is the editor of:

20 Active Training Programs, vol. I (Pfeiffer & Co., 1992)
20 Active Training Programs, vol. II (Pfeiffer & Co., 1994)
20 Active Training Programs, vol. III (Pfeiffer & Co., 1997)
The 1996 McGraw-Hill Training and Performance Sourcebook
The 1996 McGraw-Hill Team and Organization Development Sourcebook

Mel has consulted for hundreds of corporate, governmental, educational, and human service organizations worldwide. His recent clients include:

AT&T International
Merrill Lynch
Automated Data Processing
Bristol Myers-Squibb
Devereux Foundation
Hoffman-LaRoche
Bell Atlantic
ARCO Chemical

Midlantic Bank
Texas Instruments
Meridian Bank
Franklin Quest
J. P. Morgan, Inc.
U.S. Army
Hospital of the University of PA
Penn State University

He is also a popular speaker at professional conferences.

Carol Auerbach is an independent management consultant (609 Kingston Rd., Baltimore, MD 21212, 410-377-9257, cauerbach@aol.com). A former trainer for Mellon Bank and CIGNA Corporation, she now designs and conducts training on a wide variety of topics. Carol collaborated with Mel previously on *Active Training* and served as the assistant editor of *The 1996 McGraw-Hill Training and Performance Sourcebook* and *The 1996 McGraw-Hill Team and Organization Development Sourcebook.*

Are you interested in being a contributor to *The 1998 McGraw-Hill Training and Performance Sourcebook?*

In the course of your professional work, you have probably developed exercises, handouts, instruments, short articles, and other printed materials that could be useful to a wide audience of consultants, trainers, and performance specialists. Consider your favorite piece of work for publication. The *1998 Sourcebook* will contain another 40 practical tools to improve learning and performance. Would you like to contribute one of them? Join our impressive list of contributors.

For more information, contact:

Mel Silberman, Editor
The McGraw-Hill Training and Performance Sourcebook
c/o Active Training
26 Linden Lane
Princeton, NJ 08540
609-924-8157
609-924-4250 fax
mel@tigger.jvnc.net